T0386261

BORODINO
FIELD *1812 & 1941*

BORODINO FIELD *1812 & 1941*

How Napoleon and Hitler Met Their Matches Outside Moscow

Robert Kershaw

This book is dedicated to my grandsons Elijah, Finley and Freddie
and my granddaughter India

First published 2021

The History Press
97 St George's Place, Cheltenham,
Gloucestershire, GL50 3QB
www.thehistorypress.co.uk

© Robert Kershaw, 2021

Maps by Tim Mitchell © Piernine Ltd

British Library Cataloguing in Publication Data.
A catalogue record for this book is available from the British Library.

ISBN 978 0 7509 9595 5

Typesetting and origination by The History Press
Printed and bound in Great Britain by TJ Books Limited, Padstow, Cornwall.

Trees for Life

Contents

Acknowledgements

I am especially grateful to John Badgery for his assistance in translating many of the Russian 1941 personal accounts and in particular helping, through his former military expertise, in interpreting Russian maps and place names. Vladimir Kroupnik identified and translated a number of especially interesting Russian personal accounts also relating to Borodino in 1941 and advised on their context. George Falco de Mats, a fellow battlefield tourer, helped to guide me through the intricacies of Napoleonic rearguard actions on the Russian side in 1812. My wife, as ever, beavered constantly in the background, enabling me to write, and my thanks also to my agent Charlie Viney for his encouragement and enthusiasm in sponsoring a slightly unusual project.

Prologue

On 10 October 1941 a black locomotive, emblazoned with a distinctive Soviet red star, puffed into the busy station siding encased in swirling steam. As it came to a squealing, grinding halt, the flatcars behind clanked and buffeted each other to a standstill. It was becoming dark. A chorus of urgent directives and shouted commands rang out amid the bustle of ramps pushed up against flatcar sides. Wedges were hammered out and knocked clear amid the rattle of collapsing chains. Russian soldiers jumped down as vehicle engines aboard began to whine and turn over before firing into life, raising clouds of grey exhaust smoke. Soldiers were not allowed to speak to inquisitive civilians looking on. The priority was to get the reconnaissance vehicles off, followed by tanks and armoured vehicles.

Colonel Victor Polosukhin's car was escorted from these sidings at Dorokhovo railway station, 60 miles west of Moscow. German *Luftwaffe* air raids had wrecked the main Mozhaisk station, 11 miles further down the track. Gangs of labourers were industriously filling bomb craters and re-laying twisted and contorted rail track further west to enable a more efficient unloading operation. The colonel wanted to reach Borodino some 25 miles to the west, about a thirty-six-minute drive by car. In so doing he was driving against the main flow of refugees choking the roads heading east to Moscow. Polosukhin needed to see the rapidly developing situation up front for himself, and left the busy rail yard behind. The leading echelons of his command, the 32nd Rifle Division, were already unloading vehicles from stationary flatcars.

Local civilians realised such urgent activity did not bode well. Historian Dr Peter Miller, who commented on everyday life in Moscow, wrote in his diary three days before that 'there is a feeling of approaching catastrophe in the air and endless rumours'. Shops were empty, 'Orel has been surrendered, Vyazma has been surrendered, and the Germans have got to Maloyaroslavets'.[1] These place names had an eerie atmospheric Napoleonic ring to them. Polosukhin had only a sketchy idea of what was going on. His division had entrained from the Leningrad reserve further north, after arriving earlier that summer. As his small staff group drove westward, the front grumbled intermittently 70 miles away in the distance. Unbeknown to him, three German tank groups or *Panzergruppen* had torn a 300-mile gap in the Moscow outer defence line. Five to six Russian armies were surrounded at Vyazma on the Smolensk to Moscow road ahead and another three further south at Bryansk. Although the news was disturbing, Polosukhin had yet to fully comprehend how catastrophic it was. Rumours abounded that German advance forces were nearing Gzhatsk (present-day Gagarin), just 114 miles from Moscow.

The colonel appreciated history. Place names like Vyazma, Gzhatsk, Maloyaroslavets and Borodino were the 1812 milestones that signposted Napoleon's *Grande Armée* approach route to Moscow, now seemingly replicated by Hitler's *Wehrmacht*. Polosukhin's 32nd Rifle Division was one of the oldest in the Red Army and was descended from one of the first regiments of the Petrograd (now Leningrad) Workers in 1917. The division was not tainted by the opprobrium of the earlier Soviet defeats along the frontier that accompanied the opening of Operation *Barbarossa*, Hitler's surprise attack on the Soviet Union. It was an undeclared war, breaking the former Russo-German Non-Aggression Pact, signed barely two years before. Polosukhin's division had, by contrast, recently distinguished itself during intense fighting against the Japanese at Lake Khasan in 1938, for which it was awarded the Order of the Red Banner. The 32nd Division was at high pre-war strength standards, common among the Far Eastern forces, where they had been stationed the past ten years. When alerted for action in late September 1941, the division was already fully mobilised with its 14,500 men, 872 vehicles, 444 machine guns and 286 artillery and heavy mortar pieces. Labelled a 'Siberian' division, it was formed from the Volga Military District in 1922, primarily recruiting soldiers from the north-east, which included the Western Siberian Oblasts (or Districts).

Polosukhin sought to get as far forward at Borodino as possible, to view his sector of the so-called 'Mozhaisk defensive line'. This fortified zone followed an arc from the small city of Volkalamsk in the north, crossed the 1812 Borodino battlefield west of Mozhaisk and extended south to the confluence of the Ugra and Oka rivers. It was about 143 miles wide and between 38 to 50 miles deep, but only 40 per cent of its foreseen bunkers and firing positions had been completed. Due to be manned by 150 battalions, only about forty-five were in situ. The Mozhaisk defensive line was the innermost of three shielding Moscow. The first at Vyazma and Bryansk had already been breached. Behind Mozhaisk was the Moscow Control Zone, comprising urban sectors prepared for the defence of the city itself. Some 200,000 of its residents were compulsorily called out and brought forward to build the Mozhaisk line, and had laboured for the past two months. The plan was that each defending battalion would be provided with four pillboxes housing 45mm guns, two with 76mm guns and twelve for machine guns, all able to fire on fixed lines. Sir John Russell, a member of the British Embassy staff, recalled the sheer extent of the effort, observing:

> This great tank trap they were digging outside Moscow, and one saw what looked like ants moving around, in fact the entire civil population of Moscow, every man, woman and child was out there digging.[2]

Trainloads of Moscow militia, factory workers and residents came out to Borodino, not as they did before the war to enjoy a traditional Sunday picnic, but to dig. Most of them were women. Seamstress Antonia Savina was conscripted several times to dig anti-tank ditches, sustained by a sausage and one small bread roll each day. She and the others slept in local clubs at nights and had to provide their own blankets and cushions. It was not long before she and they were infested with lice. Vasili Pronin, the Chairman of the Moscow City Council, remembered looking inside an anti-tank ditch on one occasion, where 'in glutinous mud, we saw about

50 wet figures'. Sliding down to talk with them, he discovered they were professional artists and workers from the Bolshoi and other Moscow theatres, with 'faces tired and wet'. They gathered around and 'all asked one thing only: What's happening at the front?' Sympathising with their plight, he offered to replace them with other more menial workers, but their indignant response was: 'Do you take us for deserters? It's worse at the front!' They assured him they were prepared to 'put up with everything, so long as our people can hold Moscow'.[3]

When Colonel Polosukhin reached the western end of the Borodino battlefield he observed the progress that these pressed labour gangs had made on the watercourses that ran broadly north to south. The Kolocha river, the Kamenka and Semenovska streams and the Voina and Stonets had their slopes steepened to create precipitous anti-tank traps. Hillocks and woods that had witnessed Napoleon's battle in 1812 had again been transformed into defence lines, this time with concrete bunkers as well as earth emplacements. Traversing the ground with binoculars from left to right, he picked out likely German approach routes. Some fifty-three concrete pillboxes, barbed-wire entanglements, seven minefields and 9 miles of anti-tank ditches had been erected to interdict and canalise these potential lines of advance.

It seemed likely that the Germans would approach his position in much the same way the French had done in 1812. Vulnerable points and gaps were identified from his map reconnaissance, in particular battalion areas labelled 8 to 14, from the village of Kovalyovo to the north of the Mozhaisk road, to Elnya straddling the Minsk highway to Moscow further south. There were no significant natural obstacles between battalion areas 28 and 29, around the villages of Artyomki and Tatarinovo, that might impede a panzer advance. Polosukhin had 23,000 men at his disposal, 14,500 from his own division and others from attached units, to hold a line that conventionally needed five more divisions to man. He accepted he could not cover all the defence zones, and concentrated on the main roads traversing the old Napoleonic battlefield. These were the Mozhaisk and Minsk highways and other likely tank approach routes.

John Russell, from the British Embassy, observing the defence preparations, remarked:

I think they did tap every emotional resource that was available to them. I remember for instance a lot of churches being opened again, which had been shut for a long time.

The Tsarist Russian commander Kututzov had similarly sought to inspire his men when he paraded the Icon of the Black Virgin from Smolensk before his assembled troops, to fire up religious fervour prior to battle in 1812. It was becoming increasingly apparent that the typical Red Army soldier was more prepared to fight for 'Mother Russia' than Comrade Premier Joseph Stalin. Polosukhin visited a concrete pillbox at the foot of the Raevsky redoubt where Tolstoy's fictional Pierre Bezukhov had witnessed bloody French assaults in September 1812. Grigouri Tokati, an Ossetian aeronautical engineer, summed up what likely went through the division commander's mind in October 1941, after so many military defeats:

In that very situation something else appeared among us, the tradition of Borodino. Borodino is the place where Napoleon was defeated, this suddenly released feelings appearing from nowhere that helped to unite people.[4]

In 1812 about 130,000 Frenchmen and their allies with 587 artillery pieces faced perhaps 150,000 Russians with 624 guns along a 2½- to 5-mile front in a climactic 'Battle of the Giants'. It is estimated that 100 artillery rounds boomed and 2,330 musket shots spat out each minute for up to ten hours. Men fell at the rate of 6,500 per hour, or about 108 men struck each minute. Three to four cannon and seventy-seven muskets fired each second to create an unbelievable level of noise. Figures are inconclusive, but available data suggests that 239 local village houses were destroyed during the battle and, in the summer of 1813, records show 52,048 corpses and 41,700 horse carcasses were recovered for burial.[5]

Napoleon attacked the Russian centre, despite identifying a weakness on the left. Colonel Polosukhin also had an exposed left; his right, as in 1812, was protected by the steep banks of the Kolocha river, freshly fortified with concrete bunkers. All he could do in 1941 was cover the two main roads approaching from the west, the same that Napoleon used.

Although they favoured an armoured approach, the woods that screened the front of his fortified zone would canalise the panzers. A further change was the railway line, constructed in the 1860s, which traversed the middle of Borodino field, just off centre from Napoleon's original line of attack in 1812. The railway track ran over embankments, through shallow cuttings and across swampy areas, mostly screened by trees, which tended to impede any north–south passage of armour.

After his initial reconnaissance, the commander of the 32nd Rifle Division likely appreciated that, like Kututzov in 1812, he was also fighting to bar the gates of Moscow to a western invader. The Germans were coming from broadly the same direction and the Russian defence would need to be conducted from similar locations. The forty memorial monuments and plinths erected, dedicated to units and individuals that fought in 1812, indicated as much. The historical Borodino Field Park established by the Tsar in 1912, which he was surveying, covered nearly 70 square miles.

Colonel Polosukhin also took the opportunity to stop by the old Borodino museum building, which had been opened by the Tsar during the first centenary celebration. He was probably the final formal visitor before its subsequent destruction. Museum staff were bustling about, urgently packing exhibits into cases, which were earmarked for transportation well to the rear at Alma-Ata in Kazakhstan. Staff regarded the grim-faced senior Red Army officer with some trepidation. He wrote something in the visitor's book before leaving. Curious, they checked the ledger and found, under the column 'Purpose of Visit', he had written:

I have come to defend the battlefield.[6]

PART ONE

THE APPROACH TO BORODINO

1

The Road by Vyazma

147 Miles to Moscow

The Vyazma Pocket, 6–8 October 1941

On 6 October 1941 the vanguard of the *Das Reich SS* Division was driving northwards along the road from Juchnow, towards Dubna and Gzhatsk. This minor road skirted the outline of a vast pocket coalescing around the trapped elements of the Soviet 16th, 19th, 20th and 30th armies to the west. Motorcyclists and four-wheeled light armoured cars were the first vehicles to appear, from the *Aufklärungs Abteilung* or Reconnaissance battalion. They paused repeatedly, observed the road ahead with binoculars, and drove off rapidly. These vehicles were the 'eyes' of the following advance, which as *SS Sturmmann* (Corporal) Helmut Günther remembered, 'simply had to be everywhere'. Günther, a veteran since the invasion of Yugoslavia, belonged to the division's *Kradschützen* or motorcycle battalion.

Behind them came a mix of *Kubelwagen* jeeps, light Krupp 1-ton *Schnauzer* trucks, so called because of their duckbill-shaped bonnets, medium Mercedez-Benz and Opel *Blitz* trucks towing anti-tank and infantry guns as well as medium trucks festooned with assault pioneers transporting engineer equipment. The *SS* soldiers, dressed in distinctive camouflage smock tunics, kept a wary eye to their left, where in the middle distance the front line sparkled, cracked and grumbled as Russian anti–tank guns duelled with panzers. 'That was what was so unnerving about this land and its people,' Günther recalled, 'suddenly danger would threaten from some place where one would least expect it.' Blazing villages produced distinctive smoke columns, curling languidly into the grey sky across a vast panorama of treetops, adding to the general obscuration over the *Kessel* 'cauldron' pocket, being steadily compressed on their left flank. *Stuka* dive-bombers circled overhead like vultures, monitoring the flashing, spluttering conflagration below.

Two *Sturmgeschütz* III self-propelled guns clattered by, followed closely by the first company vehicle packets from the *Reich* Infantry Regiment *Deutschland*. Groups of 1½-ton Mercedes and Krupp medium trucks roared by, some towing guns and trailers, all carrying *SS* infantry. Each company packet numbered two dozen or more vehicles. On board, the men complained of sore backsides, 'as if someone had rubbed pepper under my skin,' Günther complained. 'The stench of exhaust gases wiped out attentiveness and deadened nerves' as they bumped and jolted along. 'Just the 500 vehicles of our battalion alone made a fearsome racket,' remembered Günther.

Ten minutes later another column hove into sight. Mile-long traffic jams began to build up, following the 'pick-pock' sounds of skirmishing rifle fire ahead, interspersed with machine-gun bursts that sounded like ripping canvas. Nuisance strafing runs by suddenly appearing Red Air Force aircraft caused swarms of trucks and jeeps to race madly off the road. This caused delays before the line could be reassembled.

Vehicles were grossly overloaded. Not only did they expect to fight, the vanguard had to be logistically self-sufficient. 'You would not believe everything that we hauled along with us!' recalled Günther: behind the spare tyre on the sidecars 'were pots and skillets, which beat a wild tune during the movement!'

Here and there an accordion or guitar bore witness to the musical talents of the crew. The sidecars themselves were stuffed to overflowing with ammunition boxes, machine gun belts, hollow charges, hand grenades and similar novelty items. Then there was the personal gear of the crew. The rider in the sidecar had to perch with one ass cheek on the edge, because there was simply no other place left.

Günther remembered one motorcyclist wore a top hat: 'Where that guy had got it, heaven only knows.' Others sported red bandana neckerchiefs. 'No wonder that we were maligned as "gypsies" by starchy Wehrmacht officers who disapproved of such individual frippery.'[1]

The *Das Reich* Division had been tasked to skirt the east side of the Vyazma pocket and move north to cut the highway that led north-east to Moscow. Just north of the intersection was the town of Gzhatsk, which needed to be secured before an advance along the Moscow highway. *Panzergruppe* 3, which included the 6th and 7th Panzer Divisions alongside two motorised divisions, was engaged in a broad sweeping advance around the north, or other side, of the emerging Vyazma pocket. *Panzergruppe* 4, including the 10th Panzer Division, was leading the advance up from the south side to complete the encirclement. *Das Reich* would provide the motorised infantry cement needed to secure the panzer ring sealing the pocket. If not required, it was to continue the advance down the Moscow highway towards Borodino and Mozhaisk, 80 and 70 miles respectively from the Russian capital. A bridge sign erected by the 48th Pioneer Battalion across the Dvina river signposted the way 'to the last race' for the advancing 10th Panzer. They were nearly there. Operation *Typhoon*, the final and unexpected autumn German offensive on Moscow, was the final opportunity that year to take the capital and follow in Napoleon's footsteps.

The muddy road to Gzhatsk was beginning to fall apart under the constant procession of heavy vehicles. Trucks, despite the weather, were often open topped. The infantry inside observed the wood line to their left for signs of movement as well as scanning low cloud for signs of approaching Soviet aircraft. *SS Sturmmann* Ludwig Hümmer, with the 3rd Company of the 1st Battalion *Deutschland* Regiment, was a veteran of France and the Low Countries. This was his second day of driving with the vanguard. 'Often our column came to a halt,' he recalled, when the indicators of crumbling Soviet resistance to their left became ever more apparent. 'Some vehicle-borne enemy soldiers were surprised in our immediate vicinity by our rapid advance,' he recalled.

'They came directly at our column, mistaking us in our camouflaged jackets in the distance to be retreating Russians.' Once they realised their mistake, they turned about and drove back. 'But too late, there was no escape.' They were swept up by jeeps and motorcyclists, who pursued immediately 'and most gave up without any exchanges of fire once they appreciated the hopelessness of their situation'. Many Russian prisoners were taken and the captured vehicles added to the column.

'Once again we were in the middle of the action,' Hümmer reflected, 'when at that moment it had appeared so harmless.' The rest days after Kiev had been only too brief. They sensed they would not sit on their vehicles for long 'because in the distance we could already hear the sounds of fighting'. Rain had transitioned to sleet and then wet snow the day before. Operation *Typhoon* had begun optimistically enough five days before, with warm autumn sunshine on their backs. Now, as each vehicle passed, snow squalls cloaked churned-up muddy wheel ruts beneath a sanitising mantle of white.[2]

The road eventually became impassable for wheeled vehicles so Hümmer's company had to dismount and continued the advance on foot. They marched a further 6 miles through woods and small villages before halting at nightfall. 'Apparently leaderless Russians were roaming about in the area,' he remembered, 'and were picked up and made prisoner.' Eggs and potatoes, 'farmer's breakfast', were fried that night, during a welcome pause. All the evidence suggested the last Soviet line barring their approach to Moscow was crumbling. Next morning they were ordered to 'mount up' again on trucks, with some urgency, because 'we had to get to the Smolensk, Vyazma to Moscow highway,' Hümmer recalled, 'and in driving snow we climbed up and drove forward'. This time 'our battalion took over point' for the advance; they were the lead troops.[3]

'Providing security' for the advance was not, as Helmut Günther with the motorcycle battalion explained, 'something that smacks of guard duty'. The battalion was 'outfitted with substantial firepower':

> 'Security' usually meant combat against a numerically superior attacker who knew full well that he had found a soft spot and believed that he now held the trump cards in his hand. It was our outfit's mission to dispel that belief and enable the division to roll on in its mission unimpeded.

Like Napoleon's Imperial Guard, SS formations regarded themselves as a special elite. Volunteers came from all over Germany and at this stage of the war needed to prove untainted Aryan descent to their great grand-parents. Günther's recruit-training platoon, for example, came from every corner of the *Reich*, including young men from Pomerania, Swabia, the North Sea coast, the Ruhr Basin, the Rhine region, and as far removed as Transylvania, the Black Forest and Bavaria. Most joined not to shirk national duty, others did not want to be left out, and some were idealis-tic. Racial purity meant they were bound by blood and they considered themselves superior. The blood group tattooed on their upper arm signi-fied a tangible form of pseudo blood-brotherhood.

Uwe Timm researched his older brother Karl Heinz, who had joined the *SS*, after the war. He remembered him as an unremarkable, quiet, 'brave', steady lad, a sapper in the *Totenkopf* 'death's head' Division. His sparse one-line diary entries read mainly about waiting for action, loot and an acceptance that death and killing had become an everyday occur-rence. One brief entry recalled, 'Ivan 75 meters away is smoking cigarettes,' adding simply 'fodder for my machinegun'. This was less about being cal-lous, more an absence of empathy towards the deaths that were occurring regularly around them. Killing civilians who got in the way was rarely recorded because it was hardly noteworthy.

Modern conflict fought by democracies more recently show evi-dence of similar callous attitudes, often misinterpreted, because few today have experienced the rigours of military service beyond the era of mass conscription. Warfare for German soldiers during the Second World War, as often for the Allies, involved the adventure of pseudo military tourism. Bizarrely, this included killing the enemy, often in strangely exotic locations.

SS soldiers were not necessarily more politically motivated or indoctri-nated than their *Wehrmacht* counterparts: both were educated and raised within a National Socialist society. 'What did we know about the big politi-cal picture?' Helmut Günther asked rhetorically. His unit was as surprised as many others by the decision to invade the Soviet Union – making this a two-front war that had resulted in catastrophe during the First World War. 'Political indoctrination? Don't make me laugh!' Günther exclaimed:

We mostly read the newspapers to learn what film was playing in the city we were in or which watering hole had something going on.

When their more politically aware company commanders gathered them together on a Sunday morning to explain war news, 'the time was used to catch up on sleep behind the back of the man in front'. The typical *SS* trooper viewpoint of Russia was that it was huge, had immense grain and mineral resources, the people were obliging, the roads impassable, the weather terrible and it was plagued by lice and fleas. The East meant *Lebensraum*, 'living space', for retired veterans, who might settle after the war, like the ancient Roman Legionaries.[4]

There was often friction between *SS* and *Wehrmacht* army units. The classic *Wehrmacht* view was that the *SS* had an inflated view of their prowess, with 'fat head' officers leading unprofessional Nazi soldiers. The *SS* felt the *Wehrmacht* were the direct descendants of the Kaiser's Imperial Army, with all the negatives that implied: decrepit old generals and officers that had purchased commissions. *SS* military performance in Poland in 1939 was regarded as questionable. *SS* General Sepp Dietrich's *Leibstandarte* Regiment had to be rescued by a regular infantry regiment when surrounded by Polish forces at Pabianice. Their performance in France and the Low Countries was commendable, but offset by brutal atrocities, and the *SS* was still cold-shouldered by *OKW* (Supreme Command) after the campaign. By early 1941 the *SS* had expanded to six divisions. Ill will dogged army–*SS* relations in Yugoslavia and the Balkans, but a single *SS* officer had secured the Serbian capitulation of Belgrade with only a handful of men. By late 1941 the rigours of the *Barbarossa* campaign in Russia, the longest to date, was earning the *SS* grudging respect and more recently, following the southwards advance to Kiev, some praise.

The truth lay in between. At first the army mocked the *SS* camouflage tunics, labelling them 'tree frogs' and claiming they were inadequately trained. Conversely, the *SS* criticised the *Wehrmacht*'s lukewarm morale, which was becoming a factor in this bloody campaign of attrition. Bravery might be measured in casualties, and in this the *SS* were considered 'bullish' extremists, carrying on missions regardless of cost. Analysis of casualty figures, however, suggests *SS* casualties were broadly similar to *Wehrmacht* panzer divisions and *Luftwaffe Fallschirmjäger* (Paratrooper) units. The 10th Panzer Division lost 12 per cent of its strength in the first five weeks of the Russian campaign: a total of 1,778 men. The *Deutschland* Regiment of *Das Reich* lost a similar proportion: 1,519 men from the start of the invasion to the eve of Operation *Typhoon*. The army suspected the *SS* were beginning to receive better equipment, vehicles and rations as well as a preponderance of the best 'human material' for its recruits. Yet certain elite *Wehrmacht* units like the *Grossdeutschland*, the *Luftwaffe Fallschirmjäger* and the *Hermann Göring* Panzer Division also received like privileges.[5]

The intense bloodletting of the Russian campaign brought the two sides closer together. *SS* soldiers defined the *Waffen-SS* as being an integral part of the ruling national party, whereas army units saw the *Wehrmacht* as part of the division of power in German society. Such differences, however, became irrelevant during the day-to-day business of simply staying alive on the Russian front. The official history of the 10th Panzer Division records that troops of the *SS Reich* Division became 'old acquaintances' due to the frequency with which they had fought and bled together after the invasion's launch on the Bug river to Jelnya, a particularly hard fought attritional engagement on the edge of the Smolensk pocket. 'As a result,' according to a 10th Panzer account, 'an unspoken comradeship had developed between the men of the two units.' This was about to be reforged. Whenever the two units came together on operations 'they knew that they could depend on their neighbours'.[6]

Napoleon took just over seventy days to reach Vyazma, whereas Hitler's *Wehrmacht* needed almost 100 days. The Germans were involved in intense costly fighting the moment they crossed the line of the Bug river on 22 June 1941. Napoleon, by contrast, marched and manoeuvred after crossing the Nieman river, reached by the *Wehrmacht* on their first day. He successfully blocked a union of the two primary Western Russian armies led by Generals Barclay de Tolly and Bagration, but was unable to bring either successfully to battle. Successive rearguard actions kept Napoleon at arm's length. By contrast, the Germans fought a series of encircling actions which inflicted 3 to 4 million casualties on the Russians at a cost of half a million to the invasion force of 3.6 million men. The average experience of the *Grand Armée* soldier up to Vyazma was to march through a landscape devastated by 'scorched-earth' measures inflicted by the retreating Tsarist armies. German soldiers in 1941 ironically spent more time defending rather than attacking during their advance. This was because short sharp manoeuvres to encircle Soviet armies became hard-fought defensive engagements to keep them inside thereafter. The Germans had, moreover, to face in two directions, first to contain Soviet forces inside the pockets and then to fight off rescue attempts from outside, often at the same time.

Although the encirclement battles leading to the two rings at Vyazma and Bryansk in early October 1941 were conducted by fully motorised panzer and infantry troops, these represented just under 30 per cent of the total Army Group Centre strength. Overall the invading German army in 1941 was only 22 per cent mechanised, the remainder being marching foot infantry supported by horse-drawn artillery and logistics. As for Napoleon, the momentum of *Blitzkrieg* or so-called 'Lightning War' depended upon the speed of marching man and the horse. Only these foot-borne infantry divisions, supported by the real 'killers' of the campaign – the division and corps horse-drawn artillery – possessed the combat power needed to overwhelm the Soviet pockets. Unlike the previous experience in Poland, the West and the Balkans, the Russians once surrounded chose not to surrender, but to fight to the death.

Ironically, Napoleon's *Grande Armée* made better time in 1812. Hitler's *Blitzkrieg* reached Smolensk, covering a remarkable 412 miles in twenty-seven days, compared with Napoleon's fifty-four. But by the time both armies were approaching Vyazma, at about the 500-mile point, the Germans had diverted south to the Ukraine, to reduce the massive Kiev pocket, and were some thirty days behind. What Napoleon's forces were not able to replicate was the speed of the vehicle-borne panzer and motorised infantry vanguards, which were able, with *Luftwaffe* air ascendency, to speedily bypass and surround Soviet formations.

As the *Das Reich* Division was moving north towards the key arterial highway linking Minsk and Smolensk to Moscow during the first week of October, it skirted the developing pocket on the east side. Nine panzer and motorised divisions were completing a double encirclement at Vyazma, netting six Soviet armies, and at Bryansk, where they contained another three. Eventually twenty-five German infantry divisions had to march up to coil python-like around and squeeze the life out of these trapped Russian divisions. This tied up most of the combat power of German Army Group Centre, leaving just half a dozen mobile divisions to press on to Moscow 147 miles away. Each of these mobile divisions had start states of about 16,800 men and 2,400 vehicles, representing ten to fifteen times more combat power, man for man, than the 1812 Napoleonic equivalents.

At daybreak on 2 October, the 10th Panzer Division with *Panzergruppe* 4 began its encirclement operation with an assault crossing of the Desna river, a tributary of the Dnieper. Thrusting rapidly deep into the Soviet lines, its battle groups soon found themselves spread over 60 miles of roads that were deteriorating rapidly in rain and sleet. Lack of fuel and blown bridges and other crossing points unable to support armour further slowed momentum. It formed the south side of the pocket, aiming to swing north to link with the 7th Panzer Division from *Panzergruppe* 3, attacking south and east beyond Vyazma. Both sought to cut the Moscow highway link and trap Soviet Marshal Timoshenko's Western Front armies inside the pocket.

As darkness fell during the evening of 6 October, a reinforced tank platoon from the 10th Panzer unexpectedly burst into the southern suburbs of Vyazma and seized the bridges leading into the city. Another panzer company rushed up to secure this coup to develop and reinforce the vulnerable bridgeheads gained. At 7.30 a.m. the division's II Panzer *Abteilung* (battalion) drove through the city itself and captured the bridge spanning the Vyazma river on the north-west side. Within ninety minutes they had reached the bridge ramp and began cautiously observing grey vehicles and tanks they saw on the opposite bank. On closer examination through binoculars it became apparent they were likely German. White recognition flares shot up from both sides, followed by relieved handshaking on the bridge with the men from the 7th Panzer battle group. The huge pocket was finally sealed.

'I was 15 years when the Fascists came,' remembered Alexander Igorowitsch Kristakow, living with his parents in a small village near Vyazma. 'We had geese, hens, two pigs and a cow, not much, but enough for us to live, and we were satisfied,' he recalled. When the first air attacks started he helped with the evacuation of the village cattle to a nearby collective at Gorki. 'Time and time again the Germans shot us up in low-level strafing attacks,' but 'I was lucky and managed to return to the village'.

Life changed irreversibly at the beginning of October 'when the Germans came and first of all took all the geese and hens away and scoffed the lot'. Both pigs and the cow – all they had left – were taken in 1942. Vyazma had a population of about 35,000 when the Germans marched in, living in 5,500 houses. After it was liberated on 13 March 1943 only

5,000 inhabitants remained sheltering in fifty-one houses. Alexander Kristakow detonated a German mine the day after the liberation and was blinded. This interview was conducted wearing dark glasses.[7]

Eighteen-year-old Soviet artilleryman Viktor Strazdovski's unit, trapped inside the pocket, was equipped with 60mm guns, 'trophies left from World War I,' he recalled, and 'they didn't have modern sighting devices'. His gun crew had only one rifle between five soldiers. The dramatic loss of Kiev in the southern Ukraine just weeks before had left them bewildered and fearful:

> We simply kept wondering why our army was surrendering one town after another. It was a real tragedy. It's difficult to express in words how we lived through that.

Strazdovski had only just joined his artillery unit, which was badly equipped and poorly trained. Their rapid and unexpected envelopment within the new pocket meant 'we were face to face with the Germans, and we had to use these primitive weapons in actual combat'. They were hardly confident at the likely outcome.

Unteroffizier Ludwig Horn, a 22-year-old NCO in charge of a six-man gun crew, was with Artillery Regiment 90 from the 10th Panzer Division. They were confident and closed up fast against the trapped Soviet troops. 'I enjoyed the strength of our army,' he recalled at the outset of the invasion at the Bug river, 'sending thousands of shells into the Russian border defences.' He shared the view of many of his countrymen that they were racially, technically and tactically superior to the Soviets. 'It was partly,' he explained, 'a great feeling about power being unleashed against a dubious and despicable enemy.'

The campaign thus far had been an exhilarating succession of victories. The disintegration of complete Soviet units around the Vyazma pocket appeared to confirm and magnify their feeling of innate technological ascendency. 'When I was sent to the place where the Germans broke our defence line, you can imagine how we felt,' recalled Viktor Strazdovski, 'we felt we were doomed.'

'The Russians didn't believe we would attack at this time of the year,' *Feldwebel* (Sergeant) Karl Fuchs with the 7th Panzer Division wrote to his new wife, 'when the cold weather is settling in.' Rising ground fog, a consequence of rain and sleet, obscured visibility inside the pocket.

'Once the fog lifted from the valley, we really let them have it with every barrel,' Fuchs recalled. 'Tanks, anti-aircraft guns, trucks and the infantry fired on everything in sight.'

'There were four of us,' Soviet artilleryman Strazdovski remembered:

with two rifles between us, and we didn't know in which direction we would run into the Germans. The woods around us were ablaze. On the one hand we couldn't disobey our order, but on the other hand we felt doomed.

Walter Schaefer-Kehnert, an officer with the 11th Panzer Division, regarded the low-level mist hanging eerily over the valley below from high ground to the east of the pocket. 'When the fog came up it was like a herd of men and vehicles coming up by the thousand,' he recalled, 'and it made your blood freeze.'

Russian vehicles were bogged down in the swampy conditions below. 'Then the people came on to us like a herd of sheep.' He shouted to his men, 'Let them come, let them get nearer, let them come on!' They held fire until the last moment before ripping the approaching masses of men apart with concentrated 20mm cannon and machine-gun fire.

'What happened there is like a mincing machine,' remembered Strazdovski, 'when people are sent to a sure death, unarmed to fight a well trained army.'[8]

Ludwig Horn was ecstatic at the fearful destruction their artillery was wreaking on the pocket. 'We could all communicate all the time easily,' he explained, so each descending salvo was calculated mathematically. 'It was one big advantage,' he explained, 'that the attack was so co-ordinated.'

This was to be the last *Blitzkrieg* success, fast-moving panzer groups supported by motorised infantry and artillery, under the umbrella of overwhelming *Luftwaffe* air superiority. Columns of blazing vehicles and seemingly panic-stricken assaults by infantry to break through, led to desperate bizarrely fought actions, as the loose German perimeters attempted to contain break-out attempts. Horn witnessed 'waves and waves of advancing soldiers' coming at them:

The first row was mown down, then the second bent down and took
up the guns of the dead and continued to move forward until they were
mown down also.

The irrational attacks were 'incredible for us, but it seemed normal for
them,' he claimed. It promoted an arrogant feeling of dispassionate dis-
dain among the German defenders, who regarded these senseless suicide
attacks as inhuman. Horn was wounded by splinters from a Soviet hand
grenade when they ambushed a Russian truck. The dismounting Russians
rushed at them with bayonets and he 'threw my hand grenades' and 'shot
them from the hip'. Tensed up, they saw that some of the Russians had
crouched petrified behind their truck, playing dead. 'Hands up!' they
shouted, but got no response. 'We started shooting them, naturally,' and,
'under the impact of the bullets they wavered and shook a bit,' but refused
to surrender. 'We shot them all,' he recalled.

Such behaviour from the Soviets was incomprehensible. 'They are
cowards,' Horn rationalised, 'they didn't deserve any better anyhow.' He
believed he killed perhaps twenty to thirty Red Army men during this
skirmish, 'the most exciting night of his life'.

'No German soldier would have attacked without any weapon,' he
insisted. 'We would never have done that, crouching and doing nothing.'
Ironically, if the Russians had surrendered, they would likely not have
survived. Horn's lieutenant ordered the prisoners to be shot – equally
incomprehensible he thought. Not only was this action 'un-chivalrous',
it was 'stupid' because 'Russians hiding in the forest might have seen the
prisoners being shot and so they might fight better the next time.'[9]

Fuchs remembered the grim fight with some alacrity, because his battalion had to cling precariously to the ridges west of Vyazma 'with great
tenacity'. They were committed against heavy superior KV or T-34 Soviet
tank types.

'Wherever there is a hot spot,' he wrote to his father, also serving on
the Russian front, 'we appear like ghosts' wreathed in the prevailing fog
'and engage the enemy in battle', It was a costly struggle: 'My brave young
friend Roland just died of severe wounds,' he wrote to his wife. 'Why did
he have to give his life now, with the end practically in sight?'

Having witnessed the total collapse of between seven and nine armies, German soldiers advancing on Moscow began to feel the Russians would never recover from this. 'The battle of Vyazma is over,' Fuchs assured his wife, 'and the last elite troops of the Bolsheviks have been destroyed.' Ivan, in his opinion, was finished.

Leutnant Schaefer-Kehnert, overlooking the devastated, noticed:

Some Russian girls – I will never forget them – in trousers dressed like soldiers. They got in a cart, with a horse, and had a barrel of water and then went around giving water to the dying Russian soldiers lying on that field … They were lying there by the thousand, like the battlefield of old history.

'A life wasn't worth much for the Russians,' he surmised, echoing Horn's view, who concluded, 'Their deaths were not taken as seriously as with us.' Like the majority of German soldiers, 'We were of the belief that there shouldn't be much left of the Red Army now.'

Ludwig Horn was a keen photographer and went on to explore the town of Vyazma. He took enough pictures to later fill nine photograph albums with *Kriegs errinerungen*, or wartime memories, of Russia and other campaigns. He took a snap of two German infantrymen passing Lenin's statue delivering a symbolic oration in the main square, while keeping a watchful eye out for snipers. 'Most civilians seem to have evacuated,' he observed beneath the photo caption. 'I can find a clean shirt I can use, but nothing useful, and nothing to eat.' Pickings were sparse.

The way to Moscow, now only 147 miles away, seemed open. Fuchs, regarding the carnage, believed, 'From now on, their opposition will not be comparable to previous encounters.' They had defeated the last armies of the Red Army standing before Moscow: 673,000 prisoners and 1,300 tanks were taken, more than at Kiev a few weeks before. 'All we have to do now,' Fuchs assured his young wife, 'is to roll on, for the opposition will be minor.' He looked forward to getting back home; he had not yet seen his newborn son, and never would. When he dispatched these letters home he had barely a month to live.[10]

'A feast of Church Towers', Vyazma, 29–31 August 1812

Napoleon's *Grand Armée* in 1812 was about a calendar month ahead of
the *Wehrmacht*'s 1941 progress when it approached Vyazma in stifling heat.
Private Jakob Walter, marching with the German Württemberg contingent
in Marshal Ney's III Corps, recalled their tortuous progress, 'because the
closed ranks forced all to go in columns; and the heat and dust flared up
into our eyes as if from smoking coal heaps'. The weather had been hot
and sultry since they had left Smolensk ten days before. Napoleon's aide,
Phillipe-Paul *Comte de* Ségur, described how 'our army was crossing the
broad plains of the province of Vyazma marching at top speed across the
fields, several regiments abreast'. This claustrophobic formation required
the infantry to march in short compact columns, as many as eighty men
abreast. The road alongside was for the exclusive use of hundreds of horse-
drawn wagons and artillery caissons, which churned it into a fine powdery
dust. Masses of cavalry likewise raised huge suffocating clouds of dust as
they trailed past the compacted infantry, screening them on both sides.
Jakob Walter's original company of about 100 Württembergers was reduced
to just twenty-five men on leaving Smolensk. Spare shirts and underwear
had long since been jettisoned by the men in the intense heat, which did
not augur well for the approaching autumn and winter. 'The march up to
there,' on nearing Vyazma, he recalled, 'as far as it was a march is indescribable, and inconceivable for people who have not seen anything of it.'[11]

Captain Heinrich von Brandt, a Polish officer with the 2nd Vistula
Regiment, recalled, 'The heat was extreme,' and, 'furious gusts of wind
swirled up such dense clouds of dust that often we could no longer see the
great trees which lined the road'.

'The main Moscow road we were on is sandy,' remembered
Captain Girod de l'Ain with the 4th Division:

> and the army marching in several serried columns abreast, raised such
> clouds of dust that we could not see one another two yards away and our
> eyes, ears and nostrils were full of it, and our faces encrusted.

The thirst was so bad, 'will you believe me,' he insisted, 'when I say that
I saw men lying on their bellies to drink horse's urine in the gutter'.

Poor visibility dogged the column progress constantly. Lieutenant Karl von Suckow, with the Württemberg Guard, remembered they stationed a drummer 'to beat the drum all the time' to prevent exhausted soldiers from taking the wrong turning. 'This fact alone will indicate just how dense the clouds of dust were.'

The *Grand Armée* advanced its corps in diamond formation, space permitting, with one division marching at point, two following on the flanks and the fourth division coming up in reserve. This meant a two-division front could face any unexpected appearance of the enemy. The infantry suffered considerably in the midst of these huge marching columns. As von Brandt explained:

> The constant burning dust was a real torment. So as to protect at least their eyes, many soldiers improvised dark spectacles out of bits of window glass. Others carried their shakos under their arms and wrapped a handkerchief round their heads, tearing only a hole large enough for seeing the way and breathing. Others made garlands of foliage.

Jakob Walter complained 'the dust was like a thick fog' exacerbated by 'the closed line of march in columns, and the putrid water from holes filled with dead people' and 'eye pains, fatigue, thirst and hunger tormented everybody'.[12]

Marching through Russia had been more costly than a series of battles. Napoleon pushed his armies hard, seeking by a succession of manoeuvres to bring the separated retreating Russian armies to decisive battle. The only strategic success to date was in preventing a union of the two main Russian Western armies before Smolensk. There were no pitched battles; the French columns were always kept at arm's length by repeated short, sharp and bitterly contested Russian rearguard actions. The huge invading force that crossed the Nieman river on 24 June had shrivelled from over half a million men to around 190,000 by the time they left Smolensk. The *Grande Armée* had withered, dissipated by the need to hive off forces to garrison depots, protect its flanks as it penetrated deeper into Russia, and screen the main advance. Most men had simply succumbed to terrain and weather. Lance Corporal Wilhelm Heinemann, with the Brunswick Chasseurs, had begun to notice: 'Up to now we'd been marching in the van with the strongest, who'd no inkling of what a dissolving army looks like.' Accidentally shot in the foot, he was now hobbling at the rear and appreciated:

> These were no longer the same columns. Already they were beaten men, looking only for a spot on this foreign soil to lie down and die.

Now, as the weary columns trudged by, he realised the physical change that had come over the army:

> First came the strongest, and then the weaker, then others whose strength was almost at an end. And last of all the dying, dragging themselves along at the tail. If any sank down, the thick dust soon covered him like a pall over a bier.

The army was visibly disintegrating. Bread was scarce and the intermittent supplies of food provided through foraging came from captured livestock and what could be found in peasant houses or dug up from the fields. Jakob Walter described how 'most of the men could no longer digest pure meat, diarrhoea seized many, and they had to be abandoned'. Water was often drawn from swamp pools. Holes were sunk 3ft deep and brackish water extracted amid swarms of midges, mosquitoes and flies. 'The water was very warm,' Walter recalled, heated by bacterial decomposition, and was 'reddish brown with millions of little red worms'. The only way it could be consumed was 'bound in linen and sucked through the mouth', with predictable consequences. Major Heinrich von Roos, the senior doctor with the Württemberger Chasseurs, cast a professional eye over the ownership of campsites belonging to the retreating Russian army and compared them to their own. 'The excreta left by men and animals behind the Russian front indicted a good state of health,' he observed. 'Whereas ours [showed] the clearest signs that the entire army, men and horses alike, must have been suffering from diarrhoea.'[13]

On 29 August, thumping cannon reports up ahead heralded the arrival of Marshal Joachim Murat's cavalry vanguard, ahead of Marshal Davout's I Corps, at Vyazma. The rest of the army following up heard the familiar sounds of yet another rearguard action, the intensity of firing suggesting intermittent skirmishing rather than a pitched battle. The town's population of between 10,000 and 15,000 lay alongside the serpentine Vyazma river, seated on a plateau that dominated the surrounding valleys and gullies and the defile through which the Moscow road passed. Since Smolensk, Jakob Walter had become accustomed to a bleak road where 'the war displayed its horrible work of destruction':

> All the roads, fields, and woods lay as though sown with dead people, horses, wagons, burned villages and cities.

The Russians appeared to be pursuing a 'scorched-earth' policy as they withdrew. 'Everything looked like the complete ruin of all that lived,' Walter recalled, but the town coming into view appeared different. Chasseur Lieutenant Maurice de Tascher thought the settlement 'a superb town, which at a distance appears to be a feast of church towers'. The countryside nearing Moscow appeared more prosperous. Césare de Laugier, with Prince Eugène's IV Corps, enthusiastically counted thirty-two spires; none of them had 'seen anything so beautiful or inviting since Vitebsk', now a month past. There was some dismay, therefore, when smoke began to rise and shroud the golden domes of the oriental churches and convents. Albrecht Adam, with Eugène's staff, watched the fires take hold. 'Although we were by now used to seeing such sights,' he admitted, 'we could not help but be overwhelmed by a sense of pity on this unfortunate city of 10,000 souls.' Two battalions of the 25th Line were dispatched into the city to fight the flames, much enthused at the prospect of being the first in to loot.[14]

General Armand de Caulaincourt, Napoleon's Grand Equerry, entered the city the following day with the Emperor. 'Several people believed,' he recalled, 'that this burning of the towns and villages we entered was due as much to the disorderly conduct of our advance guard as to the rearguard of the Cossacks, who did not spare Russia.' The sharp engagement with the Russian rearguard had given the Cossacks the opportunity to ignite many fires. The civilian population fled towards Moscow, swelling the vast numbers of refugees already surging towards the capital. This unheralded Russian behaviour was incomprehensible. Until now it was thought the incendiary measures were not ordered or prepared in advance. Napoleon dismissively joked about 'these people who burn their houses in order to prevent us from sleeping a night there'. Yet the ominous behaviour was beginning to depress the soldiers. 'Everybody was struck by the fact,' de Caulaincourt observed. They inspired 'solemn reflections which these terrible measures provoked, about the results and length of a war in which the enemy was making such sacrifices from the very start'.[15]

The first mass civilian deaths had occurred at Smolensk, during the assault and burning of the city. The crossing of the Dnieper river signified entry into the Russian heartland, raising patriotic and nationalist fervour. Nobody had successfully invaded Russia this far since the Mongols and Tatars, 300 years ago. Atrocities and excesses committed by the *Grande Armée's* foraging robber bands, left, right and ahead of the orderly marching columns, turned native serfs against the French. Revolutionary fervour, previously exported by France, fell on the deaf ears of a peasantry who could neither read nor write. Some 30,000 starving deserters scattered as far back as Minsk were violently pillaging a peasantry who increasingly fought back. Members of Jakob Walter's company had fired on a group of fifty peasants who had rushed them during a foraging expedition near Plotsk. 'What could we do but shoot at them?' he asked ruefully. The local peasants used ingenious ploys to hide their supplies. He remarked disingenuously:

> If they had voluntarily removed the simple covers, much of the household furniture would have remained unspoiled, for it was necessary to raise the floors and the beams in order to find anything and to turn upside down everything that was covered.

The invading French Army was likened to a swarm of locusts. Ensign Rafail Mikhaylovich Zotov, with the St Petersburg Militia, recalled 'outrage at the audacious invasion of the foreigners', and that 'on the streets, in every community, in the family circle, there was no other topic of conversation but the "people's war"'.[16]

Both Napoleon and later Hitler were much influenced by their previous victories over the Russians, both feeling they knew the psyche of the ordinary Russian soldier. Napoleon's experience of the Russian debacle at Austerlitz in 1805 influenced his perceptions like Hitler's view of the lacklustre Soviet performance against the Finns during the 1939–40 Winter War. The Führer was convinced that the poor performance of the Red Army during the summer frontier *Blitzkrieg* meant one more 'kick in the door' would bring down the whole Jewish-tainted Bolshevik edifice 'like a pack of cards'. Both the Tsarist and the Soviet Russian soldiers were enigmatic figures.

Major General Sir Robert Wilson, serving as the British military commissioner with the 1812 Russian Headquarters, felt he knew the Russian soldier well. 'The infantry,' he recalled, 'is generally composed of athletic men between the ages of 18 and 40, endowed with great bodily strength' and 'inured to the extremes of weather and hardship'. He could march days and nights on the 'scantiest food' with six hours on the road against four of rest. He was 'ferocious, but disciplined' and 'obstinately brave', being totally 'devoted to their sovereign, their chief, and their country'.

Wilson thought them admirable soldiers 'possessing all the energetic characteristics of a barbarian people with the advantages engrafted by civilization'. It was not enough to simply kill Russians, British soldiers later discovered in the Crimea: 'you had to knock them down as well'. Lieutenant Ilya Radozhitsky, with a light artillery company retreating through 'unbearable summer heat', believed:

Our men and horses endured these hardships better than the enemy since they were born in this particular climate and were accustomed to a rough life.

Like many of his Russian contemporaries, Radozhitsky was dispirited by the constant withdrawals: 'No matter how strong Russian spirits were, their physical strength was sapped from continuous exertion.' Trudging along the sandy tracks and roads and wading swamps, like the pursuing *Grande Armée*, 'could wear soldiers out and leave considerable numbers of the fatigued stragglers to the enemy'. Despite his misgivings, Russian rearguards seemed to efficiently sweep them up. Russian General Peter Bagration, commanding the Second Western Army, was dismayed at the seeming national betrayal the long retreat suggested. 'Honest to God,' he confessed to the Chief of Staff of the First Army to his north, 'I feel sick and cannot breathe out of anguish, misery and embarrassment.' Lieutenant Radozhitsky lamented, 'The retreat of our two armies from the borders of the empire to Smolensk allowed the enemy to seize a vast territory, some 530 miles wide, almost without a fight.'

'I am ashamed to be wearing this uniform,' Bagration admitted, 'honest to God, and I am sick because of it.' He vowed to leave the army after this.[17]

One of Marshal Berthier's aides, Colonel François Lejeune, had come to admire the effectiveness of the Russian rearguards, which 'withdrawing in admirable good order', tended 'to defend all positions that offer any advantage'. This meant advancing French cavalry had to constantly form and reform and shake out into attack columns supported by artillery, 'which only conquered a little ground after exchanging many discharges of grape and attacks with the sabre'.

Whatever preconceived notions Napoleon may have had about the Russian fighting man, the lower ranks in the *Grande Armée* were starting to realise he was a formidable adversary. Delaying tactics 'meant a lot of time was being consumed in making but little progress,' Lejeune commented. The Russians were steadily wearing them down. Albrecht Adam, with Eugène's staff, recalled a Russian prisoner brought into IV Corps Headquarters, who 'by his singular conduct, attracted universal attention'. He was totally unabashed, displaying 'pluck as almost bordered on temerity'. Not unsurprisingly, he absconded the first night.[18]

For many Russian soldiers, the French invasion was not just a galvanising national call to arms; it also represented a personal catastrophe. The service term was twenty-five years and conscript families knew that, short of a miracle, they would never see their menfolk again. Recruits had their foreheads and beards shaved to mark ownership by the military, which also proved illegitimacy should they desert. Soldier Pamfil Nazarov admitted he 'cried bitter tears' at 'the terrible news' of his conscription. Ivan Menshoy, drafted into the Leib-Guard Dragoon Regiment, echoed 'how terrible was that minute!' 'I remember how my family wept, and my sister Pelagoya cried the most.'

Family celebrations on departure were conducted as a form of wake. It was the worst thing that could happen. Family bonds cemented society together, psychologically as well as for physical wellbeing. 'Tears flowed for three days before my departure for Tula,' the recruit assembly point,

Menshoy remembered. He reflected on the common saying among serfs, 'that the gates to the soldiery were wide, but the gates to the return were narrow'. Allegiance to family shifted to the regiment, the new provider that underpinned sustenance and life. It was this emotive bond, as strong as family, that lay at the core of the fighting qualities of the Russian soldier.[19]

Despite the long retreat that gave up vast tracts of Russian territory, the average Russian soldier was in better physical and psychological shape than his *Grande Armée* counterparts. Young artillery Lieutenant Ilya Radozhitsky, with the 11th Artillery Brigade, recalled, 'We received news that the French army was already suffering from a major lack of supplies.' By contrast, their own 'provisions were in abundance, and the canteen keepers even satisfied our whims for luxury products'. Even so, 'We frequently encountered fatigued horses collapsing on the road and, in swampy places, several of them lay together,' holding up the artillery train. Anton Antonovskii, an officer with the 26th *Jäger* Regiment, was able to purloin 'ample spirits' for his men on the line of march 'which rejuvenated our soldiers':

> They forgot the weight of their loads, the exhausting marches, and by their talk scorned the imminent danger. Singing broke out in our ranks. The more fanciful started dancing, entertaining themselves and cheering up the others.

Conditions could have been worse. Pamfil Nazarov, on the march with the Finland Regiment, recalled, 'We were given carts for our muskets and knapsacks, but the rest of our kit was ours to carry.'

'As we abandoned the countryside to the enemy,' Radozhitsky remembered, 'we intentionally devastated it to make it more difficult for the enemy to live off it,' because 'marching in our wake, they certainly would have been desperate for provisions'. Everything that had to be left behind was systematically destroyed:

> We mercilessly trampled the tall and dense green grains of various kinds. Our infantry marching always in divisional columns on both sides of the road left behind a wide trail of trampled and devastated crops. The army left behind it entire stretches of land that were as if they had been scorched by terrible bolts of lightning.

Cossacks burned whatever was left.[20]

The *Grande Armée* that crossed the Nieman river in June with half a million men was an amalgam of many of the nations that made up nineteenth-century Europe. As many as twenty different languages were spoken in its ranks, which included Prussians, Austrians, Poles, Italians, Bavarians, Westphalians, Croats, Dalmatians, Saxons, Württembergers, Spanish and Portuguese regiments and even Mameluke cavalry from Egypt. Hitler similarly cloaked the *Wehrmacht* in a form of pseudo pan-Europeanism in 1941. The invasion was rationalised as a 'crusade' to cleanse the East from Bolshevik–Soviet communism. Italians, Romanians and Hungarians participated in Operation *Barbarossa*, and the Spanish Blue Division earmarked for the Moscow front had only just been diverted towards Leningrad. Nordic Dutch, French and Belgian volunteers back home were being actively recruited for the fight against World Bolshevism.

Napoleon's invasion force in 1812 contained some 250,000 French national troops. Conscription had dampened the ardour of the previous French revolutionary armies and the new men were not the equals of the soldiers at Austerlitz in 1805, who had extensively trained at Boulogne in 1803, waiting for the postponed invasion of England. Napoleon had already eaten into his capital of conscripted manpower reserves by 1812. Major C.F.M. le Roy, with the 85th Line, recalled his battalion 'consisted entirely of young soldiers needing a lot of care', and many of them had already fallen out of the line of march. Cavalry General Count Dejean, who raised 40,000 new troopers from Alsace, felt they were too full of striplings and complained to Napoleon, 'Half of them hadn't the necessary vigour to wield a sabre.'

'But for your Majesty's express orders,' he confessed, 'I'd have sent them back to the depots.'

Veterans were scarcer. 'You could make them out by the martial cast of their features,' observed Napoleon's aide de Ségur:

> and the way they talked. War was the only thing they remembered and it was all they could look forward to. They had no other topic of conversation.

It was generally the veterans and natural survivors – practical men who could look after themselves in the field – that had managed to march this far. Survival was virtually by natural selection. Watching the 2nd Vistula cross the Nieman at the outset of the campaign, Napoleon remarked, 'I find these young men too young,' adding, 'What I need is people who can stand the fatigues. Men who're too young only fill the hospitals.'[21]

Despite the pan-European character of the *Grande Armée*, its soldiers served their Emperor well or indifferently. Jakob Walter, with the Württemberg contingent, had little to do with French glories, or Polish or Russian patriotism. Napoleon perceptively appreciated the Germans were reluctant allies, and after this campaign they would rise against him. Walter's diary makes no political comment about the invasion; like the infantry generally, he is indifferent. The entries are about the hardships and dangers they all faced; all he wanted to do was safely return home. Like the *Wehrmacht*'s slightly superior view of its allies in 1941, French soldiers were, as Württemberg Lieutenant Heinrich Vossler observed, 'apt to regard their comrades of the Rhenish Federation with a good deal of condescension'.

A German officer serving in Russia in 1941 could just as equally have written Vossler's diary comments. The passage through Poland was described as 'wretched' and 'desolate', with villages 'whose houses resembled our pig-sties back at home' disfiguring the landscape. He remarked on the 'all pervading filth [that] encrusted practically every peasant dwelling'.

In 1812 there was friction with the French from the very beginning. 'We had been warned repeatedly to avoid quarrels with them' but 'encounters occurred'. On one occasion Vossler remembered French conscripts, 'apparently to try the Germans' patience, might have provoked a serious incident but for the firmness [with] which our admirable Sergeant Major Beck handled the situation'.[22]

The point at issue was the masterful way French veterans and soldiers foraged the countryside, often to the detriment of their foreign allies. German brigade commander General von Scheler, in Ney's Corps, reckoned 'the French soldier revealed an extraordinary knack' of methodically looting while on marauding detachments, providing 'for the good of his comrades, while almost ignoring his own welfare'. This was accomplished speedily and efficiently, even if it cost a night's rest. German detachments, by contrast, were not so well organised or led, 'so the soldier, left to his own devices, thought first of filling his own belly when he found something to eat'. This was not the best way to survive in the field. They were too slow and 'wanted to cook everything properly' instead of snatching 'quick refreshment'. 'After twelve hours on guard duty, he wanted to sleep for another twelve,' consequently never catching up with his regiment. He 'turned marauder and stayed in the rear, or else threw his booty away to lighten the load', which meant re-joining the regiment with nothing. French veterans appreciated the Russians were not the only enemy. 'We are all very keen that the Russians should stand and fight,' wrote infantry Lieutenant Charles Fare with the Imperial Guard. 'So far they have made war only on our legs and our stomachs.' The Germans were losing this fight. Von Scheler accepted 'the temperament of the German soldier was not suited to conducting this foraging with the same cunning speed, self-sacrifice and camaraderie' as their French allies, 'when swift marches and few halts were customary'. It was the robust and field-savvy soldiers that had got as far as Vyazma.[23]

The deeper the French penetrated Russia, the more ominous the lack of concerted resistance. 'Whenever a house is found it is empty and dark,' recalled Westphalian infantryman Johann Andreas Wärncke as he approached Vyazma:

All is burnt and the Russian has carried off all subjects, as they had such a fear of us, and there is no food to be found because nobody is to be found in any town.

'The countryside adjoining the main road, along which our army was advancing was deserted even before we arrived,' Lieutenant Heinrich Vossler recalled. 'We found no supplies or provisions of any kind.'

'Not a soul in sight,' echoed Lieutenant von Suckow. It had been so since crossing the Nieman river. 'I remember that we were all struck by the absence of any birds flying up at our approach.'

The march into the Russian heartland was becoming foreboding; soldiers were depressed and a little fearful at the sparsely populated desolation they trudged through. 'During the whole of this period of rapid movement from the 13th August to the 6th September,' Vossler recalled:

We had no encounter of any consequence with the enemy, and only a few forays against our van and rear by skirmishers and irregulars betrayed his presence.[24]

Artillery Lieutenant Christian Faber du Faur's spirits soared as they approached one of the repaired bridges spanning the Vyazma river. The town coming up was more opulent than those they were used to seeing:

> It was lit up by the magnificent rays of the sun, which played on the golden domes of the oriental churches and convents, making them seem to rear up above the still-smoking ruins of burnt houses.

Depressingly, the Cossacks would try to fire this town as well. When, on 30 August, his unit marched through, many of its buildings were in ruins. 'We had in the last few days, caught sight of the Emperor more and more,' he remembered, 'something which always suggested an imminent battle.'[25]

2

The Road by Gzhatsk (Gagarin)

114 Miles to Moscow

The Moscow Highway, 8–11 October 1941

During the early hours of 8 October 1941, *SS-Obergruppenführer* (General) Hausser's mobile division command group, mounted on Horsch KFZ 15 heavy jeeps, received new orders. The *SS Reich* Division was to capture Gzhatsk, which had been identified by the commanding XXXX Panzer Corps as a vital prerequisite for any further advance on Moscow. The town, with about 7,000 inhabitants in 1,600 dwellings, was an important road and rail junction, and telephone and telegraph centre, for Moscow. The new directive confirmed Hausser's expectation that his division would not now be required to seal the Vyazma pocket; the successful link-up between the 7th and 10th Panzer Divisions had already occurred.

His lead regiment, the *Deutschland*, was already on its way. *SS-Sturmmann* (Corporal) Ludwig Hümmer's 3rd Company drove through intermittent snow and sleet. 'Mount up,' they were told after the midday meal. 'We've got to advance to the Smolensk, Vyazma, Moscow highway.' Thick driving snow reduced visibility as Russian resistance increased perceptibly. Up ahead, the *Sturmgeschütz III* self-propelled gun battery worked in pairs, alongside the *Aufklärungs* Reconnaissance battalion, providing routes for the advance. The battery commander's gun *Prinz Eugen* commanded by

SS-Hauptsturmführer (Captain) Günster was hit on the driver's periscope and gunsight by a concealed Russian anti-tank gun and ground to a halt. It took an hour to repair but progress continued with the III Battalion *Deutschland* infantry leading until Günster managed to close up again. On arrival he dispatched two well-camouflaged Russian anti-aircraft guns with several rounds, but then inadvertently drove into an ambush. Once again, a Russian shell punched through the armour near the driver's periscope, this time killing Günster, his gunner and driver, with only the loader managing to bail out with minor injuries. The supporting *Sturmgeschütz*, *Derfflinger*, had bogged down in swampy ground and had to be rescued by another self-propelled gun, the *Schill*, which closed up and towed them clear under fire. The advance resumed with the *Schill* until it too was ambushed, hit and the crew bailed out. The *SS* infantry continued forward doggedly as yet another self-propelled gun, the *Blücher*, rolled up to take its place.

In all the confusion and fighting amid snow squalls, Hümmer's company overshot the vital Moscow road without even noticing it. 'According to local inhabitants,' the I Battalion *Deutschland* reported to Hausser, 'we have gone three kilometres past the highway.' It was getting dark and Hümmer recalled, 'We immediately lost two killed on the road, where we received fire up front from enemy flak and tank guns.' One of the recent new replacements from Nürnberg was killed and others lightly wounded as resistance on the outskirts of Gzhatsk thickened perceptibly. 'We have identified infantry screening the road,' Hümmer's battalion reported, 'with light machine guns right and left of the road every 200 metres.' German maps were found to be inaccurate: an interrogation of local civilians revealed they were 200 metres off course. The III Battalion *Deutschland* coming up behind closed the vital highway.

'Suddenly in the darkness,' Hümmer's company 'heard engine noises coming towards us'. They kept quiet as a Russian truck drove out of the gloom and halted nearby. Two soldiers jumped down from the cab and spoke with those in the back until interrupted by a peremptory order, 'hands up!' Shots rang out as they scattered 'but they were so surprised that they were overcome by us with no casualties,' Hümmer recalled. The truck, another captured Russian Ford, was added to the battalion's logistics train. The *Deutschland* Regiment had captured seven anti-aircraft guns, five trucks, twenty-three machine guns and 335 prisoners of war during this first day's advance on Gzhatsk.[1]

One recurring dilemma for soldiers fighting in alternating conditions of sleet and snow was greatcoats – on or off? Despite the wet and cold, greatcoats hindered flexibility of movement in combat, especially when attacking. Contemporary photographs often show German infantry attacking at this time dressed only in summer tunics, scarves around their necks, wearing gloves and woollen ear protection beneath helmets. Long dress greatcoats slowed movement and the thickness of the additional padding of clothing interfered with the dexterity required for rapid snap shooting with rifles. Layers of congealed mud on the frock snagged leg movement, added weight and could even suck off boots. Wet socks had to be festooned around the body beneath tunics to dry them out with body warmth. Carrying ammunition boxes and heavy weapons on the run or laboriously wheeling anti-tank guns forward by hand was hot, sweaty work, particularly when wearing a heavy greatcoat. If platoon administration was weak, coats and packs left with vehicles during an attack may not be brought up in time, or could be pinned to the rear by enemy harassing fire. Once the adrenalin of the action ceased to flow, soldiers were left soaked in perspiration by their efforts and subject to chills, and then froze. Energy-sapping influenza or diarrhoea from poor food further accelerated development of hypothermia, which often caused more casualties than the enemy. 'Greatcoats on or off', therefore, was an important tactical decision and only the veterans generally got it right.

Then, on 9 October, 'at about 10 a.m. we attacked [Gzhatsk] through sleet and driving snow,' Hümmer recalled, 'coming under heavy enemy fire'. Low-flying Soviet aircraft harassed the advance. The objective was the railway embankment running through the town, which was attacked with two battalions forward, the I Battalion left and the III right. Catching the Russians unaware, good progress was made until a wood line 1km south of the track where they launched was reached. The Soviets, interrupted as they occupied their prepared positions, fought back fiercely and inflicted heavy casualties on Hümmer's sister company, the 2nd, which beat back three successive Russian counter-attacks. The wood line was eventually enveloped from the right when the I Battalion crossed the railway embankment, killing seventy Russians before proceeding to mop up the eastern sector of the town. Following closely behind was the III Battalion, which also penetrated the southern suburbs so that by 1 p.m. Gzhatsk was firmly in German hands. In the marketplace they found twenty hanged Russian civilians. Eighteen months later only 300 of its 1,600 buildings would be left standing.

Ludwig Hümmer's ninth section broke into a canteen-like building and found a huge metal cauldron on the boil, which 'steamed and smelt like good food'. Peering inside, they relished what the Russians had cooked 'for us'. 'We had arrived just at the right time,' he recalled, 'the meal with rice and meat is ready!' As the company started to arrive, plates were handed out and they sat at a long table. 'After their efforts that day it tasted good, and the Russian cook received a lot of praise.' It was such incongruous incidents that provided the more memorable days of the campaign. 'The population seemed openly friendly and received us like liberators!' Hümmer observed, filling his flask with fresh milk from one of the local houses. He was much impressed by the quality of the furnishings. It seemed to indicate they were getting closer to Moscow. His section was dispatched to a neighbouring village to check out and monitor enemy movement.[2]

Hausser's division command group moved forward in its heavy Horsch jeeps. They were repeatedly attacked during the day by Russian fighter aircraft, but nobody was hit. Even so, the liberal peppering of holes along vehicle sides prompted sober reflection. 'During these days, at least in the area the division was fighting,' the official *Reich* history recalled, 'the Russians clearly controlled the skies.' The Red Air Force was able to use its hardened-surface air bases around Moscow.

Hausser was an inspirational commander, who liked to be seen well forward by his soldiers. *SS-Hauptsturmführer* Dr Windisch, on his staff, described how 'many times we crawled or crept up to the most forward foxholes, because the division commander wanted a better view of the terrain and enemy positions'.

Windisch was the intelligence officer and got most of his information at this time from abandoned Soviet artillery vehicles. 'Interrogation of prisoners was often not very productive,' he commented, whereas there 'were excellent maps of the best quality and accuracy'. Although he concentrated on captured officers and NCOs, he admitted 'the poor devils did not know much anyway'. What was clearly apparent, however, was that many Russians were fleeing eastwards, while resistance in that direction was increasing perceptibly.[3]

Helmut Günther's *SS-Kradschützen* (motorcycle) Battalion *Reich* also had problems detecting the main west–east arterial highway to Moscow through sleet and snow. 'We could distinctly hear that there must be a road in front of us,' he recalled:

> Faintly but unmistakably, the wind carried the sound of fast-moving vehicles to us. The road had to be there!

'We were right in the enemy's rear!' he realised. Russian vehicles were using the last available route open to them to escape eastwards. 'What ensued could have come straight out of a manual on the employment of motorcycle troops,' Günther remembered. PAK anti-tank guns were man-handled on to the high ground to cover the road through the trees, while riflemen moved stealthily forward beneath the low-hanging branches alongside the highway:

> Several trucks emerged from where they had disappeared behind a gentle curve. They were packed with standing Russian soldiers. They moved pretty fast; they were in a mighty hurry.

The first PAK gun barked out, sending a brightly lit red tracer shell screeching through the leading truck's engine compartment. The vehicle 'swerved to the side, turned over and the Ivans flew high into the air from the truck bed' as it exploded. The following truck's cab blew up and pro-duced similar results, which effectively blocked the road. Anti-tank gunfire then shifted to the rear of the road bend, trapping a segment of the convoy. 'The vehicles that followed couldn't go forward, but neither could they go back,' said Günther. Machine-gun and rifle fire raked the length of the convoy in a 'gruesome song'. Caught unawares, the Russians were unable to offer organised resistance. 'It was pointless,' Günther recalled. Fleeing Soviets scattered through the bushes but most raised their hands. German motorcycles roared off to block the road to the east and west. 'The Vyazma pocket was sealed!' Günther recalled. 'Now it was a matter of holding the positions long enough until reinforcements came up.'

As the fighting died away, Günther noticed a throng of SS riflemen surrounding one of the trucks, passing mess tins around. A *Sturmmann*

(Corporal) stood theatrically on the captured Soviet mess truck waving his ladle and announcing: 'Who wants some? Come and get it you people.' This type of booty was more significant to the average soldier than the accomplishment of the next tactical objective. Everyone crowded round 'and spooned up first-class noodle soup in which pieces of chicken were swimming around'. Getting hot food during an advance was an exceptional occurrence; Russian soldiers, nearer their logistic hubs, were eating better than them, the SS soldiers realised. 'Now who says the Ivans had no chow!' Günther exclaimed triumphantly.[4]

SS-Untersturmführer (Second Lieutenant) Hugo Landgraf was a *Kriegsberichter* (war correspondent) with the 1st Platoon of the *SS Propaganda Kompanie*. On 9 October he made a dramatic sound recording for the *Reichs Rundfunk* radio company, the equivalent of the BBC, back home in Germany. 'The weather is miserable and unfriendly,' he commentated, 'but for us a proud day, because our *Waffen-SS* Division attacked up to the *autostrasse* that leads up to Moscow.' He was with the *Reich's Aufklärungs* Reconnaissance Battalion. 'Months before,' he reported, 'we had reached this road by Smolensk, now we're 200 kilometres further eastwards towards Moscow.'

As the noise of an aircraft passing overhead receded into the background of the recording, he announced that a Messerschmitt fighter plane was heading towards the Russians 'to impede their movement' on the road. 'Now the rain is turning into sleet,' he announced, with the noise of battle crackling and thudding in the distance, 'but this does not concern us.' Artillery bursts are clearly audible on the recording, which he described rhetorically as 'distant detonations like gigantic hammer blows, striking the gates of Moscow'.

Landgraf drove further with the reconnaissance unit to Romoschkova village, a quiet place where soldiers and inhabitants, eager to co-operate, were surrendering. His report was chronicling the collapse of Soviet resistance to the listeners back home. 'Many reserves have been sent to the front without any weapons,' he observed. Then, after a brief pause, he announced dramatically:

> Within an hour of filing this report, we have just received a radio message stating one of our regiments has taken Gzhatsk during the course of the day, which also gives us possession of the *autostrasse*.

This was precisely what the Ministry of Propaganda wanted civilians, seated expectantly around their radio sets in the *Reich*, to hear. With the taking of this 'important life road', Landgraf informed his audience proudly, 'a glance at the map shows we have reached the furthest point towards Moscow that any other unit has reached'.[5]

As early as the morning of 5 October, a Russian fighter pilot with the 120th Fighter Regiment had spotted a long ominous column of German panzer and motorised troops moving north from Juchnow. This was to the rear of the Soviet Western Front armies east of Vyazma. Many of the *Reich* troopers had commented on the frequency of Russian overflights and harassing strafing attacks as they bypassed Vyazma to the east on this road. The Red pilot's report was greeted with incredulity in Moscow and a repeat sortie was ordered. This time the pilot took a closer look and came back peppered with machine-gun holes. Air Force General Telegin was told the bad news, which he nervously passed on to Shaposhnikov, Stalin's Chief of General Staff. He was equally sceptical and a third aircraft was dispatched, which again came back full of holes. Stalin was informed and he promptly castigated Telegin and told him not to believe every bit of information he received. The air commander delivering the bad news was arrested and handed over to the *NKVD*. Colonel Sbytov, the regimental commander, was informed his pilots were panic-mongers and cowards, and he was personally threatened with a court martial.[6]

Unwelcome though the news was, the Germans had certainly occupied Juchnow, the jumping-off point for the *Das Reich* Division. Clearly, the Germans had broken through and were on their way to encircle Moscow. One flank of von Bock's Army Group Centre with part of the Third Panzer Army and Ninth Army was poised to strike towards the capital from Kalinin in the north-west, while General Guderian's Second Panzer Army was in a position to threaten Tula and approach from the south. Stalin had no idea his Bryansk, Western and Reserve Fronts had lost a total of sixty-four rifle divisions, eleven tank brigades and fifty artillery regiments, even more catastrophic than the losses at Minsk and Kiev that summer. Stalin summoned an emergency session of the *GKO*, the State Committee for Defence. Fortunately for them, the German pursuit was executed in intermittent fits and starts, because 60 per cent of Army Group Centre's offensive power was wrapped up trying to reduce stubborn Soviet pockets fighting to the death.

On 5 October, General Georgy Zhukov, having just ruthlessly stabilised the Leningrad front, was summoned to Moscow. Five days later he was given command of a newly formed Western Front made up from scraped-up reserves from the former Western and Reserve Fronts. He replaced a despairing Konev, fully expecting to be shot over the debacle at Vyazma and Bryansk. Despite Stalin wanting his head, Zhukov kept him on as an able deputy. Konev told him that Gzhatsk, just off the Moscow–Minsk highway, was in the path of the *SS Reich* Division advance, and was only defended by remnants of 50th Rifle Division. Zhukov gives the impression in his memoirs that he quickly took control of the situation and began to stabilise the front, but his role at this stage, having just arrived, was to listen and advise. Much of the credit should actually go elsewhere.

Colonel Semyon Bogdanov, a Red Army tank officer who had fought his way out of the Minsk pocket that summer, was in the process of forming new tank brigades in the Moscow Military District when Operation *Typhoon* broke. At his own initiative, he dispatched the first two formations: Alexsandr Druzhinina's 18th Tank Brigade and Ivan Troitsky's 17th Tank Brigade, forward to aid the visibly ailing Western Front. *Stavka* General Headquarters also decided to re-form the Fifth Army, formerly destroyed in the Kiev pocket, under Major General Lelyushenko. It was set up as a command cadre at Mozhaisk to co-ordinate the arrival of reinforcements. Druzhinina was deployed to Gzhatsk, to block the *SS Reich* advance, and Troitsky south towards Maloyaroslavets, to delay von Kuntzen's *LVII Armeekorps*, which had captured an intact bridge at Yukhnov over the Ugra river. Bogdanov sent a further three Soviet tank brigades – the 9th, 19th and 20th – to reinforce the first two. Without tanks, the Germans could not be stopped. These decisions to delay with armoured units were made before Zhukov arrived. He was to play a major role in the winter offensive that would follow two months later, but not at this stage. The measures were taken without Stavka approval, and uncharacteristically by a mere colonel. The impact would be far reaching.

On 7 October, Druzhinina's 18th Tank Brigade was unloading from flatcars in rain under leaden grey skies about a mile short of Mozhaisk railway station, already severely damaged by the *Luftwaffe*. The brigade, although incomplete, could field sixty-three tanks grouped into two tank and one motorised battalion with 1,400 troops. Only twenty-nine new

T-34 tanks were included; the rest were light and somewhat obsolescent BT light tanks and, like the single T-26, drawn from repair depots. Even so, they were better equipped and trained than those which had succumbed in the pocket fighting. Under the cover of low cloud and drizzle and sleet, Druzhinina moved his armour into the woods near Gzhatsk. They began to prepare for battle and set up blocking ambush positions near the village of Budayevo, 7 miles east of the town, along the Moscow highway. Like the other four Soviet tank brigades steadily moved forward to reinforce the Mozhaisk line, the ambush positions in effect represented a light armoured screen, lacking infantry and substantial artillery support.

Aleksandr Bodnar had barely graduated as a lieutenant from the Ulyanovsk tank school before being sent to Vladimir, 115 miles east of Moscow. His 20th Tank Brigade was forming up after the rapid departure of the 18th. He was placed in command of a KV (Klim-Voroshulov) heavy tank, a 45-ton monolith mounting a 76mm gun. With 3½in of armour protecting the front glacis plate, it was the superior of any German tank. 'They let us get inside the heavy tank and drive it to the Lenin Monument in the Lenin Square above the Volga at Ulyanovsk,' he recalled, this being the only familiarisation he received:

> To drive it to the Lenin monument, put it in reverse gear and drive back, to go one more time to the Lenin monument … switch from first gear to second and come back.

That was the only training they received. 'The war taught me the rest,' he recalled. The new brigade had '7 KV tanks, no more than 20 T-34s, and the rest were T-60s, BTs and T-26s; so the brigade was fairly weak'. They were ready inside a week, 'assembled from everything that could have come together from the nearest directions'. They loaded the flatcars on 9 October. After the brigade was presented with a new banner, 'We marched around town, the townspeople applauded us, loaded us up and sent us on our way to Moscow'. On arrival the brigade drove out to an assembly area near Borodino.[7]

Ludwig Hümmer's 3rd Company discovered and occupied some abandoned Russian field positions during the night of 10 October. They were fortunate: it had begun to snow with temperatures well below freezing and the ground was frozen hard, too difficult to dig in. Inside they found an underground bakery, the ovens still hot, left by the fleeing Russians. 'Once again the Russians had baked for us!' he recalled gleefully as fresh bread was cheerfully handed out. Soldiers were able to spend a comfortable night sleeping in heated bunkers. Morale soared at these unexpected luxuries and the knowledge that only the lucky few with the 3rd were able to benefit. 'Unfortunately we had to leave these excellent positions,' Hümmer recalled, because at dawn, 'we got the order *prepare to move*'. Once again the company took the lead, following the railway line running north of the Moscow highway out of Gzhatsk toward Staraja, Doronino and Mozhaisk.[8]

Resistance all along the line stiffened perceptively as the division began its advance to the east, two regiments forward, *Deutschland* to the left and *Der Führer* right. Even as the move commenced, reports trickled back that an armoured train had gone beyond the Koloch railway halt, north of the village of Yelnya on the Moscow highway, and was coming their way. The rail line had already been cut south-east of Gzhatsk and the *Deutschland*'s Assault Pioneers were dispatched to blow the track at the Holesniki stop to prevent the train's retreat.

The *Sturmgeschütz Lützow* lurking in the trees by the track suddenly emerged from its ambush position as the armoured colossus approached and the duel began. Shell after 75mm shell crashed into the armoured skirts protecting the locomotive while its armoured turrets and quad machine guns returned fire. It puffed slowly rearwards, cascades of steam hissing out of the punctured engine. The *SS* Artillery *Reich* batteries attached to *Deutschland* closed to within 1,600yd of the train and bracketed the carriages and weapon mounts with salvo after salvo of shell bursts. The 4th Battery closed to within 400yd or more and fired directly over open sights. The locomotive, hissing furiously through repeated strikes, came to a gradual creaking halt, whereupon the whole length of the train was subjected to punishing fire. It was all over by midday, with the train out of action and abandoned by its crew.

Der Führer, meanwhile, on the right continued the advance until it was brought to a halt by heavy fighting outside a wood line that straddled both sides of the Moscow highway. Awful road conditions slowed momentum. General Gotthard Heinrici, with the XXXXIII Army Corps, complained, 'The weather has thrown a spanner in the works, which nobody expected':

It is becoming a real inconvenience for us. No one back home could imagine the state the roads are in now. A thick mush runs several feet deep on their surface and is then pushed like a wall of mud in front of cars until they can no longer move.[9]

Quite often the *Reich*'s self-propelled guns were seen towing two trucks, and sometimes a motorcycle combination in tandem, through the worst stretches of the morass. It was at this stage that *Der Führer* came up against the light BT and heavier T-34 tanks of Druzhinina's 18th Tank Brigade, ensconced in the woods near the village of Budayevo. The Soviet tankers waited until the *Waffen-SS* vanguard, led by armoured cars and motorcycle troops, closed up, before opening a devastating fire at virtually point-blank range. Well-camouflaged machine guns spat out through the trees as *Der Führer*'s advance was bracketed in the open by repeated salvos of Russian artillery. The deep-throated roar of tank engines starting up sounded like the harbinger of doom to the vulnerable *SS* infantry on foot. The new Soviet T-34 was virtually impervious to German anti-tank fire, as one veteran attested:

Use your rifle? You might as well turn round and fart at it. Besides, it never comes into your head to shoot; you just have to stay still as a mouse, or you'll yell with terror. You won't stir your little finger, for fear of annoying it. Then you tell yourself you may be lucky, perhaps it hasn't spotted you, perhaps its attention has turned to something else. But on the other hand perhaps your luck's right out and the thing is coming straight for you, till you lose sight and hearing in your hole.

The options for the *SS* infantry caught in the clearing before the woods either side of the highway were not great. The standard drill was to call up the manhandled light anti-tank guns, the 37mm PAK, contemptuously referred to as the 'door knocker', because of the tendency of the rounds to simply bounce off Russian tanks. Veteran soldiers were aware of the limitations for tank commanders and drivers viewing through small letter box-size vision slits. Immediate action on the appearance of tanks was to call for artillery or *Luftwaffe* support, and force the tank crews to close down and attempt to separate tanks from their accompanying infantry.

'That's when you need nerves like steel wire, I can tell you,' reiterated the German infantry veteran:

> I saw Hansmann of the Ninth get under the tracks of a T-34, and he hadn't dug his hole deep enough; he had been too tired to shovel. The tank just turned a bit off course, that skidded just enough of the ground away. It had him. The next minute there he was flattened out like a bit of dog's shit you accidently put your foot in.[10]

SS troopers had to operate in close combat teams in order to survive. They stealthily approached isolated tanks to engage with crudely shaped explosive charges. These might be bundled hand grenades, *Teller* plate mines with slow-burning fuses, activated before being thrown upon engine decks, and even petrol jerry cans with grenades strapped to them. 'Throwers' generally stripped off their equipment harnesses, because they had to crawl rapidly from cover to cover to approach the short-sighted monoliths, supported by 'coverers', who protected them with machine pistols or rifles. One option was to 'blind' the tank's vision blocks by throwing two phosphorous grenades joined together with extended wire, thrown to snag the gun barrel and other protrusions. Occasionally they might intimidate a crew into bailing out by suffocation or set oily surfaces like the engine decks alight. A thermite poultice stuck on the rear deck could also melt through protective armour and disable the engine.

Artillery officer *Leutnant* Wigand Wüster later recalled the difference that formal *Panzernahkampflehrgang* (tank close combat courses) could have upon an individual's ability to combat a tank. 'It helped diminish the fear of tanks, at least relatively,' he explained. They were instructed how to be rolled over by tanks in foxholes, but still felt helpless and unprotected 'exposed to the weapons and observation slits of a tank'. These perceptions changed, he explained, once they were invited to ride inside a tank during a mock practice attack:

> Now the feeling of inferiority was with the tank crew. Nothing could be seen or heard. If a foxhole was even noticed, it could already be too late. Perhaps a figure would be seen scampering past, then the dull impacts of

an anti-tank mine on the rear deck behind the turret, would be heard. Too late! The effect of smoke pots and smoke grenades when combatting tanks was surprising. Visibility was not only taken from the tank crew, but the incendiary combustion also deprived them of oxygen. The crew had to bail out immediately if they did not want to suffocate.[11]

Russian T-34 commanders had only a single vision slit and traversable periscope. Attackers would close in from the rear or sides and at the last moment heave a heavy mine on to the back of the engine deck, or leave it on the track of a stationary tank to cut the caterpillar tread. Such close combat required steely courage, 'do-or-die' fanatical determination, and was costly. Groups of enemy tanks would cover each other by spraying each other with machine =-gun fire to brush off boarders, or when lurking silhouettes suggested a threat. Only cold nerves and teamwork succeeded. *Teller* mines slung beneath turret overhangs or engine decks could stun the crew within from the shockwave of the explosion. This broke off jagged metal scabs that ricocheted inside, around the crew compartment, lacerating men and often setting off ammunition fires. Cutting a track at least immobilised the vehicle, but did not prevent it from continuing to fire. The *Der Führer* soldiers were caught off balance by the emergence of Druzhinina's tank blocks, which exacted fearsome damage before the stunned *SS* troopers combined to fight back effectively. Only the fact that they were fighting inside woods, with protection from trees and reduced vision, meant that they managed to escape being overrun.

Hümmer, with the *Deutschland* Regiment, had been making steady progress when 'suddenly to our left several tanks emerged from the woods ahead of us!' They were pinned until a PAK anti-tank gun was manhandled up to them 'but the shells did not penetrate through, they bounced off'. The village they had just passed through was soon blazing from the tank tracer overshoots. The attack ground to a halt, 'but luckily, to our right were two substantial ravines that lay parallel to the enemy, which gave us good cover'. The rest of the I Battalion and the III Battalion following on behind suffered casualties from 'tank rounds swishing over our heads'. As darkness fell they could pick out 'the steel colossuses remaining in the same stretch of woods in the half light'. When it finally got dark, meals were brought forward 'and our greatcoats for the cold'; they had attacked in light equipment to retain mobility and flexibility during the assault. They could not dig in because the ground was frozen solid.

The reconnaissance section sheltered just under a ravine overhang. 'We didn't need to go off and scout,' Hümmer recalled, 'because the enemy was directly under our noses.' Their company commander came forward to see what was happening and to lend moral support. 'He was much loved by us all with a personal affiliation with each man, and was like a father.' He led them with a steady veteran's hand 'and I learnt unfortunately,' Hümmer recalled, 'that only too often many of our chiefs left us, falling at the head of our company, or were seriously wounded'. Helmut Günther, with the motorcycle battalion, remembered his *Deutschland* company commanders were 'all sharp tough cookies'. Most of the idealists had long since fallen. 'Exaggerated coolness under fire had already changed the status of some soldiers from living to dead,' he remembered. What remained now were the seasoned practical survivors. Hümmer's company commander was in this league. Experienced leaders were not just revered because they led by example: they also made rapid decisions under fire, often the difference between life and death, as their subordinates were only too aware. Günter's hard-headed appreciation of the regimental company commanders was that they 'were not to be trifled with'. In his opinion, they 'were all men who could summon the devil out of hell' and 'their later careers proved it'.

Hümmer's company commander 'had been ill for several days and was running a fever'. He was seen 'clenching his teeth and would not have it that he had developed a serious cold'. They moved back through the ambient light of the blazing village. 'Virtually everything had been destroyed in the fire, because nobody was playing the fire brigade,' behind them. He observed ironically how often their unit had been called upon as a 'fire brigade' for action. This time they were not in a position where 'it burned' to deploy and 'put it out'. At least the fire warmed one side of their bodies this frosty night.[12]

The *Das Reich* Division had ground to a halt on the Moscow highway. *SS* General Hausser realised casualties were very heavy up front, maybe hundreds, blocked by the 18th Brigade tanks, firmly ensconced in the wood lines around Budayevo. Hausser's *Waffen-SS* division was a strong motorised formation with nine infantry battalions, a motorcycle and reconnaissance battalions, but his only integral armoured support was a *Sturmgeschütz* battery with six self-propelled guns. Von Bock, the Army Group Centre commander, was completely engrossed in reducing the Vyazma pocket, which was absorbing 60 per cent of his offensive potential. He had paid scant attention to providing Hausser's vanguard with the necessary supplies or reinforcements to maintain a thrust towards Moscow. As Kutuzov's Tsarist army discovered in 1812, there are few natural terrain options able to favourably sustain a defensive line before Moscow. The Red Army's decision 129 years later was also to include the area around Borodino as part of the 1941 Mozhaisk line.

The woods 7 miles east of Gzhatsk appeared to be hiding as many as fifty tanks around the Moscow highway. Hausser therefore requested armoured support from his parent superior headquarters, von Stumme's *XXXX Armeekorps*, to get himself out of a bloody fix. Further south Troitsky's 17th Tank Brigade was similarly blunting the lead elements of von Kuntzen's corps north-east of Yukhnov; *Oberst* Horst von Wolff's Infantry Regiment 478 had already received a severe mauling. This was also General Zhukov's first day on assuming command of the newly constituted Soviet Western Front. With the Vyazma pocket virtually at the point of collapse, the 10th Panzer Division was instructed to send a Panzer Regiment 7 armoured *Kampfgruppe* under von Hauenschild with motorised infantry, *Schützen* Regiment 86, to aid Hausser's breakthrough attempts.

Ludwig Hümmer heard the rumour from the rear *Tross* logistics train that panzers were on the way. As in the case of his company commander, it appeared that illness, exhaustion and casualties were sapping professional expertise where it was needed, at the front level of operational and tactical decision-making. Both the major spearheads heading towards the Russian capital during the crucial period of 7–12 October, while the Vyazma and Bryansk pockets were collapsing, were led by motorised infantry divisions, with negligible panzer support. Meanwhile, the Russian Western Front had managed to scrape together over 200 tanks, including about sixty T-34s on the main approaches to Moscow. The arrival of the 18th and 19th Tank Brigades before Borodino and the 17th and 9th to block at Maloyaroslavets, resonated with Napoleonic precedence, with this thickening of the Mozhaisk line.

Auftragstaktik, the German term for mission-orientated tactics promoted and taught by the German General Staff, was losing some of its edge by this stage of the campaign. It was reliant upon the personal energy and initiative of the myriad of German junior commanders who had already become casualties in this successful but pyrrhic campaign. *Totsiegen* was an expression used increasingly to describe the advance of Army Group Centre; it meant they were literally 'victoring themselves to death'. The innate sharp and creative aggressiveness of junior commanders was being haemorrhaged away by exhaustion, sickness or death. About one-third of the veteran junior officer and NCO leadership had perished since the start of the *Barbarossa* campaign. The loss of this command 'seed corn' was starting to influence drive and momentum. German command inactivity during the crucial days between 10 and 11 October represented the equivalent of a Soviet tactical victory.[13]

'The Pretty Little Town of Gzhatsk', 31 August–5 September 1812

'It's already autumn here, no longer summer,' Napoleon wrote home to his wife Marie-Louise, because on 29 August 1812 the weather broke. Cold rains descended suddenly, lashing the previously hot French columns, which had been labouring forward in torrid weather. The changed conditions caused 'both men and horses to sicken,' Napoleon observed. Colonel François Lejeune, one of Marshal Berthier's aides, recalled they were 'stuck in the mud at every step'. It rained for several days, and Berthier remembered 'discouragement seemed to be overwhelming the army':

> In the evening overwhelmed by fatigue, soaked to the bone and filthy, we halted in a wretched bivouac that offered no shelter and where the suffering caused by the cold stormy night was added to those from all kinds of privations.

The gloomy Berthier, Napoleon's Chief of Staff, 'though very timid about proffering his advice,' according to Lejeune, 'made so bold as to counsel the Emperor to retreat'. Napoleon and he worked closely together, inside the dripping mobile headquarters carriage. The Emperor was unimpressed and 'took this proposal very much amiss, and told him he could clear out if he was tired'. The onset of the first autumn rains was very unwelcome: the year was starting to draw out, and still Napoleon had failed to draw the Russians into a decisive battle.[14]

'From Vyazma onwards the land became more fertile,' artillery Lieutenant Faber du Faur recalled, 'and our march through Gzhatsk took us through rolling countryside and well-constructed villages,' As the columns of the *Grande Armée* approached 'the pretty little town of Gzhatsk', Major Eugène Labaune, with IV Corps, described it as 'the most important one on the Smolensk–Moscow road, bisected by the little river of the same name'. Banging cannon reports and spluttering musketry in the distance suggested the Russian rearguards were not going to abandon it without a fight. The triangular-shaped town sat across the road with one side parallel to the north–south course of the Gzhat river; another followed the vital road itself and the third segment combined the two. A strong rearguard commanded by General Konovitsyn contested the approaches for thirteen hours. Labaume remembered the town was 'surrounded by streams flowing through small lakes', so 'measures are taken to enter it at a rush before it can be put to the torch'. Major Le Roy, advancing with the 85th Line, saw the eastern side of the town was ablaze, 'unfortunately the side with the bazaar and merchants'. Napoleon's aide, Philipe-Paul de Ségur, saw 'the Russian rearguard, protected by the river, had the time to burn all that quarter; only Murat's prompt action saved the rest of the city'. Despite heavy Russian cannon fire, cavalry commander Murat and Eugène followed the 85th Line advance at a deliberate walk, 'even though,' Labaune observed, 'they calmly see several of their entourage fall under the enemy shots', trying to demonstrate they were less concerned than the other. It was still raining.

The lead elements crossed the Gzhat river as best they could, wading or using small boats, and pursued the Russians into the flames and beyond. 'One of the inhabitants came running towards them,' de Ségur remembered, 'shouting that he was French.' Upon being questioned by Marshal Davout, the I Corps commander, they heard 'according to the man's story, The Russian Army had undergone a complete change'. It was said General Mikhail Kutuzov had taken command of the Tsar's army two days before at the nearby village of Tsaryovo-Zamische. He was replacing General Barclay de Tolly, who had masterminded the Russian retreat so far. 'They are asking,' according to the civilian informant, 'why they must have this foreigner?'

'Bagration's insubordination and the general outcry had gained the desired result,' de Ségur acknowledged. 'Kutuzov and a battle!' It appeared the Tsar had succumbed to popular and senior army commander pressure to replace him. 'To save Russia, it will take a Russian!' their informant insisted. The news appeared to be confirmed by a later Russian envoy, who approached under a flag of truce. Somewhat arrogant, he was asked what the *Grande Armée* might find between Vyazma and Moscow. 'Poltava!' was the impudent response (where Charles XII of Sweden was decisively beaten by Peter the Great of Russia.) 'This answer promised a battle and pleased our generals,' de Ségur recalled, 'who appreciated a ready rejoinder.' The news coincided with the first sunlight that had been seen in days and augured well. 'The sky turned blue,' Labaune remembered, and ended the despairing speculation about retiring back to Smolensk. It appeared Gzhatsk might be the only town that stood between the *Grande Armée* and the Russian Army assembling at Borodino on the Kolocha river.[15]

The vagaries of Russian weather and climate had the same impact in 1812 as they did in 1941. On both occasions they sapped the strength and momentum of the invader. Both Napoleon and Hitler enjoyed an especially high standing among their troops, which was tested severely by the geography and epic land mass of Russia. One anonymous German soldier describing his 1941 experience in Russia could have just as easily been speaking about 1812. 'The immense space,' he emphasised, 'was so immense that we had many soldiers who became melancholy':

> Flat valleys, flat hills, flat valleys, flat hills, endless, endless, there was no limit, we could not see an end … and it was so disconsolate.[16]

Hitler conquered Poland in four weeks, the Balkans in over three weeks, while France, which had not succumbed in four years of attritional warfare between 1914 and 1918, fell in just six. The enormous Russian land mass was different. Napoleon took twelve weeks to cover the 570 miles to reach Gzhatsk; Hitler's *Wehrmacht* reached the same point in over fourteen weeks, having envisaged a campaign lasting eight to ten weeks. The immensity of the area of operations in 1941 was startling. Three army groups started on an attack frontage of 620 miles, which opened to a width of 1,000 miles just short of Moscow. This conventionally required a frontage of some

280 divisions, while Hitler attacked with 127. Napoleon's advance could be likened to an arrow shot into a massive interior. His right flank was partially protected by the Pripet Marshes, but in taking the traditional 'land bridge' invasion route over Minsk and Smolensk to Moscow, he had to shed strength to protect distant flanks the whole way. Moscow, moreover, is only one-seventh of the way into the full extent of the Russian land mass. Both Hitler and Napoleon obsessed over reaching this point. Destruction of Soviet armies appeared to have no political impact and likewise Napoleon was unable to bring the main Russian armies to battle. From Vitebsk onwards, there were misgivings in the *Grande Armée* about their depth of penetration. Pierre Daru, Napoleon's accompanying Secretary of State, had to remind him:

> War's a game you're good at. But here we aren't fighting men, we're fighting nature.

Hitler and Napoleon were both convinced by the infallibility of their decision-making. Napoleon 'believes there'll be a battle because he wants one,' de Ségur recalled, 'and believes he'll win it because it's essential he shall. No amount of reasoning can enlighten him.' His soldiers continued to follow where he led:

> The spectacle of his soldiers, their enthusiasm at the sight of him, the reviews and parades, and above all the King of Naples' and certain other generals' frequently coloured reports have gone to his head.[17]

Hitler, at the height of his power and reputation, would brook no criticism. *Barbarossa* had decimated the Soviet frontier armies in *Blitzkrieg* encirclement all conducted in fine *Führer* weather. His surprising move south into the Ukraine had confounded Soviet expectations and resulted in the largest encirclement battle recorded in history. Leningrad was besieged and now Moscow beckoned. Despite harsh fighting lying ahead, the typical German *Landser* (equivalent to the British 'Tommy') was convinced their *Führer* 'had it in hand' and they would soon be wintering in Moscow. Hitler, in their estimation, could always be relied upon to pull the proverbial rabbit out of the hat.

Leading the advance east beyond Gzhatsk towards Borodino in 1941 was Hitler's *Waffen-SS*. Like Napoleon's Imperial Guard, they had begun life as showpiece 'asphalt soldiers', providing ceremonial guards at headquarters, formal occasions and places of residence. By the time of the Russian campaign, the *Waffen-SS* were developing a ruthless reputation as highly effective shock troops, regarding themselves as an elite. Napoleon's Imperial Guard formed from the old Consular Guard was a personal creation of the Emperor. He vetted its recruitment, promotion, privileges, duties and uniform. Like the emerging divisions of the *Waffen-SS* in 1941, it became an army within the army with its own infantry, chasseurs and foot grenadiers, heavy and light cavalry all supported by foot and horse artillery. It also included the whole spectrum of gendarmerie, marines, engineers and logistic trains. Subsequent expansion to up to 56,000 in 1812 diluted earlier stringent entry requirements, which was also the case with the *Waffen-SS* from 1942 onwards. The Imperial Guard was subdivided on expansion into the Middle Guard and Young Guard, which distinguished them from the founding Old Guard.

The Old Guard had mounted sentry at the Emperor's palace, covered duty at state banquets and guarded Napoleon's headquarters in the field, as it was doing in Russia. They were Napoleon's 'children': he knew hundreds of them by name amd remembered faces when he stopped to speak with them on picket duty or lined up for battle. He admonished and rewarded them like any company commander and attracted absolute devotion in return. They did not address him as 'Your Majesty' or 'Sire' but simply as '*Mon Emperor*'.

The Guard was paid double that of line regiments and each Guard rank was one higher. They had the best accommodation, better food, their own civilian cooks and their own unique supply train in the field, whereas the line regiments had to forage. Other regiments had to give way to Guard regiments on the march and even salute as they went past, for which they generally received only cursory acknowledgement. One line officer referred to them bitterly as the 'Janissaries of the Depot' because they:

> were extremely arrogant towards the other troops; they repelled with disdain all commerce and contact with other brands of the service; and were justly detested by them.

Friction therefore existed not simply between the national contingents making up the *Grande Armée*, but also between the French themselves. The standing joke in line regiments was that even the 'Guard asses have the rank of mules'.

The Old Guard was particularly proud of its distinctive role as Napoleon's shock troops, and they were not to be trifled with; they looked the part. Alessandro Barbero, an Italian historian, described them as hardened veterans, confident to the point of arrogance, with 'skin covered with tattoos, and large gold earrings hanging from their ears, giving them the look of old time pirates'. Some 13,932 Guard infantry marched with the columns, with 4,930 cavalry and 109-crewed cannon. Bernard Hayden, a British historian, had seen them on duty at Fontainebleau and was impressed by their towering bearskins, magnificent curling moustaches and high-quality uniforms and equipment. 'More dreadful looking fellows than Napoleon's Guard I have never seen,' he admitted:

> They had the look of thoroughbred veteran disciplined banditii.
> Depravity, recklessness and bloodthirstiness were burned into their faces.

Napoleon husbanded them carefully. Their function was to deliver the knock-out blow in the coming battle, or in the event of a crisis, they would form a bastion. As a consequence, they rarely fought and came to be caustically named 'The Immortals' by the rest of the army, because they never died.[18]

Napoleon was frustrated by Russian rearguards denying him the opportunity of administering a decisive blow at every step of the campaign thus far. Even after the Russian armies combined they had fought three set-piece rearguard actions and a fourth group of skirmishes between Smolensk and Gzhatsk. Another would be fought at Gzhatsk and two more before Borodino. To withdraw in contact with the enemy is one of the most difficult phases of war. The Russians had excelled, despite Napoleon not particularly rating Russian military prowess at the outset. Middle-ranking commanders, who had fought these bitterly contested skirmishes, were revising their opinion of their adversary and beginning to regard them with some respect. The whole point of the rearguard was to tire the enemy and make him wary of rushing ahead too boldly, by constant harassment and counter-attacks. Small easy victories energised the retreating Russians and compensated for the long morale-sapping retreat. It generally needed four to six regiments of light Russian cavalry and Cossacks with some four battalions of light infantry, in fit condition for fast marches, with no wagons with pack mule-borne supplies. This and a few light artillery caissons kept the advancing invaders at bay.

The French cavalry, with their large western European horses, were ill-adapted to harsh Russian field conditions; they were worked hard with little feed and fared badly. 'Every day from five o'clock in the morning we skirmished with the Cossacks,' remembered Captain Victor Dupuy, with the 7th Hussars, in pursuit of the Russians, 'and sometimes this lasted until ten or eleven at night.' Villages in their path were burned as they withdrew:

If, by a bold manoeuvre or a sharp attack, we did not allow them time for this, their artillery would fire incendiary shells, which produced the same result, setting alight the thatched roofs.

'This method of waging war we found very prejudicial,' explained Dupuy. 'After days spent entirely in fights and fatigues, we could scarcely find enough to eat and often had nothing to give the horses, whose number dwindled every day in alarming fashion.' Horses 'dropped with fatigue and hunger,' Dupuy complained, primarily he believed because Mutat over-taxed the pursuing cavalry and did not resupply them properly. On the eve of battle approaching Borodino 'our division, which had numbered 7,500 at the crossing of the Nieman, had not even one thousand, and this immense gap was certainly not caused by the enemy's fire'.[19]

Pickets were left standing and campfires burned until dawn when the main Russian army departed, under cover of darkness or poor weather. Ruse and deception were employed by Cossacks, who maintained fleeting contacts and skirmished along the withdrawal route, before veering off to lure the pursuit in the wrong direction. Such measures were reliant upon good control and communications, which was not always the case. There was a mix-up between the First and Second withdrawing Russian armies retreating from Dorogobuzh, after a successful withdrawal battle fought at Valentuno after they had left Smolensk. Major General Panchulidzev's Dragoon rearguard failed to inform General Platov's Cossacks he was leaving. As a consequence 'the enemy immediately seized a position on our rearguard's flank,' explained Aleksey Yermolov, the First Army's Chief of Staff, enabling the French cavalry to 'observe our movements'. Ruses only worked for about twenty-four hours at most. The French aim was to identify the direction of retreat and then pin the rearguard, so that they might be bypassed and then fall on the main retreating army's flanks. 'The enemy soon confused their roads,' Yermolov explained, and 'inadvertently got ahead of Panchulidzev and found itself between him and our army'. The lesson was to maintain contact, but more importantly co-ordinate countermeasures. 'The encounter was sudden so Panchulidzev and the French cavalry let each other pass,' the Chief of Staff recalled, 'without firing a single shot.'[20]

Russian rearguard commanders, with their light infantry, cavalry and horse-drawn artillery, generally marched slightly ahead of their cavalry screens. They were constantly on the lookout for places to make a stand: favourable terrain like hilly ground across Moscow Road, a village at a river crossing point, gorges, broken ground or wooded areas. Gzhatsk was chosen as such a location and, like the rearguard at Dorogobuzh, earned some breathing space for the main army withdrawal. The intent was to defend with sufficient force to oblige the advancing vanguard to deploy its infantry. Yermolov remembered their *jägers* (light infantry) 'earned respect from the French and taught them another lesson in prudence'. At Dorogobuzh 'after numerous vain attempts and heavy casualties, the enemy stopped attacking', as more force had to deploy to overcome the opposition. 'The rearguard remained in position and retreated only once the army had covered some distance.'

All this was constantly draining the resources of the French cavalry. 'The cavalry melted very quickly thanks to the engagements and exces-sive marches imposed upon it every day,' remembered an officer with the 16th Regiment of *Chasseurs á Cheval*. He complained about the 'neglect and selfishness' of his senior officers, namely Murat, the commander of cavalry. 'We marched all day,' he recalled with exasperation, 'and halted for an hour at a time, often for two hours, during which it would have been possible to cool off some of the horses.' But they were not allowed to unsaddle. 'Next day we had to march and fight just as though we had been short of nothing,' having bivouacked all night with no water or forage nearby; 'death resulted'.[21]

After over seventy days retreating, the Russian army faced the dilemma that only 114 miles remained before Moscow. It would have to stand somewhere, but where? The risky conundrum ran in parallel with the leadership crisis. Colonel Carl von Clausewitz, serving on the Russian staff, explained, 'Russia is very poor in positions.' In October 1941 Soviet armoured screens attempting to fight rearguards in the forests 7 miles east of Gzhatsk faced the same shortfalls von Clausewitz observed in 1812:

> Where the great morasses prevail, the country is so wooded that one has trouble to find room for a considerable number of troops. Where the forests are thinner, as between Smolensk and Moscow, the ground is level without any decided mountain ridges and without any deep hollows.

The Vyazma–Bryansk defence line was rapidly bypassed by the panzers, creating catastrophic encirclement battles. There were no natural obstacles to exploit until some dominating ground, criss-crossed by stream gullies by the villages of Shevardino and Semyonovskoe to the rear, near Borodino. This was why the terrain had been incorporated into the Mozhaisk defence line. Von Clausewitz further assessed:

> The fields are without enclosures, therefore everywhere easy to be passed; the villages of woods and so ill adapted for defence.

'There is therefore,' he concluded, and he could just as easily have been referring to 1941, 'little choice of positions.' General Peter Bagration, commanding the Tsar's Second Western Army, recalled, 'as usual we have yet to make a decision where and when to give battle.' This huge risk had to be faced at the very time a new supreme Russian commander, Field Marshal Prince Kutuzov, was appointed. 'We are still selecting places and are finding each new one to be worse than the previous,' complained Bagration.[22]

The disappointed General Barclay de Tolly received the stark news of his replacement as he was marching through Vyazma. Von Clausewitz reckoned, 'Barclay was rather a cold man, not readily accessible to other people's ideas, and it is difficult to win the confidence of men of this sort.' The timing was unfortunate, just as de Tolly's developed policy of drawing Napoleon into the interior was showing results and the *Grande Armée*'s superiority in numbers had been significantly reduced. Nevertheless, the nation faced a crisis, and as von Clausewitz commented, 'All were in agreement that at such a time it was essential to have a brave Russian at the top, a pupil of Suvorov, rather than a foreigner.' The Tsar had disliked Kutuzov since the debacle at Austerlitz in 1805 and had been pressured by public opinion to grant the appointment. 'The public wanted Kutuzov,' he confided to his aide, and as far as he was concerned, 'I wash my hands of it.' Kutuzov, who had as many detractors as admirers, was no fool. Beneath the apparent drowsy absent-minded facade, there lurked cunning, patience and keen judgement.[23]

Kutuzov had seen a lot of active campaigning in Poland and against the Turks. His primary value to the army was probably his judgement, not at the tactical level, but more from the morale boost he provided for his Russian soldiers at a vulnerable moment. Field Marshal Suvorov thought, 'He is very shrewd, no one can trick him.' He 'knew Russians and how to handle them,' von Clausewitz recalled. 'How can one go on retreating with young lads like these?' Kutuzov is alleged to have remarked astutely on meeting his new honour guard at Tsarevo-Zaimishe, knowing full well the comment would be repeated from mouth to mouth on every soldier's lips within hours. But at age 65, despite being hale and hearty, he was corpulent and unwieldy on horseback – so much so, he often moved about the field driven in a *droshky* light four-wheeled carriage. Englishman Sir Robert Wilson, accompanying the staff, described him as:

> more disposed to trust to diplomacy for his success than to martial prowess, for which by his age and the state of his constitution he was no longer qualified.[24]

The retreats to the very gates of Moscow in 1812 and 1941 had both precipitated crisis replacements of senior Tsarist and Soviet generals. Kutuzov was appointed to overall command within days of the decisive battle the Russians had sought, until now, to avoid. He had grown stouter since Austerlitz in 1805 and had been engaged on only administrative duties since. The Russian army had, meanwhile, modernised since then, with in particular its artillery and cavalry arms much improved. Relentless rearguard actions had sapped morale and promoted national indignation, but the retreat had sharpened up the practical skills of the soldiers and junior leaders who had conducted it. Kutuzov had played no part in this and had arrived fresh at the field in a rapidly developing operational situation. Likewise, Marshal Zhukov was to appear fresh on the scene 129 years later, abruptly transferred from the situation he had stabilised at Leningrad and parachuted into a similar unknown perilous command situation. Both men were required to offer immediate advice and direction in a deteriorating situation. Zhukov's predecessor, General Dimitry Pavlov, had been shot two months before, alongside his Western Front Chiefs of Staff in communications, artillery and aviation, as well as mechanised corps and division commanders. Like Kutuzov, there was simply no time to offer little more than immediate advice for the battles that would shortly be fought in and around Borodino.

In 1812, the first conundrum was where to fight the decisive battle. Barclay de Tolly remembered that on arrival at Gzhatsk 'the Prince [Kutuzov] found a local position advantageous and ordered the construction of a few fortifications'. It was his Chief of Staff General Bennigsen's suggestion to move on, citing a forest nearby that would cloak the enemy's movements. De Tolly retorted 'that if we were to follow his thinking, there would not be a single acceptable position in all of Russia'. Bennigsen's observations were 'dreadful', de Tolly recalled:

> And so our armies wandered around like the sons of Israel in the deserts of Arabia, from [one] position to another, without any arrangements, until fate led them to the position at Borodino.

Fortifications were started at Fedorovskoe but abandoned, due to a lack of drinking water and the marshy ground that would have inundated the left wing. Another site was investigated near Tsarevo-Zaimishe, where Kutuzov assumed command, attracting further engineering works before it too was rejected. Kutuzov favoured the ground near Kolotsk Monastery, optimistically at first, but then declaring it 'is very good, but also too vast for our army and could expose one of the flanks'. As with the other rejected alternatives, a rearguard was left behind and the army moved on yet again. 'After so many preparations for battle,' recalled Aleksey Yermolov, the first Army Chief of Staff, 'the army refused to believe that a decisive one would ever be fought, although it eagerly awaited combat.' They were fast running out of space.

On 3 September the army retreated back to the area near Borodino and set up camp. Colonel Karl Toll, the Quartermaster-General, consistently engaged with seeking out the succession of aborted locations, now suggested Borodino. Kutuzov disapproved, then hedged his bets, weighing the flaws and advantages of the position until persuaded by Toll to accept. Von Clausewitz looked at it and assessed it was 'a deceptive one, for it promises at first sight more than it performs'. Barclay de Tolly thought it 'favourable in the centre and on the right flank, but the left flank was exposed'. He was right. Kutuzov, nevertheless, took the strategic decision, but his two army commanders, de Tolly and Bagration, would have to carry the fight. Bagration felt his Second Army, which would be on the left, would be the most threatened. The decision had been taken. A battle would be fought here at Borodino, on the lower stretch of the Kolocha river, across the numerous north–south stream gullies that criss-crossed the area between the village and the Moscow river.[25]

Meanwhile, the 'pretty little town of Gzhatsk' described by Major le Roy, with the 85th Line, was no more. As artillery Lieutenant Faber du Faur recalled:

> The fields cultivated with so much care, the houses so clean and tidy, and the château, so charming and fine, all bore testament to the affluence and wealth of the inhabitants, all of whom had fled. Within one day of our arrival, all this property had vanished, destroyed and trampled by our troops.

Major Eugène Labaune, with the IV Corps, had seen the transformation from 'a well laid out park, beautiful long alleys', with 'newly built pavilions evincing the owner's good taste' reduced to 'the most horrible devastation'. Now:

> Everywhere we saw only shattered furniture, bits of precious porcelain strewn about the garden and expensive engravings ripped out of their frames and scattered to the winds.

The army was looking for and found plentiful stocks of corn and forage.

Lieutenant du Faur recalled, 'The entire army had concentrated around Gzhatsk, having heard Kutuzov had been appointed commander of the Russian Army – which suggested that they would offer battle.' Captain Heinrich von Brandt had also heard 'old Kutuzov', nicknamed 'the runaway of Austerlitz', was now in charge. 'This change seemed to augur well for us,' he remembered. 'They would likely fight.'

Napoleon declared a few days' rest, now that a decisive battle was at hand, to enable stragglers to close and reorganise. 'In their present condition,' du Faur with III Corps assessed, 'our units no longer made tactical sense.' Their three brigades 'barely furnished three battalions, namely one light battalion and two line battalions'. Two Portuguese regiments were encamped nearby and their numbers had 'seriously diminished' since crossing the Nieman. They 'more than perhaps any other unit had suffered at the hands of the intemperate climate and the general want of everything', thinned further by casualties at Smolensk and the bitterly fought Russian rearguard at Valutina. Watching them relax amid the ambient glow of campfires, 'we could see how few of them remained with their colours'.

'The Russian army had come to a stop at last!' announced Napoleon's aide de Ségur. They would get their battle. They learned that some 16,000 Russian recruits 'and a multitude of peasants carrying crosses and shouting *God wills it*' had arrived at Kutuzov's camp. Napoleon adroitly observed that 'on the whole he was more able courtier than general'. His significance lay in the surge of nationalist fervour he was able to engender. 'In Moscow,' de Ségur heard, 'the people completely carried away in their elation, kissed each other in the streets and believed that they were saved.'

'The peaceful interlude was of but brief duration,' du Faur remembered: the *Grande Armée* was on the move again between 4 and 5 September. Smoke billowed up from the fires raging in the western suburbs of Gzhatsk as they marched through. 'Carelessness, on the part of soldiers inexperienced in the art of heating and lighting houses constructed out of wood, was largely to blame,' du Faur recalled. The irony was 'that we had managed to extinguish a fire started by the Russians on entering'; now, on leaving, 'despite ourselves we had managed to accomplish their task'.

'The road leading out of Gzhatsk was closed off by a most singular barrier,' du Faur observed. It was a sentry box painted in chequered black and white pattern and the barrier's palisade in Russian national colours had two mobile spiked *chevaux-de-frise* hinged on a wheel, which could be opened and closed. 'The barrier witnessed the movement of massive numbers of troops' traversing through towards Borodino. 'It was an almost continual procession of soldiers of all kinds,' du Faur recalled, 'and you could see men drawn from every nation of Europe jostling each other in their hurry to get to the fore.' Once through, they passed a succession of elegant windmills but 'the area round about was completely devoid of life'. Du Faur's artillery battery was following up the bulk of the army, already well ahead. 'Only a few signs marked the passing of the great mass – dead horses, stragglers and cautious inhabitants emerging from their hideaways.'[26]

The weather had dawned chilly and foggy with drizzling rain. Only through lifting mist patches could Belgian captain François Dumonceau with the 2nd 'Red' Lancers 'see our immense column stretching away as far as the eye could reach' as it crossed 'an open slightly undulating plain'. Chasseur Lieutenant Heinrich Vossler, with the Württemberg contingent, had noticed the 'sharp changes in temperature' after the stifling humidity of the weeks before, which was 'beginning to affect our health and, to a much greater degree, that of the army as a whole'. He marched by soldiers who 'had dropped by the roadside from sheer exhaustion' and then perished from exposure.[27]

Napoleon, as impatient as ever to get to grips with the enemy before it was too late again, castigated his staff constantly over the large numbers of officers' carriages, whose placid progress appeared to impede the line of march. Coming across one such fine yellow carriage, mixed in with the artillery train, he ordered it burned. It belonged to one of his aides, Count Louis de Narbonne, who pointed out it might mean stranding some officer who had lost a leg in the battle. 'It'll cost me even more tomorrow if I've no artillery!' the visibly irate Napoleon responded, ordering escorting chasseurs to set fire to it. The emperor waited for the carriage to catch fire before riding on again. As soon as he was out of sight, the fire was extinguished by the same escort that had set light to it, allegedly paid 10 louis by Narbonne himself to save it.[28]

It became increasingly apparent that the usual hasty ill-prepared attacks on the Russian rearguards were being met with unusual violence. The 11th Hussars, exploiting forward, received a considerable mauling, as did the

3rd Italian Chasseurs, whose withdrawal after a 'terrible scrum' was seen off by Russian infantry and artillery fire. The devastation seen by the approaching *Grande Armée* seemed even more pronounced. One soldier recalled the Russians had 'laid waste the entire plain we were obliged to camp on':

> They'd mown the long grass, felled the woods, burnt down the villages. In a word, had left us nothing to eat, nothing to keep our horses alive, nothing to shelter us.

'How gladly would I renounce for my whole life the warm food so common at home,' declared Private Jakob Walter with the Württemberg contingent in Ney's III Corps, 'if I only did not lack good bread and beer now.' The homesick soldier recalled, 'The thought of my brothers and sisters so far away added to my pain.' This was a common thought, and significant, as they were deep in Russia. What would become of them if they were wounded at this late stage of the campaign so far from home? 'Where ever I looked,' he recalled, 'I saw the soldiers with dead, half desperate faces.' They could not afford to lose.

Everybody was aware the Russians were waiting only a couple hours of march away. De Ségur remembered:

> We were told that they were turning up the whole plain of Borodino, throwing up breastworks and digging in with the evident intention of not retreating another inch.

This is what they all wanted: seventy-six tortuous days marching 590 miles had brought them to within 84 miles of Moscow. They were confident they would win, end the war and spend the winter quartered in Moscow. But having penetrated so deeply into the Russian heartland, they were betting all. One French major, aide to one of the cavalry corps commanders, confided to a Württemberg artillery friend:

> If we don't win a battle so decisively that we capture two hundred guns from the enemy, then our whole army is done for.[29]

3

The Road from Gzhatsk to Borodino

From 114 to 83 Miles to Moscow

Moscow Behind Us! 11–14 October 1941

More and more Soviet trains were heading west converging on Moscow, so many that locomotive drivers followed the lights of the last carriage from the train in front. Freight train vans might be equipped with bunk beds, but most simply had a small stove installed in the centre. Each goods carriage was designed to carry twenty horses or forty men; the latter would relieve themselves by the track or empty buckets at every station stop, taking on hot food. Conversations with wounded heading east told men how long units had been in action and did not augur well. Infantryman Vladimir Boukhenko remembered, 'We gradually began to understand that, at best, we'd be in hospital within a couple of months.'[1]

Wide-ranging *Luftwaffe* air attacks meant units had to disembark further and further away from Borodino and Mozhaisk. Thirty-one-year-old Ivan Barchuk, with 322 Regiment, detrained at dawn on 14 October with the 32nd Division and recalled, 'the day before our arrival Nazi aircraft had bombed the tracks at the station.' The destination had been Mozhaisk, but they had to unload at Dorokhovo, 25 miles short of Borodino, and 60 miles west of Moscow. Three days earlier, Captain Mikhail Kazmirov's 2nd Battalion with the 17th Regiment did arrive closer, at Mozhaisk.

Just before they pulled in, 'German aviation tried several times to bomb the town, but were driven off by anti-aircraft fire', he recalled. They hastily cleared the train and the command post was 'quickly set up,' he remembered, with some urgency, 'and swiftly camouflaged against air attack'. The battalion assembled quickly 'because they could not exclude the threat of a repeat air raid' and joined streams of refugees thronging the roads. 'People were leaving on carts, without their possessions, on hand carts and with children in their arms,' Kazmirov remembered. Barchuk and his companions were 'warned not to talk or ask questions of any people moving out on the highway'.

Colonel Polosukhin's 32nd Division arrived piecemeal over a four-day period starting on 10 October. Unloading during the first forty-eight hours was conducted in vulnerable and tense conditions; nobody knew where the Germans were. Artillery Captain Petrovich Nechaiev recalled the rumours as they approached Mozhaisk. 'In the town there was unease,' with residents fleeing eastward. 'There were rumours that the Germans had captured Gzhatsk,' but they could not be certain. Overhead were constant overflights of German aircraft giving the impression 'the enemy was tearing toward our capital Moscow'. 'Where are the Germans? Where is the front?' Barchuk overheard, 'everyone wanted to know.' Kazmirov's 2nd Battalion unloaded without incident and was immediately ordered to 'force march' to Borodino and 'occupy a defence in the fortified area constructed by engineers at upper and lower Yelnya at the edge of the Minsk highway'. The mission was to delay a German breakthrough.[2]

Polosukhin managed to rapidly hustle two of his infantry regiments forward to the edge of the former 1812 Borodino battlefield site. The 322 Regiment would be to the north or right of the railway line now traversing the former parkland, with 17 Regiment to its left or south. The 113th Rifle and the 133rd Light Artillery and 154 Howitzer regiments were in the process of following. Division headquarters was established in the woods south-east of the village of Novaya Derevnya, north of the Mozhaisk road.

Barchuk's battalion was soon force marching in the direction of Mozhaisk and Borodino. 'A foot soldier is loaded like a donkey,' infantryman Efim Golbraikh later recalled, carrying:

trench coat, backpack, damn gas mask stuffed with hand grenades, a steel helmet, entrenching tool, mess tin, map case and several ammo pouches plus a rifle or machine gun. You're sweating all over. White salt stains would appear on your blouse – you'd take it off and it would stand upright on its own.

On arrival they would freeze all night. 'On their shoulders was 32 kilo-grams of kit,' Barchuk remembered, 'and we were rushing to the front.' The 'main effort was: get a move on! Get a move on!' amid roads crowded with civilians and marching troops, a bizarre mix:

> Within these crowds there were workers in forage caps and without, in Gym clothing and with greatcoats over their shoulders. They were taking cows and goats.

Barchuk realised there were two or three former soldiers in the ranks, whom they did not recognise. 'They were in uniform, but of an undisciplined sort, with hats on a slant', probably 'some sort of youth organization'. 'Comrades, how are things at the front?' they asked them. 'Go ahead, go ahead, go quickly,' was the wry response, 'and you too will run like us,' which added to the atmosphere of fear and uncertainty that was starting to pervade the marching troops. The column was brought to an abrupt halt.

'Repeat what you just said,' a captain demanded, which they did, with some defiance. He peremptorily ordered them to turn about and announced sonorously, 'For the spreading of false rumours and for the betrayal of the nation, you are condemned', whereupon he shot them both in the back of the head on the highway. Wheeling around to the horrified troops, he next demanded with some menace, 'Whoever asked the question – step forward.' Nobody moved, so he repeated it three times. 'Alright,' he accepted, 'if you listen to such questions you are all provocateurs.'

With an abrupt '*right turn – quick march!*' the matter was over. 'There was complete silence for the next two or three kilometres,' Barchuk remembered, until at the next halt a babble of conversation broke out, with guarded comments and pronouncements of, 'Look, you can be shot without a court or its deliberations'.

'Let's see how he conducts himself in battle at the front,' was the murmured conclusion. However, the NKVD officer was gone and not seen again. It had been a sobering experience.[3]

Politburo member Lavrenti Beria, the head of the NKVD, was informed by a confidential October document that Special Sections 'have held 657,364 servicemen separated from their units and running away from the front'. Their actions resulted in 25,878 arrests, of which 10,201 were shot. Those remaining were formed up in units and sent back to the front. NKVD Lieutenant Vladimir Ogryzko commanded such a section operating around Moscow. He was totally uncompromising when dealing with any form of wavering allegiance to the regime. 'Panic was spread by diversionary groups and spies,' he explained, 'who had broken through Moscow's defences':

> There were robberies – everything you can imagine happened – because as usual the people lost their heads … the ill-educated ones. The scum of the earth did show its face. It seeped through.

Beria heard that 4,013 such arrests were made on the Western Front alone, of which 2,136 were liquidated. 'It isn't peacetime,' Ogryzko maintained:

> You're not going to say 'Stop or I'll shoot!' a thousand times before you shoot, nor are you going to shoot in the air. Of course not. You shoot them on the spot. It was a tough command.

He was equally scathing about fleeing Muscovite civilians. 'They are running away,' he explained, 'they were marauders, bastards who thought they'd stay alive at the end of the day.' He frequently ordered their cars overturned into roadside ditches and 'if the driver was crushed, well even better'. Ogryzko identified the core of resistance, the 'beautiful measures' that held the front together. If all else failed there was fear. It was not about human rights and the measures employed 'are neither cruel or mad'. He rationalised, 'Had there not been such a tough order, there would have been total panic.' Of 686 people arrested in front of the Central Sector, 346 were shot; 799 were detained around Bryansk, of which 389 were executed. Ogryzko explained:

Anybody who resisted and didn't obey orders on demand – especially if they moved away or opened their mouths – was eliminated on the spot without further ado.

Moreover this 'was considered a truly heroic act, you were killing the enemy'.[4]

By the time Barchuk's unit reached Volkhovo, 'heads were shaking through the lack of sleep and the weight of helmets', and by dusk soldiers 'were on their knees'. They crossed the Komsomol Square in Mozhaisk shortly before midnight, where loudspeakers were still mechanically intoning the latest news. 'Every soldier greedily lapped up every word,' Barchuk remembered. With bloody defensive battles being waged around Vyazma and Yelnya, 'It was clear that the enemy was in strength and close by.'

The grumble of artillery further west added audible emphasis to the reports as light tanks joined the column on the road. At about the same time, Captain Kazmirov's battalion was moving into its defensive positions near the villages of Yelnya and Rogachyovo. By daylight 'all the sub units were at their camouflaged positions, and in our sector there was a deathly silence'. 'The only thing that could be heard,' Barchuk remembered, 'was the artillery preparing their fire positions.' It had been tricky negotiating a myriad of ditches and obstacles in darkness as they occupied the forward edge of the Mozhaisk defence line near the highway. 'At the exit from the town they warned us: there are anti-tank ditches here, there are minefields we would have to cross by planks thrown across between anti-tank ditches.' Red Army engineers provided guides.

As they started to dig they found 'the water was squelching under our knees'. It could not be done: 'water was oozing from the soil' and it was too dark to see; they needed daylight to reconnoitre their new defensive positions effectively. Where they had arrived 'was equivalent to lying in water'. Commanders conferred urgently and they were moved even further forward, closer to the advancing enemy. Tents and packs were left behind, so they could fight light. They could only change their underwear and take clean spare puttees forward alongside their first-line ammunition scales. Nerves were on edge. 'You cannot die seven deaths,' the proverb was bandied around, 'but you cannot escape one.'[5]

On 11 October the Stavka recalled Major General Lelyushenko from Mtensk to take command of the newly formed Fifth Army at Mozhaisk, but only two regiments from the 32nd Division had begun to occupy the fortified positions around Borodino and Yelnya. Lieutenant Aleksandr Bodnar's KV-1 heavy tank was guided into its assembly area position the night before. He recalled the underlying tension. News came only from scattered fleeing remnants that had broken out of the German encirclement at Vyazma, and none of it was good. Bodnar's brigade commander, Colonel Orlenko, had driven out on to the old Smolensk road, which ran through the 1812 battlefield site, looking for potential tank positions. 'A car with lights on drove up to us at high speed,' Bodnar remembered, 'from the direction of Gzhatsk.' The glare from its blazing headlights compromised their night vision. Orlenko angrily motioned the car to stop, waving his pistol, and approached the occupants, some Red Army soldiers and their lieutenant. 'How dare you violate the blackout!' he hissed with exasperation, at which point 'a shot rang out and the brigade commander fell, and the car sped away'.

'That was our first serious defeat,' Bodnar recalled, not even having closed with the enemy. They were shocked and dumbfounded: 'No one realised anything.'[6]

NKVD Lieutenant Ogryzko targeted such deserters. 'It was right to execute the people who didn't understand their position at a time which had become more cruel for their country,' he insisted. But it was not fear of draconian discipline alone that was motivating the soldiers of the 17th and 322 Regiments, hastily occupying positions under the threat of imminent heavy attack. Colonel Polosukhin's 32nd Siberian Division was a veteran Red Banner unit that had fought the Japanese at Lake Khasan two years before. It was probably the steadiest formation left between the Germans and Moscow at this time, at full strength and with all its equipment. These soldiers had come from the Far East with no comprehension of the horrific casualties suffered by the Red Army to date. They were, moreover, untarnished by the negative fallout from these failures. There was effective unit cohesion. Artillery Captain Nechaiev recalled his Civil War commander Colonel Nikolai Polyansky, who had:

methodically taught his subunit the requirements necessary for war. The regiment conducted marches of many kilometres in severe Far East

conditions. Each of these marches and every tactical exercise concluded
with combat firing.

Despite illness, Polyansky had refused all medical treatment at this crisis
hour. He had a considerable reputation as a crack shot and was acknowledged as an outstanding practical trainer with considerable battle
experience. As one Soviet T-34 crew member testified:

> There was no despair or feeling of being doomed. We were all 20 years
> old, all patriots brought up by the Soviet Union in a fanatical spirit.

Even after the horrors of famine and Stalin's political purges, genuine
affection still remained for the ideals of the Socialist Revolution. One
elderly Tsarist general had confided to German Panzer General Guderian,
when captured at Orel at the beginning of the month:

> We were just beginning to get on our feet and now you arrive and
> throw us back twenty years, so that we will have to start from the begin-
> ning all over again.[7]

The perfidious German invasion the previous June, in the face of the
Non-Aggression Pact of 1939, had aroused deep indignation alongside
the surprise. Anger at this underhand treachery aroused rabid patriotism,
which went hand in hand with a confidence that the Red Army, with its
glorious traditions and modern equipment, would soon see the Germans
off the field. How could the Soviet government have allowed itself to be
so taken by surprise? Many wondered, but wisely kept their opinion to
themselves. Stalin insisted shrewdly, despite his reported shock at the invasion, that Molotov the Foreign Minister, who had actually signed the pact,
should be the one to publicly broadcast they were at war.

Political commissars attached to units occupied staff positions.
Information and political directives often came to soldiers through leaflets
or word of mouth. Obedience was an integral facet in any army. T-34 tank
commander Vladimir Alexeev accepted, 'When a commander sets a task, I
must do as I am told.' He was perceptive enough to appreciate that commissar approval would be a vital prerequisite for future promotion. 'They

sought out brave people,' he explained, and encouraged them to join the Communist Party. They were purveyors of influence, not repression.

Infantry junior officer Anatoly Kozlov recognised the combined effect of fierce discipline, stoic acceptance of one's lot and intense patriotism as important motivators. 'A person only lives once,' Alexeev commented. Soldiers appreciated that commanders would not necessarily be governed by an overriding imperative to avoid or reduce casualties if failure was staring them in the face. Arrest followed by a posting to a penal battalion was 'for the sort of people who had failed to accomplish some mission or who had shot themselves to avoid fighting,' remembered infantry officer Ivan Malyeshev. The main influence exerted by commissars was more their ability to bring pressure to bear on families back home in the event of questionable behaviour by the unit in the line. Both Alexeev and Kozlov agreed most soldiers followed a 'live and let die' philosophy, accepting 'authority only became menacing if things went wrong'. This constrained initiative; nobody wanted to stand out in case of failure.[8]

Excesses committed on Russian soil by invaders in both 1812 and 1941 hardened the resolve to resist. When the *Grande Armée* approached Borodino in early September, stories of French marauders being coura-geously repelled by local villagers spread rapidly through the Tsar's army. Russian soldier Pavel Pushin, with the Semyonovsky Guard Regiment, heard forty-five enemy soldiers were killed and fifty captured during a vil-lage raid where even the women fought back fiercely:

> One 18-year-old girl fought with particular gallantry. Despite receiving a mortal blow, she was so strong in spirit that, with her last breath, she still managed to thrust her knife into the Frenchman who shot her.

Exaggerated or not, Russian soldiers were incensed by such stories and sought revenge.

'When we marched into the Soviet Union,' in 1941, declared junior infantry officer Hans von Bittenfeld:

> We were regarded initially as liberators and greeted with bread and salt. Farmers shared the little they had with us.

All this changed in a self-perpetuating spiral of atrocities and revenge attacks, with rural villagers caught up in the middle. 'The disaster was the Nazis succeeded in driving people who were willing to co-operate with us back into the arms of Stalin,' von Bittenfeld felt. 'We lost because of the bad handling of the Soviet populace.'[9]

The town of Rzhev north of Gzhatsk was bombed heavily by the *Luftwaffe* on the morning of 10 October. 'Awful,' Nina Semjonowa wrote in her diary, 'what lies before us?' Four days later, 'The Fascists have occupied the town,' and the following day she saw the first German columns passing her house. The Lenin statue standing in the main square was removed and gallows erected in its place. The night of 20 October was, she recorded, a sleepless one. 'Gestapo people came and asked everyone the same; they want to know where all the Communists have disappeared to.' Corpses were dangling from the gallows by November 'because they had listened to the radio and because they were Russian and not frightened to demonstrate this to the enemy'. By 28 January 1942 Nina Semjonowa had succumbed to starvation.

In 1812 the destruction of Smolensk heralded the first major loss of civilian lives. De Tolly's Chief of Staff Yermolov remembered it as 'a completely new feeling, which wars outside your native land cannot inspire'. It changed things; the enemy was now laying waste to the Russian heartland:

> I have never witnessed the destruction of my native land or seen burning cities of my motherland. For the first time in my life, my ears heard the moans of my compatriots and for the first time did my eyes see the horror of their terrible conditions.

Russian soldier Fedor Glinka told the story of 'two young peasant girls who were wounded to their hands' while trying to protect their grandfather near Borodino. 'The other killed a Frenchman who injured her mother.' Innocent girls having to fight off the French while the army retreated was particularly emotive.[10]

In 1941 revenge massacres following partisan atrocities on German soldiers produced even more senseless violence. 'We of the SS may be ruthless,' explained Peter Neumann, an officer serving with the 5th SS *Wiking* Division, 'but the partisans also wage an inhuman war and show no mercy':

Perhaps we cannot blame them for wishing to defend their own land, but all the same, it is clearly our duty to destroy them ... where does true justice lie?

Soviet soldiers were aware of the inhumane German treatment of prisoners of war. It is believed that as many as 2 million of the 3 million Red Army men taken since June had perished by October. The Germans could barely logistically sustain the extent of their own advance, let alone feed the additional forty-nine enemy division mouth equivalents they had captured. *Schütze* (Private) Benno Zeiser, guarding one of the camps, described the extent of the neglect:

> Nearly every day we had men die of exhaustion. The others would take their dead back to camp, to bury them there. They would take turns carrying corpses and never seemed in the least moved by them. The camp graveyard was very large; the number of men under the ground must have been greater than that of those still among the living.[11]

For the 32nd Division soldiers, hatred of the Germans became synonymous with the spirit of 1812, described as such in many post-war Soviet histories. It resonates with the significance of the term 'Borodino Field', still emotionally important for the average Russian citizen today. The issue in 1941 was, however, less clear cut. The parents of these soldiers had been brought up following the traditions of the Tsar: absolute loyalty to an autocratic regime supported by the Orthodox faith. Most peasant dwellings displayed a picture of the Tsar alongside a religious icon. Hundreds of thousands of this older generation were consumed in the fires, purges and famines engineered during the emergence of the Socialist Communist State. Their serving sons, by contrast, were developed and educated by the new regime. Comrade Stalin's portrait now hung on the wall. He had ostensibly been hoodwinked by the Nazi Non-Aggression Pact and at present seemed to offer little relief against the fascist hordes rushing up to the very gates of Moscow. The catastrophic series of events appeared inexplicable to those raised to a pitch of social optimism by years of Soviet propaganda. Most people were simply bewildered at events and craved for the government to tell them what to do. Both the regime and general

populace faced the dilemma of what they were prepared to sacrifice for –
Stalin or Russia?

'At the Borodino battlefields the soldiers of the 32nd Red banner
Division saw first many monuments,' recalled artillery Captain Petrovich
Nechaiev, 'towering like sentries, reminiscent of the former motherland.'
Curious soldiers 'went up to the majestic monuments to read the words'.
Colonel Polyansky, his regimental commander, had established his command post in the village of Semyonovskoe, where General Bagration, the
commander of the Second Army in 1812, had set up his headquarters.
It was just a short walk down the road from the museum that division
commander Polosukhin had visited on arrival, and sworn to defend on
the battlefield. Nechaiev saw the unit commissar Ivan Bakanov addressing
soldiers from the 5th Company of 322 Regiment, who were providing the
reserve behind the village. 'Here, on Borodino Fields,' Bakanov announced,
'the Russian nation inflicted the fatal defeat on Napoleon's hordes paying
no heed to their casualties' – a statement as dismaying as it was inspiring.

There was some irony about what was being said because just 1,300yd
up the road was the site of the former Raevsky redoubt, a turning point
during the 1812 battle. The main monument erected to the Russian soldiers in 1839 had been pulled down by the Soviet regime in 1932 because
of its association with the Tsarist era and Orthodox Church. Tsar Nicholas
had reviewed his soldiers marching past this monument, crowned
with a cross, at the battle's first centenary in 1912, six years before the
Revolution. A walk further to the south would have revealed the site of
a 'Grateful Russia to its Defenders' monument, unveiled during the same
visit. Thousands of Russian defenders had perished here heroically holding the Bagration *flèches* to the death. The regime had ordered it destroyed
during the aftermath of the Revolution in 1920. Nevertheless, Commissar
Bakanov emphasised the sacrifice of the Russian soldiers of 1812:

> On the Russian field of Borodino the legend of the invincible
> Napoleonic Army was dispelled. The Russian Army showed itself capa-
> ble of routing any invader.

Clearly they were being invited to emulate the former epic outcome.
Nechaiev continued to watch as, at the foot of the surviving monument to

the 53rd Volinsky Regiment, 'Red Army soldiers took an oath of loyalty to the homeland, the Communist Party and the Soviet Nation.'

These gatherings and small morale-boosting ceremonies were going on all over the old battlefield. Captain Mikhail Kazmirov, with the 17th Regiment, on the highway near Yelnya, which Poniatoski's V Polish Corps had passed through in 1812, remembered: 'The political officers and the companies talked to the soldiers about the immortal heritage of the past, of 1812.' The mood, he recalled, 'was earnest'. The old traditions and religion were not totally eradicated by the Russian Revolution. Helmut Günther, with the *Das Reich*, recalled finding icons in all the Russian huts he entered in the countryside and 'at first, we were rather amazed at that':

> The animosity to religion of the Bolshevik regime apparently had been unable to 're-educate' the people, at least in the country. Again and again we discovered that the average Russian is an outspokenly deeply devout man. The fact that the beautiful churches were being used as warehouses, especially in their cities, was no fault of the locals.

In the midst of a deep national crisis, the Soviet authorities perceived that dying for comrade Stalin did not resonate in the same way that Kazmirov heard the commissar offer. 'Today's men' had 'their fighting tradition and love of the motherland'. Political workers now 'spoke of the protection of Moscow' and a new term, 'the Great Patriotic War'. There were contradictions in this. The Borodino church was, for example, dedicated to the Smolensk Icon of the Virgin, revered as a protector against Russia's enemies from the West. It too had been vandalised during the period after the Revolution.

Artillery Lieutenant Vasily Zapragaev took his soldiers to the dull pink obelisk erected to the artillerymen of the 12th Battery Company that had defended the Shevardino redoubt in 1812. As they dwelt on the inscription 'To the Glory of the Forefathers, 12th Battery, Life Guards of the 3rd Artillery Brigade', the commissar, Nechaiev appreciated, was becoming exasperated by questions from the 'inquisitive intelligence officer Ivan Skiba'. Why 'Life Guards?' he asked, why 'Battery Company?' Questions were not welcome; 'The Russian nation never forgets the feats of its heroes,' the commissar insisted. It is difficult to disentangle the effect the monuments may have had upon the men's morale. The Raevsky mound monument was not restored until 1987, and the rebuild of 'Grateful Russia to its Defenders' waited until 1995. Ivan Barchuk's gritty account of the Borodino fighting that followed in 1941 made no mention of the ghosts of 1812. Battalion and company commanders used every psychological aid at their disposal in order to harden resolve for the coming fight. Nechaiev's battalion commander Captain Sherbakov's appeal was simple and uncomplicated: 'Lads! Is Moscow behind us? Give your life for the sake of Moscow.' Fighting for the Motherland crossed all political and ideological divides. The fact they even had the luxury to pause and consider this was due to the rearguard actions being fought out desperately in the woods to the west. Waves of rolling noise coming from these clashes, accompanied by outbursts of firing away to their front and intermittent tank battles, were becoming perceptibly near.[12]

Ludwig Hümmer, with the *Deutschland* Regiment, was delighted and relieved to see panzer after panzer roll up to the battered village they had occupied the night before. 'It was no rumour,' he recalled, trundling up came familiar panzer crews, men who had fought with them around the Smolensk pocket. Six days before, von Hauenstein's Panzer Regiment 7 from the 10th Panzer Division had been standing on Vyazma airfield. Its two division infantry regiments were still fighting to contain the pocket. *Gruppe Hauenstein* turned up reinforced with an infantry motorcycle battalion and its own integral self-propelled artillery battalion. It was a powerful addition for the proposed advance. Crews had barely time to perform basic maintenance and tighten tracks after ten days' fighting and marching before being dispatched again to support *Das Reich*. Fuel was in short supply, sufficient only for limited distances, and tanks were badly in need of servicing. The average distance driven by their Panzer IIs and IVs since June varied between 6,800 and 7,700 miles. Photographs of Panzer IIIs belonging to 10th Panzer Division taken at this time often show three of six road wheel rubber rims, on one side, shredded down to the metal.[13]

Hümmer's forward elements with 3rd Company were pinned down by heavy machine-gun fire in a shallow ravine, where most had spent the night. This, they identified, came from Russian tanks. 'Our panzers moved forward in the grey light of an early dawn,' he recalled. An impressive display of force, von Hauenstein had over fifty tanks at his disposal. 'We heard them long before they arrived,' Hümmer remembered; they were preceded by bellowing engines and the rattle of heavy tracks:

> From our protected ravine position we experienced a dramatic tank fight, like in a film, except here it was bitter reality. We counted about forty Russian tanks during the action, something like the number we had. A bitter tank engagement unfolded before our eyes, the like of which we had never experienced before!

It is not clear why the engagement developed into such a one-sided affair. 'Ten to twelve of the enemy tanks were soon standing in flames, others retreated,' Hümmer observed. 'A complete success for our panzers!' Druzhinina's 18th Tank Brigade was probably caught by surprise, missing the German armoured approach. Panzer Regiment 7 utilised the wooded cover and severely mauled the Russian tanks, working with *Stuka* dive-bomber attacks. Lacking infantry and artillery support, Druzhinina was caught in the flank while occupying his dispersed screen position. Soviet tank tactics in woods consisted of lying in wait in camouflaged half circles before opening fire at extreme range with their superior 76mm guns. German post-combat reports noted these could 'deliver enormous penetrating energy with high accuracy'. Wide tracks on T-34s also gave greater mobility across boggy conditions because of the dispersed reduced ground pressure. German panzer crews had learned to deal with these superior T-34 and KV-1 types through teamwork, co-operating closely with other panzers, mixing in high-velocity 88mm flak guns mounted in the ground role and aggressive supporting infantry. *SS* infantry deployed tank-hunting groups and spotted for the panzers from within the close confines of the woods. The *Deutschland's* artillery also came forward and fired armour-piercing rounds over open sights at close range.

KV-1 tank commander Aleksandr Bodnar remembered how 'firing in defence' was conducted by tanks dug in with just the gun showing. His 45-ton tank carried 114 76.2mm shells and over 3,000 7.62mm rounds in drums mounted on the three hull- and turret-mounted machine guns. The firing 'distance was checked and a reference point provided in order to have good target lines' of fire. This enabled the concealed tank to kill with the first shot. When fighting offensively, 'the commander orders the driver *short*', which meant the tank halted and the commander allowed himself no more than three to four seconds to take the shot or 'you will be hit by the enemy yourself'. Firing on the move was not considered an effective option by either side.[14]

'Our 50mm KwK tank guns can achieve penetrations only at vulnerable locations under very specially favourable conditions at very close ranges,' one 4th Panzer Division combat report noted in October. By this stage of the campaign German panzer crews had identified the vulnerable points they needed to hit to kill these superior tank types. The T-34 could be immobilised by hitting the tank treads and a direct hit on the driver's front hatch often collapsed it. Much of the driver's upper body was eviscerated by such a shot. More would follow after the distinctive strike splash on metal was observed. If there were doubts whether the vehicle was in fact permanently disabled, groups of panzers would pour in the rounds until flames were positively identified. Tanks on fire were generally irrecoverable if left to burn out.

A strike on the turret ring or armoured cupola of a KV-1 tank could jam the gun's rotation and they were prone, like the T-34, to burn out clutches, because the diesel engine was slightly underpowered. The genesis of German tactical success was close tactical teamwork. Soviet tank crews, by contrast, were often poorly led and had little time to familiarise themselves with their new tank guns or zero them in, since it was found that their fire could be very inaccurate. German tank rangefinder equipment was less effective in poor light conditions, increasingly the case with the onset of winter. In which case, German infantry might ride behind the turret or drivers to assist with target acquisition. Druzhinina may well have misjudged his moment in this battle because the Russian brigade was cut off in the woods, and he only personally escaped encirclement fighting his way out with seven tanks. His deputy commander was killed and thirty-two tanks were lost.[15]

Hümmer watched a dozen tanks knocked out around his position, with only three of their own panzers disabled by snapped tracks. The woods and ravines enabled the German crews to approach and hit the Russian tanks at close range from the flanks and rear. Dry understated combat reports do not reveal the physical and visual tension – 'like a film' – that Hümmer and his companions experienced. The sheer noise from multiple explosive impacts, accompanied by agonised screams and shrieks to get out, were disorientating. Metallic clunks signifying strikes were accompanied by series of popping cracks and bangs as ammunition fires broke out inside tanks. Turrets could be launched skyward, crashing on to their sides, spat out by the enormous uncorked pressure from burning propellant. Gushing globules of yellow and orange flame jetted 100ft into the air, through hull circles vacated by turrets, like inverted rocket exhausts. *SS* troopers hugged the ground beneath the lip of the ravine to avoid pressure waves hissing by, flinging shapeless lumps of metal that spun and gyrated in all directions

'Aim at the hatches and openings!' advised one 6th Panzer Division report during a tank-on-tank melee. A glancing hit on a hatch or other extremity might not appear serious, but the concussive impact of this release of kinetic energy could badly shake up those within. Flakes of metallic paint propelled at velocity were sufficient to pierce skin on hands and faces and draw blood. Successive impacts bludgeoned the senses and drove less-experienced crews to vacate their tanks. On emerging, they were brushed off the sides of vehicles as they scrambled out, hit by supporting tank or infantry machine-gun fire.

When the Russian tanks charged forward, the panzers would disperse off to the flanks and allow the enemy to come in between, before shooting them up from the sides. Colonel Kalihovich's 19th Tank Brigade was also forced out of the wood line, losing some twelve tanks in the process. By nightfall the II Battalion Panzer Regiment 7 and the *Deutschland* claimed forty-one enemy tanks destroyed, with two guns, twenty-seven trucks and 115 prisoners taken. Four German tanks were damaged. Every Soviet tank lost meant on average two to three severely burned or mortally wounded Russian crewmen left lying on the battlefield. Few would survive studied German indifference on capture.

There were tank-on-tank skirmishes all along the main Moscow highway as the advance continued eastwards, moving behind the withdrawing Russian infantry. Forest trails were extremely hard going, even for tanks, but a degree of momentum built up. Hümmer checked out isolated wooden settlements in the woods where they came upon 'women, children and old men' who 'came up to us directly, astounded at our appearance'. 'We were the first *Germanskis* they had seen,' he recalled. Gabbling excitedly, they indicated by raising five fingers that 'Russian soldiers, five minutes ago – gone!' There was excitement at the *SS* division's parent *XXXX Panzer Korps* headquarters, which reported 'the tanks of the 10th Panzer Division have advanced to within three miles of Yelnya', and 'has destroyed a total of 56 Russian tanks', including ten T-34s in the past twenty-four hours. They could see they were approaching the historically famous field at Borodino, but not that this was the outermost fringe of the Mozhaisk fortified zone.

Captain Mikhail Kazmirov was with the 2nd Battalion of the 17th Regiment covering the approaches to Yelnya on the Moscow highway. He recalled 'a soldier from the cavalry reconnaissance platoon rushed inside the CP to report they had clashed with an enemy company and several tanks in the area of Klemyatino', further west, and that they were 'coming towards them'. The Soviet battalion commander briskly informed all sub units by telephone and told them what had happened. 'Be on the alert,' he ordered. Then 'at around 6 p.m. the enemy in about platoon strength supported by three tanks with crosses came out of the woods,' Kazmirov remembered, 'and came towards our defended area'.[16]

The second battle of Borodino was about to begin.

Ground of 'No Particular Advantage', 5 September 1812

'When Kutuzov examined the position at Borodino for the first time,' his adjutant Alexander Golitsyn recalled, 'a large eagle soared above him.' Such a phenomenon was normally viewed by Russian (and Austrian) soldiers as the precursor to a successful fight. The men looked up and were suitably impressed. 'Wherever he went the eagle followed him.' It appeared the diplomat Ivan Anstedt, Golitsyn remembered, 'was first to notice it, and the people discussed it endlessly'. The rank and file always perked up when Kutuzov, their *batiushka*, or little father, appeared, and started to perform normally humdrum tasks at the double. 'The eagle foretold good fortune for us,' Golitsyn surmised, and set the old soldiers off reminiscing about Kutuzov's feats in the Turkish wars. Former days of humiliating retreat would now be crowned with success. The Prince wrote exultantly to the Tsar that:

The position I have taken up at Borodino four miles from Mozhaisk is one of the best you could find in this rather weak terrain. I have resorted to artifice in order to remedy the one weak sector of the line, which lies on the left. I only hope the enemy will attack us in our position: if they do, I am confident we shall win.[17]

His chosen battlefield stretched across beautiful rolling countryside broken here and there by copses or larger birch and pine woods. It had not changed much even by 1941, apart from some newly established small villages, and still held the strategic advantage of lying astride two key routes leading to Moscow. Kutuzov covered the old and new Smolensk roads, which ran east on converging courses to link at Mozhaisk behind the battlefield. The road then continued through a vast tract of forest to Moscow. Colonel Polosukhin's 32nd Division in 1941 likewise covered the Mozhaisk highway (the former new Smolensk road) to the north and the Minsk–Moscow highway running in parallel further south, from west to east. In between was a railway constructed in the 1860s.

Kutuzov's right (northern) flank was covered by the steep banks of the Kolocha river, which ran south-west to north-east towards the Moskva river. Von Clausewitz, the perceptive Prussian officer serving with Kutuzov's headquarters, remembered the road, covered by a fortified chain with twenty-six artillery pieces 'runs unfortunately not at right angles to the Kolocha, but parallel for some distance' until it 'diverges from it at an obtuse angle', where two further heavy batteries were ensconced north of the road near Gorki village. The southern flank rested in the area where several streams converged like wheel spokes to a hub, near the village of Borodino. The extreme left was anchored on a small knoll between the villages of Shevardino and Doronino. Von Clausewitz highlighted the weakness of the position, because it presented an oblique rather than right-angled block to the route towards Moscow. This meant 'the army stands obliquely to its line of retreat and exposes its left flank to the enemy'. It might enable the French to exploit the line of the old Smolensk road to the south, which led from the village of Yelnya, 'straight behind the rear of such a position'. Yermolov, Barclay de Tolly's Chief of Staff, had also noted 'the old postal road to Mozhaisk wound through the forest for one mile from the left wing, gradually skirting around our positions'. This caused particular concern to Russian General Bagration, whose Second Army was supposed to cover the weak left. He urged the construction of a redoubt on the Shevardino mound and further *flèches* to be constructed by Semyonovskoe village, to compensate.[18]

In order to achieve greater depth in 1941, engineers established the forward edge of the Mozhaisk fortified zone along the line of the Elenka river. This scoured a ravine that ran north–south from a roadblock at Golovino on the Mozhaisk road via the villages of Koloch and Rogachyovo, built since 1812, to Yelnya on the Moscow highway. The fortified strip crossed the old Smolensk road, which diverged from the highway to Utitsy and Borodino railway station. The Napoleonic front line of 1812 was 2 miles further back. The haste with which this line was chosen led to some rancour among senior officers, with many alternatives debated and disregarded. By contrast, the development of the Mozhaisk fortified line in 1941 resulted from considered engineer surveys, not conducted under time pressure. The similarity of the finished result to 1812 exemplified the universal nature of terrain advantages, despite revolutionary changes in weapons and tactics. Broadly following Kutuzov's key sites, the Soviets built concrete bunkers along the banks of the Kolocha river near the Koloch railway halt, via Aleksandrovo and Fomkino, through Borodino and Gorki villages, then north to Maloe Selo, not far from the right of the 1812 line near Maslovo. The bunkers covered the route of the Mozhaisk highway, formerly the new Smolensk road at the time of the Tsar.

The centre of the 1941 blocking zone lay astride two parallel roads leading to Moscow, at right angles to any approach from the west. It ran south from Borodino village, with its 1812 two-storey church still intact, through the site of the old Semyonovskoe village down to Borodino railway station and Utitsy village, with its distinctive mound to the southwest, to Artyomk village on the Moscow highway. Colonel Polosukhin sited his 17th Rifle Regiment left and 322 Regiment right of the railway line that ran between the two main roads leading to Moscow. His third regiment, the 113th, was sited north of the Kolocha river, also at right angles to any approach from the west.

Siting in 1812 and 1941 sought to exploit the defensive aspect of the river lines and ravines running broadly north–south. Extensive anti-tank ditches steepening and widening the streamlines produced formidable obstacles for any movement towards Moscow. Areas of high ground, characterised by isolated knolls and gentle ridgelines and escarpments, were to be crucial to both battles. A high water table precluded digging trenches or erecting fortifications in many areas, unless ditches were dug through marshy locations to produce moats. As a consequence, the villages of Yelnya, Shevardino, Semyonovskoe and Utitsy would be fiercely contested in both 1812 and 1941. Colonel Polosukhin sited his 367th Anti-Tank Battalion at Yelnya, within a cluster of concrete bunkers and as part of a fortified Artyomk village, along the Moscow highway. The 121st and 421st Anti-Tank Battalions covered the approach of the other primary road crossing the battlefield near Shevardino and Borodino and further in depth along the line of the Mozhaisk highway towards Gorki. The 316th Artillery and 154th Howitzer Battalions were sited in depth on other similarly dry spots behind the outer and middle defence zones. The depth of the Soviet line extended as far back as the villages of Gorki, Tatarinovo and Psaryovo, which was also where Kutuzov's and Barclay de Tolly's 1812 headquarters had been located.

One 17-year-old Russian ensign, Avraam Norov, recalled how in 1812 'all nearby heights were glittering with the steel of our bayonets and the copper of our guns'. The streams of the Voina, Stonets and Ognik brooks deeply scoured the ground and created steep banks, which would be a hurdle for French infantry to surmount. In the centre the Russians had occupied heights that dominated the surrounding area in all directions. Here 'the air was filled with the voices of hordes of men and the neighs of horses,' Norov remembered. Semyonovskoe village occupied a key position on a hill at the east bank of the shallow brook of the same name. Its combustible wooden houses had no defence value, so the whole village was dismantled and the material used to rivet field defences and artillery positions. 'Only two houses were still standing out of one hundred,' recalled General Bagration's adjutant Sergei Mayevskii. They were sequestered for the General and his staff.[19]

The position was strong on the right, in General Barclay de Tolly's First Army area. Kutuzov was convinced the French would make their main effort along the axis of the new Smolensk road. The Raevsky battery redoubt would remedy this, with two short side-facing openings, and two long forward-slanting parapets, meeting in a 160° 'V'. The fortification was open at the rear and was constructed, as Engineer Lieutenant Dementii Bogdanov recalled, from 'wood and iron from the nearby villages that had been dismantled'. 'Wolf pits' were dug 116yd ahead to ensnare any cavalry approach on the open rolling terrain to its front. Attackers would encounter 8ft-high palisades, inclined to 6½ft for defenders inside. Arcs of fire interlocked with other batteries at Gorki to the rear, on the opposite side of the new Smolensk road, and a sixty-gun open battery as well as the VII Corps artillery to its left. Bogdanov was well satisfied with his engineers' efforts:

> Emperor Napoleon saw a simple, open battery yesterday but his troops will find a true fortress here today; over 200 cannon protect its approaches, its ditches are of sufficient depth and width, the glacis is well done and we will have a clear sight of what is happening.[20]

It dominated the road axis that Kutuzov assessed would be the likely approach and the open ground fell away from the front of it towards Semyonovskoe, slightly forward to its left. This enabled the gunners to attain the full 'grazing' effect of bouncing projectiles at knee to chest height into the ranks of any approaching French.

The Raevsky mound, with the scar of its 1912 obelisk destroyed by the Soviets in 1932, similarly dominated the Mozhaisk highway, which followed the line of the new Smolensk road in 1941. Five formidable 76mm gun concrete bunkers supported by fifteen concreted machine-gun emplacements were clustered around the slope and south of the Kolocha river in the vicinity of the 1812 Museum, Borodino village and successive river crossing points on the road to Gorki village. They were all designed to block an advance from the west, with four concrete emplacements covering the approaches to Borodino village itself. History was repeating itself.

Bagration's Second Army deployment on the centre and left of the 1812 line was much more vulnerable by comparison. As von Clausewitz explained:

> The ground taken up by the left wing presented no particular advantages. Some hillocks with a gentle slope, and perhaps 20 feet high, together with strips of shrubby wood, formed so confused a whole, that it is difficult to pronounce which party would have the advantage of the ground.

Von Clausewitz sensed the French would see the strength of the right and be immediately attracted to press in on the left. He had correctly identified the Achilles heel of the deployment. 'Thus,' he concluded, 'the best side of the position, the right wing, could be of no avail to redeem the defects of the left.'[21]

Bagration felt he needed a redoubt at Shevardino to anchor the Russian line on the left. Lieutenant Bogdanov's thirty pioneers had been working on it since the evening before, on 4 September. Hard ground and the shortage of labour meant that seven hours' labour sufficed only to produce a foot-deep trench around walls barely 5ft high. The pentagon-shaped structure could only accommodate three guns; the remaining nine guns of the 12th Battery Company had to be unlimbered on a hill to the north side of the mound. Hastily constructed embrasures and crude earthworks compromised the effectiveness of the fire support that could be brought to bear. Moreover, the newly installed battery was within range of a hill located about 200yd to the south-west, which if taken would seriously expose the redoubt to counter-battery fire. Prince Andrey Gorchakov, the nephew of Kutuzov's prime patron, the renowned Field Marshal Suvorov, was tasked with 8,000 infantry, supported by 4,000 cavalry and thirty-six guns to defend it. They began to occupy the mound and the villages of Doronino and Shevardino, to the left and right.

The last contested Russian rearguard was fought at Gridnevo, on the new Smolensk road, coming from Gzhatsk. On the morning of 5 September, Eugène's IV Corps on the left flank of the *Grande Armée* was advancing rapidly. 'Pushing through a forest,' Albrecht Adam recalled, 'we were troubled by Cossacks but drove them back through some partially destroyed villages.' A scorched-earth policy preceded the advance, so that 'the desolation caused by these horsemen meant that it was relatively easy to follow their traces'. More firing was heard up ahead by early afternoon. Russian columns were observed winding their way towards a 'huge plateau' where 'it seemed that Prince Kutuzov was drawing up his army for a trial of strength,' Adam recalled:

On our right we could see the Kolotsk Abbey, its multitude of towers making it seem a miniature city. The domes on these towers were glittering in the sunshine and shone through the clouds of dust raised by our numerous cavalry.

A running fight developed with the final Russian rearguard, with Borodino just under 7 miles away. One Würtemberger artilleryman with the French vanguard recalled the Russians 'chose very advantageous positions'. They were fired upon by Russian artillery from the left side of the monastery, which was occupied by skirmishing light infantry *jägers*, with cavalry screening their right flank. 'We unlimbered our guns and the fighting soon turned into a hell,' he remembered. 'The Russians persisted for a quarter of an hour before they hastily retreated' with the French in hot pursuit. Russian cavalry made frequent charges to enable General Dimitry Konovitsyn's rearguard to break clean, which it did, under considerable pressure.

Meanwhile, the rest of the *Grande Armée* was closing up, moving through what Adam described as 'sombre' countryside. Before long the Russian army gradually came into view. Saxon dragoon officer von Leissing swept the field with his telescope and recalled:

> As far as my inquisitive eye could see the whole ground to the left and right was covered with a growth of hazel bushes, junipers and other brushwood, which rose to at least a man's height. To the left centre, about two thousand paces distant, stood a village [Borodino] and a nice Byzantine church which rose from a gentle tree-covered slope and had a pretty tower plated in green copper.

Adam, gazing into the distance, could see 'the plain before the Russian position was devoid of supplies'; it had been completely devastated:

> The fields had been harvested, the villages burnt to the ground and so it was that we had nothing to eat, nothing to feed our horses and nothing in which to take shelter.

This was the first time they had a view of the Russian army that had eluded them since the preceding June. Von Leissing scanned right and made out a ridge 'covered along almost all its length with masses of Russian infantry and artillery':

> As I could clearly see through my telescope the Russians had thrown up earthworks on some of the highest points of the ridge. These

fortifications were cut into notches which seemed to be embrasures for the artillery.

He could even pick out the towers and churches of Mozhaisk off to the right in the distance.[22]

The fluid rearguard action, meanwhile, increased in pace. The Russians on the plain ahead turned into the direction of fire when they saw Konovitsyn's troops come into view, pursued energetically by the French advance guard. What happened next was as swift as it was unexpected. The infantry columns were forcing the pace along the line of the new Smolensk road. Horse artillery were periodically unlimbering to fire into the pursuit, which was being contested by cavalry. Retreating artillery and transports came across the Kolocha bridge at Borodino, while the cavalry waded through the river on both sides of the village. At around 2 p.m. Prince Eugène arrived with the French advance guard to recon-noitre the Russian positions coming into view ahead. Napoleon came up and after a brief conversation ordered him to begin probing attacks towards Borodino. Eugène's 13th and 14th Divisions moved towards the heights of the Voina stream north of the village to fix and threaten the Russian right flank. The rest of the *Grande Armée* started to move up when General Montbrun, the II Cavalry Corps commander, informed his superior, Murat, that he had spotted a major fortification between the villages of Doronino and Shevardino. Captain François Dumonceau, an Imperial Guard lancer, identified:

> A broad, tall hillock, like a truncated cone, which we took for a redoubt. Some individuals were visible on its summit, probably put there to observe.

Napoleon, studying the ground, could see what appeared to be the main concentration of Russian force, and quickly discerned the vagaries of a position that was seemingly very strong on the right, with nothing on the left. He was observing from an oblique angle, which in addi-tion to obscuration from drizzle and smoke from burning villages, prevented him from seeing the entire layout. He could see nothing to the left because the redoubt was, in fact, the end of the Russian line.

It made eminent sense therefore to shift left. The redoubt was in the way. Dumonceau saw that:

> At its base and behind its flanks we could make out two black masses, which could only be the heads of the columns intended to support it.[23]

It is not clear whether Napoleon realised this was the end of the Russian line, but the redoubt would impede the drawing up of his army as he shifted left. It was mid-afternoon and he decided it should be taken before it got completely dark. As the Russians looked on, the *Grande Armée* swung perceptibly left. The Corps were approaching in diamond formation and Poniatowski's Polish V Corps was already starting to emerge on to the old Smolensk road to the left of the Russian position, while Eugène's IV Corps was in the process of pinning the Russian right in place.

French engineers were brought forward to start erecting pontoon bridges across the Kolocha river west of Borodino and its Semenovska stream tributary. Napoleon, without waiting for the rest of the I Corps divisions to arrive, ordered General Compans's 5th Division from Davout's corps to attack the redoubt they had identified from the northwest. Poniatowski's V Corps, approaching the village of Yelnya on the old Smolensk road, was to support with a flank attack from the southwest. At around 3 p.m. Compans's troops crossed the Kolocha river at Fomkino, followed by the two cavalry corps of Nansouty and Montbrun. The Russian line at this stage ran diagonally along a south-west to northeast line similar to a half-opened lid, with the left extremity at Shevardino and the right at Maslovo. The sudden move to the left by the French represented leverage by a force of 34,000 to 36,000 men supported by 194 guns, which might open the lid completely. This leftward stance was unexpected for the Russians. Napoleon had barely arrived and caught them unbalanced.

Russian militia soldier Fedor Glinka climbed the bell tower of the Church of the Nativity at Borodino as evening approached. Initial French probing attacks against the village had been repelled by Guard *Jägers* and the Elisavetgrad Hussar Regiment, supported by artillery on the Russian home bank of the river. It had turned into a beautiful evening and the unharvested fields 'waved as a golden sea and were coloured by the rays of the setting sun'. 'In the midst of this golden sea,' Glinka recalled, 'was a steel river of bayonets and muskets that glittered in the evening sun.' The height and thickness of the crops meant 'people almost could not be seen'. Glinka was oblivious to the significance of the nightmare command dilemma emerging for the Russians. Kutuzov was facing the wrong direction. The Russian army was divided into a right wing, which was almost too strong, and a left wing, which was vulnerable and over extended. The French army was ignoring the right and perceptibly shifting left. Glinka observed:

> how the entire French line narrowed in some places and swelled in another, with all these masses seemingly merging to the right, towards the old Smolensk road. It was a remarkable sight!

The commanders of Kutuzov's First and Second armies had been seriously wrong-footed by this choice of deployment, and were beginning to appreciate they must redeploy to form a right-angled block to Napoleon's approach. In so doing the centre of the Russian army's stance would have to shift between Utitsy on the left through Semyonovskoe in the middle to Borodino village on the right. The ensuing battle would then be fought on a plain no more advantageous to them as a position than any other plain in Russia. They had lost the advantage of ground.

The French were completely unaware of what had already been achieved tactically. 'It was wonderful to see the keenness of our troops,' recalled horse artillery Colonel Lubin Griois:

> The beauty of the scene was enhanced by the splendid sky and by the setting sun, which was reflected from the muskets and sabres. From its positions the rest of the army watched the troops as they marched on, proud to have been chosen as the first to come to grips with the enemy.

The telltale rattle and pick-pock of musket fire could already be heard to the south-west of the knoll, where the first of Poniatowski's V Corps men began to skirmish with Russian *jägers* ensconced among trees and the undulating scrub to the left of the redoubt. The Russians were not ready to begin a general engagement under these unexpected conditions. They needed to shift the entire line so that it faced directly west.[24]

Part One: The Approach to Borodino

Colonel Viktor Polosukhin, Commander of the 32nd Rifle Division.

'Like ants moving around': it appeared as if the whole population of Moscow was out digging for her defence.

The *Reich* advance guard: a mix of motorcycle infantry and towed heavy weapons.

Helmut Günther with the *Kradschützen* Battalion *Reich* remembered how 'suddenly danger would threaten from some place where one would least expect'.

Unteroffizier Ludwig Horn of the 10th Panzer Division: 'I enjoyed the strength of our army.'

Slaughter in the Vyazma pocket, 'a mincing machine' as one Soviet soldier remembered.

Soviet soldiers addressed by an officer beneath the Kutuzov Monument in Gorki village.

Captain Mikhail Kazmirov, with the 2nd Battalion, 17 Regiment, was to fight at Yelnya. He strolled around the 1812 monuments immediately prior to the battle.

'A feast of Church towers': Napoleon's army pauses at Vyazma at the end of August 1812. (Albrecht Adam)

The road leading out of Gzhatsk was closed off by a Tsarist Imperial barrier. Thousands of Napoleon's troops passed through it in early September, heading for Moscow. (Faber du Faur)

Albrecht Adam's depiction of the battlefield as it came into Napoleon's view on 5 September 1812, showing Borodino village church, the Russian right of the line, from which soldier Fedor Glinka watched the French advance.

General Barclay de Tolly
commanded the northern part of
the Russian line from Borodino to
Semyonovskoe village. (Military
Gallery of the Winter Palace)

General Kutuzov, commanding the
Tsar's Imperial Army, misjudged the
direction of Napoleon's approach.
(S. Troshin Moscow)

General Bagration commanded the southern sector down to Utitsy village on the old Smolensk road. (Museum of the Great Patriotic War, Moscow)

PART TWO
BORODINO FIELD

4

The Road by Rogachyovo, Yelnya and Shevardino

From 86 to 84 Miles to Moscow

Break-in, 13–14 October 1941

The first view *Oberleutnant* (Lieutenant) Lohaus had of the Mozhaisk defence line was nothing like that experienced by Napoleon's junior commanders reaching the Russian line, coming from the same road 129 years before. Lohaus, a platoon commander with the 5th Company of Panzer Regiment 7, was moving cautiously forward on foot from the village of Golovino, just north of the Koloch railway halt. He was part of the vanguard of 10th Panzer Division and conducting a joint tank/infantry recce with the 9th Company commander from the *SS Deutschland* Regiment. In 1812 they would have been able to discern the crude pentagon-shaped earth-constructed outline of the Shevardino redoubt. The only other fortifications then were similarly hastily constructed earth wall emplacements to the south at the Raevsky redoubt and the Bagration *flèches* to its left. Lohaus, by contrast, observed a modern defensive belt of concrete bunkers extending kilometres beyond to the rear. He recalled:

> The system of positions extended for the most part halfway up the slope in an arc from the north-east to the south-west as far as Rogachyovo [village] and from there to the south-west toward Yelnya.

Such an integrated defence network, clearly evident in front, would require a planned deliberate attack to overcome. It was unlikely to be pierced by a hasty attack off the line of march. All Soviet eyes were on the Moscow highway, 3 miles further south by the village of Yelnya. Lohaus commanded the panzer element of the *Reich* Division's advance, accompanying the 9th Company infantry, which had passed Golovino an hour before. Their direction of approach mirrored Napoleon's 1812 route and was totally unexpected. They had attracted desultory rifle fire on penetrating Golovino but little else. The *SS* infantry had quickly dismounted the panzers and occupied the houses. 'We observed through binoculars how the enemy was still working on his positions without the faintest idea we were there,' Lohaus subsequently wrote in his post-action report. 'He was digging trenches and in the process of building new bunkers.'

Lohaus could see a long line of pipes sticking out of the ground. These were automatic flamethrowers, dug in and initiated by covering bunkers, to douse any infantry approaches in flame. Behind them was a herringboned system of mined zigzag trenches, festooned with wooden stakes, barring the way to an immense anti-tank ditch, filled with muddy water. The idea of these so-called 'asparagus beds' was to ensnare any advancing panzers, which would then be finished off by artillery fire. Any tanks managing to get across would then face dense barbed-wire entanglements up against a belt of 'Spanish riders' or 'Czech Hedgehogs', which were railway tracks welded into asterisk-shaped obstacle clusters. Beyond these, Lohaus discerned distinctive mound-shaped concrete bunkers, with freshly dug infantry field emplacements in between. It was a formidable position, later found to be up to 14km deep.[1]

Oberleutnant Lohaus ordered three Panzer IIIs to advance south in wedge formation from the Koloch railway and halt to enter an east–west depression that offered a covered approach up to the fortifications. By so doing they avoided the obvious approach along the Mozhaisk road, the old Smolensk road in Napoleon's time. This was covered by Soviet field emplacements and bunkers along virtually its whole length as far as Borodino village. The 9th *SS* Company infantry led the advance, echeloned by platoons, maximising terrain cover, on an approach some 300–500yd wide. There was a sharp crack when the leading Panzer III approached the small bridge spanning the anti-tank ditch. Debris was flung into the air, followed by another detonation 80yd to the right as another crossing was collapsed into the ditch. Having raised their drawbridges, Russian fire gradually raised in tempo as concealed bunkers opened up against the SS infantry seeking to cross the Elenka stream bed, widened to form a steep-sided anti-tank obstacle.

Lohaus brought up two heavier Panzer IVs 'which were in position on some high ground' and 'were able to suppress that fire'. His report records that 'four enemy bunkers were destroyed in a short time'. The 9th Company infantry managed to scramble across the debris of the destroyed ditch crossing points and close in on the enemy bunkers, using tank covering fire and their 12th Company heavy machine-gun platoon, which had joined the fight. Supporting panzers fired armour-piercing rounds directly at bunker openings and observation ports. Embrasure-blasting infantry groups, supported by riflemen and machine guns from the flanks, suppressed all openings, while three to four men poked pole charges through the firing slits and placed satchel charges up against bunker walls. The shockwaves from these explosions broke off large chunks of concrete, which ricocheted around inside, propelled by the velocity of the blast, and this disabled the Soviet occupants. Infantrymen burst in to finish off any shocked survivors with grenades and automatic fire.

Lohaus climbed out of his tank with his section leader *Oberfeldwebel* (Senior Sergeant) Scholz and 'approached the stream bed under cover and after a long search located a crossing'. Meanwhile, the SS infantry had penetrated as far as the village houses in Rogachyovo further to the right and south. Enemy fire built up steadily. Lohaus appreciated they were being pinned down, recalling 'the left wing of the company hung back even more, since the high ground to the left was heavily wooded and a bunker, which had initially remained silent, opened fire'. Two resounding metallic clunks indicated that one of his Panzer IVs had been hit twice by the new bunker, before it too was put out of action by the concentrated fire of two of his other tanks. The battle was reaching a teetering point.

Urgently seeking some way to get his tanks across the ditch, Lohaus realised the Russian 'demolition had not been a complete success'. 'At that point,' he recalled, 'the ditch was only half as deep as elsewhere and could be filled up with tree trunks that were lying nearby.' This made a crossing possible, and he guided his tank platoon across the ditch, to support the *SS* making headway in Rogachyovo.

Obersturmführer (Lieutenant Colonel) Tost, the commander of the 1st Battalion *Deutschland*, came up with his men and immediately began to enlarge the penetration on the south side of the village. Sensing a break-through was imminent, *SS Oberführer* (Colonel) Bittrich decided to exploit the initial success of the 9th Company with his entire regiment. The battalions, led by the 1st, had been closing up behind in echelon, using the same covered approach found in the initial reconnaissance. Bittrich sought permission to commit the entire *Deutschland* Regiment at 1.22 p.m. and was told by his division commander, 'Approved. Advance past Yelnya to the north.' The radio message informed Bittrich, 'Der Führer will join you in the attack.' Hausser had decided to penetrate the line without pausing to set up a deliberate attack. With the arrival of fresh units, Lohaus remembered 'the command relationship of our reinforced [tank] platoon,' now in a crucial position to support, 'was not entirely clear'. Hausser ordered him to continue to support rolling up the Rogachyovo to Yelnya position, which the 1st Battalion *Deutschland* had started. Lohaus had just crossed the anti-tank ditch with his panzers when:

> I received a radio message that by order of the corps, I was to return to my company and battalion.

His tanks turned around and re-crossed the bridge, now made pass-able by *SS* engineers, to return to his company, retracing his route back through Koloch and Golovino, so audaciously reached that morning. An intensely irritated Bittrich radioed his displeasure to division headquar-ters, complaining about such incomprehensible directions. 'Pass on to corps headquarters,' he radioed at 4.40 p.m., 'infantry has broken through without heavy weapons.' He added the 'order withdrawing armour is irre-sponsible'. At the very point he had achieved a decisive penetration, his only supporting armour was taken away.[2]

The first reports coming into Soviet Colonel Polosukhin's 32nd Division headquarters were bleak. The 1st Battalion of the 17th Regiment was holding the sector the Germans were attacking, with the 3rd Battalion in depth. '1/17 and 3/17 battalions lost communications with the regiment's headquarters,' his operations diary noted, 'units acted with no concordance, and were scattered by the enemy artillery and mortar fire.' The break-in came as a complete surprise. 'They retreated eastwards by small groups towards Borodino and Artyomki' some 3 miles to the rear. Soviet communications were not working well. Polosukhin ordered the 3rd Battalion to counter-attack the penetration point at Rogachyovo, but the report read 'the attack was not well organised, came late and failed'.[3]

The 2nd Battalion 322 Regiment moved out of Semyonovskoe village to retake Rogachyovo during the afternoon and met a similar fate. Intense German mortar and machine-gun fire lashed the advance to such an extent that heavy casualties obliged the unit to stop 500m short of the village at about 4 p.m. and dig in. An hour later they were ordered to renew the assault with an additional company and an artillery battery in support. Neither the infantry and the artillery reinforcement materialised, again probably due to poor radio communications, and the attack had to be postponed.

Fighting was now verging on the area where Napoleon's first troops had entered the battle area in 1812. The area behind Rogachyovo and Yelnya villages saw the emergence of Compans's 5th Infantry Division and Mansouty and Montbaun's Cavalry Corps pouring across the Kolocha river to the north, near Fomkino and Doronino. General Poniatowski's V Polish Corps cut diagonally across the rear of the outer 1941 Soviet defence belt and passed through Yelnya, which existed as a settlement in 1812.

In 1812 the 'queen' of the battlefield and the biggest killer of men was artillery. This was replicated by the fighting around Borodino in 1941, but there the resemblance ends. The main artillery protagonists in 1812 were six-, nine- and twelve-pounder guns, which generally deployed in sight of the enemy at ranges between 400 and 1,200yd. Between 700 and 800yd combat range was the generally regarded distance for maximum effectiveness. At these ranges they could often be seen setting up, and came as no surprise. They could fire an explosive projectile, in the case of howitzers, commonly one-third heavy with gunpowder. Much of the impact came from solid shot, which was fired to 'graze' the surface of the ground to produce a glancing bounce to a man's height at between 300 and 500yd, causing gruesome head and shoulder injuries. The next graze with continuing ball momentum was at waist height at 500–800yd, which struck the body core, and if a third graze came at 800–1,000yd, it could chop soldiers over at knee and ankle height. The velocity of the tumbling ball was sufficient to dismember bodies and pulverise equipment, producing even more lethal flying debris at each graze. In 1812 shell bursts were far inferior in effect compared with 1941 equivalents.

The power of modern artillery was anything like twelve to twenty times more destructive. Polosukhin's initial operations reports mentioned the extent to which his 17th Regiment battalions 'were scattered' by incoming German artillery and mortar fire. Unlike in 1812, there was an element of surprise when it landed. German 75mm and 105mm medium guns were fired from distances varying from 7 to 11 miles, well out of sight of the intended victims. Modern artillery is rarely spotted by ground troops until the first shells arrive, when they are often vulnerable and in the open. Even two-man portable 81mm mortars, employed by both sides directly in support of infantry attacks, like those at Rogachyovo, were far superior to six or eight conventional Napoleonic artillery pieces. In 1812 artillery could manage to fire at a rate of about two rounds per minute, whereas two 81mm mortars could blanket a small confined area with twenty to twenty-four rounds per minute, at a superior range to maximum Napoleonic artillery shoots, and remain concealed. Each mortar round weighing about 7.7lb contained over 1lb of TNT explosive, far more volatile and destructive than gunpowder.

The sheer weight and rate of *SS* artillery batteries firing groups of 75mm and 105mm shells by battery fire in multiples of six could smother a defensive emplacement with sixty or twenty-four rounds respectively per minute. Each bang contained nearly 13 to 33lb of TNT. The power of this explosive mix immediately over-pressurises the air around troops caught in the open, or even under cover, with millisecond blast waves that rupture body tissue and organs in its wake. The flash of the explosion scorches skin, while flying metal shrapnel dismembers bodies, as the shockwave tears lung tissue and blood vessels. These blows impair the ability of the body to oxygenate and breathe, causing victims to suffocate or drown in their own blood. The only preventative measure is to get out of the way or take cover. Nothing can move in an artillery bombardment. Near misses knock people over and burst ear membranes, causing temporary or permanent deafness. The psychological impact of these hammer blows preceded by the howling shriek of their unexpected arrival, plus the violence of the blast, can unnerve even the most hardened veterans.

Soviet eyes were fixed on the Moscow highway, the shortest and most obvious route from Vyazma. The formidable Mozhaisk defensive line followed the line of the Elenka river, at its outer edge, from Rogachyovo to Yelnya. There were clusters of bunkers and emplacements covering the highway bridge across the Elenka. The left forward position of the 2nd Battalion of the 17th Regiment was sited here. Their right forward 1st and 3rd Battalions were already hotly engaged by the emerging *SS* Regiment *Deutschland*'s unexpected penetration. The Moscow road crested a ridgeline hill bounded by thick woods on both sides, before descending to the Elenka crossing point. This narrow highway was intersected by fire from three 45mm anti-tank guns covering from the slopes on the high side of the east bank, with three machine-gun emplacements and the left forward 5th Company's infantry trenches. The 4th Company covered the Rogachyovo direction and the 6th Company lay 1,200yd behind it in depth. This rearward company was at the southern end of Yelnya village, whose village rooftops were just visible from the road.

A 76mm bunker dominated the road at this point, with another 500yd further back, covering a long stretch of road. It was also the area where the 6th Company's trenches criss-crossed around and blocked the old Smolensk road, which led to Utitsy and Borodino railway station. The anti-tank guns were manned by 17th Regiment's Anti-Tank Battery and elements of 367 Anti-Tank Battalion, integral to 32nd Division. These guns were sited to link with 121 Anti-Tank Battalion in the area around Doronino and Shevardino villages. Only a concerted deliberate German attack could hope to prise open the highway in this sector, through which 10th Panzer Division, impeded by alternate terrain limitations, would be obliged to pass.

Coming down the road from the ridgeline on the west side of the Elenka was the III Battalion infantry *Der Führer* riding the tanks of the leading elements of the 10th Panzer Division. *SS Sturmmann* (Corporal) Ludwig Müller had started the day in a like fashion that morning, 13 October, riding panzers with the *Deutschland*. 'We sat on the tanks and the advance continued,' he recalled, 'until once again it got serious!'

We drove ahead through the middle of woods and over undulating ground with the hatches often closed down. The panzer crews had it 'good' while we had to put up with the flailing branches from on top. Despite that, we were in good heart.[4]

The leading elements of *Der Führer* halted at the top of the ridgeline before the Elenka river and then continued on down, heading toward the small bridge that spanned the river and obstacle belt. They were tracked all the way down by the Soviet anti-tank gunners and were soon in range. Tension rose on the Russian side, and engineer company commander Alexander Kolmakov, tasked with blowing the bridge, recalled 'they heard the rumble of the engines, which grew louder every minute':

Shortly after, the engineers saw enemy tanks and mechanised infantry. The enemy was getting closer and closer but the bridge was still not ready for detonation. The engineers became agitated but they did not falter, they continued to work.

The sappers were ordered to blow the bridge, but were not ready, having not finished. Once again German progress down the highway was something of a surprise.[5]

Russian eyewitness reports vary, but it appears that two tanks preceded the German column, followed by a bus, more panzers and truckloads of infantry. N.S. Selin, a scout with the 17th Regiment Anti-Tank Battery, remembered despite having loaded with armour-piercing, it was difficult to engage the advancing tanks because they were screened by the trees and knolls on the undulating road. 'The tanks got up the last knoll,' he recalled, 'and rolled down towards the bridge.' The road was severely hemmed in by thick trees either side. Tension rose even further when Selin saw 'the leading machine suddenly turned off the highway into a glade'. Once stationary, 'tank commanders gathered in a half circle and unfolded a map'. They could see the river line but had not identified the bunkers on the far bank. Battery commander P.E. Polibin ordered 'open fire' at this point, but only one gun, Selin remembered, Sergeant Ivan Kharintsev's 45mm, next to the road, had a clear line of fire. His 'gun fired, then once more in an instant and then again'. His 45mm cracked out again and again as quickly as he could reload:

Our strike was so sudden and surprising, that only the closer panzer, which stayed on the highway, managed to return fire. It fired inaccurately, while moving, and then it ceased shooting.[6]

Sapper commander Kolmakov remembered 'the gunners destroyed six enemy vehicles'. This assembly of blazing hulks momentarily blocked the road. 'The crews of the knocked out tanks tried to jump out of the top hatches,' he recalled, 'but were cut down by machine-gun fire.' The 5th Company infantry and supporting Russian artillery joined in the firefight, which led to a brief respite when the Germans withdrew.

This fierce clash attracted the attention of a number of senior German commanders, who all came forward to investigate reports of a seemingly formidable Russian position. *SS Hauptsturmführer* (Captain) Windisch, with Hausser's staff, remembered General Stumme, the corps commander, and an artillery general gathering 'in the afternoon' where 'We stood beside the main road in the protection of the woods and observed the enemy, who was racing about with tanks'. This would require a deliberate concerted attack to clear:

> A firefight began of an intensity I had not yet experienced. One battery of 88mm Flak went into position and fired on the Russian armour. One could clearly see the tracers and follow their gently curved trajectory, as they struck the armour – and ricocheted off.

Aleksandr Bodnar's KV-1 tank with the 20th Brigade was positioned near the highway, dug in to turret height:

> My KV tank had only its turret sticking out with the 76mm gun, so it was comparatively easy for me. Without any risk, I burned two armoured personnel carriers from a distance of 500 to 600 metres, and when the Germans jumped out of these carriers I kept pouring machine-gun fire on them.[7]

While watching the action, Hausser was informed, according to Windisch, that 'our grenadiers of the *SS* Infantry Regiment *Deutschland* had penetrated the enemy system of positions north of the main road'.

'They had fought their way through,' despite the withdrawal of the 10th Panzer tanks, 'in bitter costly fighting'. *Der Führer*, meanwhile, had closed up behind on the highway, with its II Battalion in the woods to the right, the III left and the I Battalion waiting in depth 2 miles to the rear. Buoyed by the news of a successful break-in to their left, Hausser ordered *Der Führer* to attack that night. Preliminary reconnaissance revealed that an approach left of the highway, deep in the woods, was the best option. The I Battalion moved up left of the established III Battalion and prepared to attack. They were to be supported by a concentration of three artillery groups: *Gruppe Hecht*, two battalions from Artillery Regiment 61, and the *Reich's* divisional artillery. The aim of the deliberate night attack was to widen the wedge shape already opened by the *Deutschland* to their left in the Soviet line.

As it grew dark, mortar and artillery fire methodically probed the Russian 17th Regiment, strung out between Rogachyovo and Yelnya. Soviet anti-tank gunner Sergeant Kharintsev and an accompanying scout moved down to one of the unburned German panzers abandoned near the entrance to the Elenka bridge in the gathering dusk. 'We found only three sets of uniforms inside it,' Selin later remembered, 'most likely meant to be used at the [victory] parade in Moscow.' The uniforms were useless, but what they did pick up was 'a downy blanket and pillows', very welcome because temperatures were once again plummeting to well below freezing at night.[8]

Ludwig Hümmer's 9th Reconnaissance Section was also on the move in the frozen night, probing ahead of the *SS Deutschland*'s penetration point. 'It was freezing again with light snowfalls,' he remembered. Their task was to pick out Soviet positions and minefields under cover of darkness. The situation ahead was confusing:

We reached a wood and heard a terrific firefight ahead. As we were at the point [front] in our sector, we couldn't work out what this fight in the wood was about.

They could have been similar patrols from *Der Führer*. It transpired the 'firefight' was in fact a horse-drawn ammunition wagon, which had been hit, 'producing a real firework display'. When they reached the next tree line they found themselves pinned down by heavy fire coming from a bunker line, but they could not quite discern the extent of the position. They lay prone until the fire died down and it grew quiet. 'Only in the distance could you hear a shell falling,' and it was so dark 'that truly, you could not see the hand in front of your face'. Stealthily they picked their way across water-filled ditches criss-crossed with barbed wire, anxiously scanning the way ahead for disturbed earth or other telltale signs of mine-fields. On nearing the Russian position, there was a bustle of movement and they heard voices. Suddenly a Very light shot up into the sky and in the scramble for cover, Schatzl, their leader, slipped in the mud and plunged into a water-filled ditch, covered in a thin layer of ice. More Very lights were fired and 'seconds became minutes' before investigative bursts of machine-gun fire swept the ground. 'They went over us,' Hümmer recalled. 'We were in dead ground.'

> We didn't realise we were lying so near their raised positions. More lights went up as we hugged the ground and again their machine guns criss-crossed the approaches to the position.

By the time the shooting ended, 'Schatzl's uniform had frozen stiff, solid in the cold'. They now had to creep back the way they had come and Schatzl could hardly walk, because the ice had made 'his uniform as stiff as a plank'. Had it not been so dangerous, Hümmer recalled, 'they would not have been able to stifle a grin'. They managed to get back safely and thaw Schatzl out over a cottage oven. The incident revealed the full extent of the Russian position, through which they must advance.[9]

Sapper commander Alexander Kolmakov, still in Rogachyovo, atmospherically recalled this suspicious night-time activity:

> The Fascists used the darkness to deploy marching columns into attack formations, and to send their commandos disguised as our soldiers and officers breaking out of encirclement, into our rear. Vehicles and tanks were noisy in the enemy's lines all night through.

As a consequence, the Russians decided to blow the small bridge spanning the Elenka river on the Moscow highway.[10]

Der Führer Regiment set up its command post just 500m back from the bridge in the protective cover of the woods. It was necessary to clear the obstruction on the highway to bring up 10th Panzer's tanks in strength. The 16th Pioneer Company worked its way forward with mine detectors, disarming mines and over fifty automatic flamethrower devices. Soviet 76mm *Ratsch-Bumm* anti-tank guns dominated the highway, so called because the *ratch* sound of the screaming incoming armour-piercing projectiles always preceded the *bumm* sound of the gun firing at source. At these ranges the first indication of danger with these high velocities was when a panzer was suddenly enveloped in flames.

Der Führer attacked on a 1,000yd sector about a mile deep into the woods on the left, moving west to east. Such an advance at night, within deliberate prescribed sectors, is a difficult operation, requiring veteran experience. The regiment had been fighting intensively day and night, in all weathers, since June. The I and III Battalions attacked in echelon across a narrow frontage and soon broke into the forward Soviet defensive positions. It was a two-stage advance; moving through the dense woods in file made it easier to control units and presented a smaller target. This 'shaking out' phase was conducted under cover of artillery and manhandled direct fire guns. The second stage, 'the development', was the deployment of platoons and squads, which stayed in column until the last moment, before spreading out and breaking into the Soviet trench system at various points. Headed by junior commanders personally directing Spandau machine guns, riflemen dashed right and left of the column point to grenade an entry point into an opposing trench. Incoming Russian fire led soldiers to advance using fire and movement in ragged skirmish lines about 5yd apart, scrambling from cover to cover. German soldiers were trained to grasp their rifle in the left hand in the attack, with grenade in the right, using the fingers of the hand clutching the rifle to pull the fuse cord of the grenade at the right moment. At the command '*Handgranaten!*' a shower of grenades would precede the final dash and leap into the trench. Contact was soon established with the *Deutschland* Regiment, who were continuing into the depth of the Soviet positions further to their left.

'By the grey dawn the break-in point together with *Der Führer* had been expanded to three kilometres,' recalled Ludwig Hümmer:

It was a costly fight on both sides, often man against man. We attacked further on and reached the edge of a wood and dug in, so far as the frozen ground allowed.

On gaining entry into the trenches, fighting became a savage melee of stabbing bayonets, grenade explosions, clubbing rifle butts, slashing and chopping with sharpened spades, and pistol work after automatic weapons and rifle magazines were expended. Men died alone and unknown, in a lurid surrealistic earthen setting, bizarrely lit by momentary grenade flashes and bangs. N.A. Ivasenko, with the 8th Company, 17th Regiment, recalled 'the action was hot, and it came out successful for our company'. He claimed, 'The enemy failed to reach the advanced line of our defence and had to withdraw to a grove edge, having lost about 20 killed and wounded.' Hümmer remembered:

> They were big strong lads equipped with long coats, pelt boots and fur hats. They were stubborn and did not know the meaning of panic. They stayed and held and let themselves be overcome. We were raked with every conceivable calibre, flak, anti-tank, *ratsch-bumm* and all sorts of mortars.

German firepower, however, took its toll. 'The panzers drove along the edges of the woods firing from all barrels,' he recalled, 'alongside machine guns and snipers and in between, low-flying aircraft.'

Kolmakov remembered the night counter-attack on Rogachyovo by the 3rd Battalion, 17 Regiment, 'silently, with no shooting on the move', which resulted in 'many killed and wounded men amassed in the trenches'. Medics were overwhelmed and 'had no time to attend those, who were coming or crawling back'. Captain Mikhail Kazmirov, with the 2nd Battalion, was sent forward to bolster resistance with the 5th Company by the highway, who were being attacked by a German break-in to their right. The Germans had already got into the trenches of the 3rd Platoon, he remembered, during a fierce struggle that raged to and fro:

> They stunned Captain Ilyashenko with a blow to his helmet and began to haul him off as a prisoner. He came to his senses and yelled 'platoon commander, fire on me!' After a long burst, everything calmed down.

When they looked up, both the company commander and his political commissar lay dead in the smoke, surrounded by German bodies. Kolmakov saw that 'having wiped out the company in their third attack, the SS men, having incurred heavy losses, broke into Rogachyovo'. Behind them, the 4th and 6th Companies still clung to the Moscow highway from their positions in their depth.[11]

The II Battalion *Der Führer* was diverted southward to cross the Moscow highway and roll up the Soviet positions on the other side, so that the panzers could be brought up in numbers. Hausser watched the progress of the battle from a position in the woods 300m ahead of the regimental command post. He was informed by corps that 'unfortunately reconnaissance indicated that it would be impossible to bring up the tank brigade of the 10th Panzer Division, since the terrain north of the highway appeared unsuitable for armour'. Hausser was concerned and frustrated at the lack of tank support he was receiving. The *XXXX Panzer Korps* diary reported, 'passage along the highway was also impossible, since there was still a Russian-occupied bunker at Yelnya', which the SS advance had yet to reach. 'That bunker kept up fire on the road and prevented improvement of the seriously damaged surface.'[12]

Hauptsturmführer Windisch was also forward with Hausser's staff that day, 14 October, watching the Russian roadblock. 'We left the motor vehicles behind and continued on foot,' he recalled, 'always trying to stay concealed along the wood line.'

They watched the combat engineers at work, seeking to repair the road bridge, while 'rounds from enemy tanks struck here and there repeatedly'. One suddenly burst among the trees in close proximity, scattering shrapnel and debris in all directions. Windisch, accompanying Hausser, saw:

Suddenly, the commander stopped and clutched at his right eye. We were frozen with horror. We ran to him immediately to be of assistance. He was severely wounded in the right half of his face and in the eye.

The commander of the *Das Reich* Division was taken out at the crisis point of the battle, and had to be immediately flown out in a light Fiesler Storch aeroplane. The facial wound was grievous; it was to cost him the sight in his right eye. 'Papa' Hausser was very much the division's father

figure and had been known by many of the *SS* recruits since the beginning
of the movement. He had been the commander at the Bad Tolz training
camp in the Bavarian Alps before the war. Barely one candidate in three
successfully completed the five-month course. Hausser dealt with the
'gentlemanly' social niceties of commanders as part of their professional
military development. Fitness and mobility were the hallmarks of a course,
designed to prepare *SS* leaders physically and mentally for rapid assaults
that would leave an enemy reeling. *Oberführer* Felix Steiner, his assistant,
recalled the course produced 'a supple adaptable type of soldier, athletic
of bearing and capable of more than average endurance'. The *Wehrmacht*
perspective was that it produced young officers prepared to expose their
units to needless losses in order to get results. Whatever the view, Hausser
was a larger than life figure.

   Much decorated in the First World War, Hausser had led the *Reich*
division through the French *Blitzkrieg*, the Balkans and up to the very
gates of Moscow. The bad news swept through the division like wildfire.
Hausser had exuded a quiet, competent permanence to men aware that
future survival in fast-moving situations was dependent upon the right
decisions. 'He had truly stamped the entire division with his personality,'
Windisch reflected later. He, like every officer, NCO and man, was shaken
at his loss. Helmut Günther, with the motorcycle battalion, remembered
his injury 'was bound to happen at some point', because he was always
forward with the troops. He took risks. 'We hoped he would make it,' he
recalled, 'there was hardly a surplus of generals like him.' SS *Oberführer*
Bittrich, who commanded the *Deutschland*, assumed command, which
meant further changes at regimental level, at the wrong time. Inevitably
there were misgivings. Veterans recognised survival was all about the
competence of the commander.[13]

   Hümmer's I Battalion had attacked at the penetration point achieved by
the 9th *SS* Company. They fought their way southward through the linear
outline of Rogachyovo village, followed closely by the III Battalion. At the
same time, the II Battalion *Deutschland* combed through the wood line
eastward from the Koloch railway halt toward the villages of Doronino
and Shevardino, a penetration of 1½ to 2 miles. 'We had big losses in the
woods,' Hümmer remembered, 'often from ricochets.' The medics could
hardly cope.

My machine gun was lying and firing a few metres away. Digging in the frozen solid ground was hardly possible. The number two [loader] at the gun gave me a sign that the number one [firer] was hit. We immediately hauled our friend out of the small depression. Head shot! Too late for any help.

Hümmer's nerves were stretched so taut he did not appreciate a bullet had shattered his left hand. 'Only when a trail of blood spurted down my wrist and the hand was paralysed did I realise I was hit – shot through!' Schatzl, his friend and section leader, bound him up and he stumbled back to the rear. He found the 2nd Platoon commander *Hauptscharführer* (Senior Sergeant) Bühl with a wounded arm waiting with the injured aboard the horse-drawn medical *panje* wagon. They took the decision to move back ahead on foot to protect the progress of the cart, Hümmer with a pistol in his uninjured right hand. 'We had hardly set off before – direct hit!' They had instinctively taken the correct course of action, 'the *panje* wagon was no more', blown to pieces with its occupants. 'Don't think about it,' Hümmer and Bühl resolved, 'but we couldn't get it out of our heads.' They moved back on foot, anticipating an ambush at every moment. Hümmer's company was already reduced to two weak platoons, having lost its commander and another platoon commander, the worst losses in the regiment. Within six days it would be further reduced to an understrength platoon of twenty-seven men.[14]

German progress was being made on the Moscow highway. The Russian 4th Company from 2nd Battalion, 17th Regiment, was caught out when the II Battalion *Der Führer* broke into its trench network, inflicting heavy casualties. The whole regiment was steadily being forced back eastwards towards Fomkino and Shevardino. German motorcyclists infiltrated along the railway line past Doronino. Counter-attacks by the 2nd and 3rd Battalions of 322 Regiment were fought to a standstill and by the end of the day they had lost 120 men killed and wounded. The highway was starting to be cleared. Russian militia units being sent forward were being 'issued with rifles picked up from the fighting,' recalled Boris Baromykin with the 32nd Division, 'many of which were encrusted with blood'. Patriotism and the spirit of 1812 was not always sufficient to hold the line. Baromykin remembered at one point, 'We were ordered to line up, and there in front of us, they put a soldier from one of the central Asian republics.' This was a sinister development: 'apparently he was guilty of having retreated without permission'. He never forgot the poignant scene:

> The poor fellow was standing just a couple of metres from me, peacefully chewing a piece of bread; he could only speak a few words of Russian and had no idea what was going on. Abruptly the major heading the military tribunal read out an order, 'Desertion from the front line – immediate execution', and went up to him and shot him in the head. The guy collapsed in front of me – it was horrible.

His blood soaked out into an ever expanding crimson patch in the snow. Baromykin, looking down, admitted 'something inside of me died when I saw that'.[15]

'What a Sham!', Shevardino, 5–6 September 1812

On 14 October 1941 *Kriegsberichter* (war correspondent) *Untersturmführer* (Second Lieutenant) Hugo Landgraf gave a live phonograph broadcast on the Moscow highway, just short of Yelnya village. It even includes the sounds of battle in the background. 'We're standing on the historical position at the famous battlefield we have all at one time or other remembered from school,' he said, 'at Borodino.'

'Now the German *Wehrmacht* is standing at this place,' he announced triumphantly, 'on the so-called autobahn to Moscow.'

The *Das Reich SS* regiments were exploiting forward, having pierced the outer defence crust on the Elenka river, and were spilling into the area where Napoleon's forces had deployed to attack the Russian redoubt at Shevardino on 5 September 1812. The village of Rogachyovo had not existed then, but General Poniatowski's 16th and 18th Divisions had passed through the Yelnya settlement to approach the redoubt from the southwest. The intention was to attack further along the old Smolensk road and maybe unhinge Prince Kutuzov's left flank. 'We have quickly driven what forces the Russians had against us back,' Landgraf recorded in 1941. 'The road behind us looks like a road of retreat, left and right are shot up tanks and guns on Soviet vehicles.' He was near the spot where 'Papa' Hausser was grievously wounded in the face by a Soviet tank shell. 'We are facing the strongly built Soviet positions at Yelnya,' he observed. The difference between this scene and that of 1812 could not be more stark.[16]

Landgraf was viewing a segment of the 6-square-mile area of action in 1812, when Davout's 5th Division under Compans advanced on the Shevardino redoubt coming from the north-west, having crossed the Kolocha river. Two cavalry corps under Nansouty and Montbrun were following on close behind. In all some 36,000 soldiers from Napoleon's *Grande Armée* with 194 cannon were manoeuvring to face about 12,000 to 18,000 Russians with thirty-six guns defending in and around the redoubt. This was in essence a crowded battlefield, where most of the deployment could be seen clearly. Six battalion columns were advanced across a front of 500yd, 600 men across and 800 men deep: densely packed masses of determined men, arrayed in straight lines wearing splendid uniforms and moving in the open. Advancing *SS* infantry, by contrast, would cover a similar area, moving tactically from cover to cover with about sixty men across wearing camouflaged helmets and tunics, with about another ninety men also moving tactically in groups. In 1812 some 54,000 men were engaged in this 6-square-mile area, whereas in 1941 about 5,000 men fought each other across the same space, where very little would actually be seen.

By 1941 the modern battlefield had become a lonely place. One Second World War veteran has accurately described the typical scene:

> It's very funny, a battlefield. The other day I was watching a duck shoot. The actual area extended to about four square miles, of which one fifth was in action, all the rest was waiting, and a battlefield is like that. It's extraordinary how inanimate the whole thing seems. A bit of action going on in the right-hand corner of some sort, the rest of the people are lying about smoking and waiting and sleeping.

Hugo Landgraf said the same of the Russian positions beyond Yelnya on 14 October 1941. 'The Russians are about 1,500 to 2,000 metres away, and the territory before us is completely devoid of people.' Just a 'few vehicles ahead of us' are visible, 'nothing seems to be happening'. Another Second World War veteran remembered:

The action is over ahead somewhere in another corner. And they ask you if you were there.

Locating the actual enemy during the Second World War was one of the most difficult tasks facing soldiers in combat. In 1812, this was rarely the case.

The arrival of Napoleon's *Grande Armée* could be seen clearly from the main Russian defence position at Borodino. As the huge French columns emerging along the new Smolensk road began to pour across the Kolocha river, heading south, it looked as though the vulnerable Russian left, anchored by the Shevardino redoubt, might be unhinged. The Russian generals had persuaded a grudging Kutuzov that they felt vulnerable to their left, but only now at this late stage was General Bagration's 2nd Western Army withdrawing troops to a line before Semyonovskoe village to face due west instead of north-west to block the emerging threat. The small 12,000-strong force under General Andrei Gorchakov could cover this move and assist the rearguard, but then the Shevardino Redoubt simply became a forward fortification that might complicate Napoleon's deployment. General Aleksey Yermolov, Barclay de Tolly's Chief of Staff, recalled how the sudden onset of fighting 'quickly escalated and no one on our side expected such a rapid onslaught by the French army'. This placed the ongoing swing of the line in jeopardy. As a consequence, 'our change of position was conducted in front of the enemy':

Notwithstanding the speed in which it was made, the enemy was presented with a chance to attack. An otherwise useless redoubt now had to be defended out of necessity, in order to give troops time to occupy their [new] positions, since the enemy could try to impede and even throw our entire army into confusion.[17]

Napoleon was unaware of the opportunity. He was simply instinctively attracted to vulnerabilities he could discern to the left of the Russian line. The Shevardino redoubt would hinder a linear deployment if it was not removed.

The village of Doronino to the left of the redoubt was soon taken and the arrival of Mansouty's and Montbaun's cavalry corps released infantry to flank the redoubt to the right. Two more infantry divisions from Davout's I Corps were preparing to cross the Kolocha river. By about 5 p.m. General Compans began to assault the Shevardino redoubt directly with four regiments forward in line. The 25th and 11th came in from the left, enfolding Shevardino village, while the 57th and the 61st attacked on the right beyond Doronino. De Ségur, Napoleon's adjutant, observed how Compans's men took advantage of the rolling terrain:

> The hillocks provided platforms from which his cannon could batter the redoubt, and sheltered the infantry as they formed their columns for attack.

Despite the punishing French fire coming from these knolls, the redoubt guns swept the open approaches, where the compact approaching columns, sixty files across and about nine ranks deep, attempted to storm their way through. Round shot pulverised bloody furrows into these blocks, which still advanced, shedding corpses and mutilated wounded in their wake. As the columns closed irresistibly, seemingly absorbing this terrible punishment by force of willpower alone, the Russian artillery switched to canister. These rounds, as the name suggests, were canvas buckets filled with over eighty 1½oz ball bearings, which sprayed out in a shotgun effect on firing. 'Despite numerous killed and wounded due to our dreadful canister fire,' artillery Major General Karl Löwenstern, looking on, recalled, 'the French advanced boldly toward our fortifications.'

The French occupation of the Doronino *kurgan*, or hill, to the southwest of the redoubt enabled a battery to sweep the interior of the redoubt constantly, and this began to shed fleeing infantry and some gun crews. The French broke in and seized it for the first time.

Löwenstern checked the retreat and redirected a counter-attack by the Russian 27th Infantry Division, which was on the lower slopes to the rear of the redoubt. It regained entry, which initiated a point-blank musketry duel between the French and the reinforcing Russian infantry lapping around the redoubt on both sides: the 25th and 11th to the left and the 57th and 61st to the right. 'A murderous fusillade' broke out, according to French soldier Gaspard Gourgaud. 'Only separated by a couple of dozen yards, the troops on either side of the wattle fences were protected from each other up to chest level.'

The first shot fired in battle by a Frenchman with his IX Charleville musket was likely to be his most accurate. Loading thereafter was often rushed, with increasing technical problems arising from misfires and jamming becoming more pronounced at each shot. 'This sanguinary fusillade lasted three-quarters of an hour,' Gourgaud reckoned:

> Its vivacity and noise made it impossible to hear the general's order to advance with the bayonet, a manoeuvre that would have cost us a lot of men.

Most observers calculate it took something like 250 musket rounds discharged in battle for every man killed. Point-blank engagements, however, produced horrific results. Musket balls inflicted massive physical damage on striking home. Soft lead bullets mushroomed on impact, causing extensive tissue damage, and could lift a man off his feet, leaving a visceral funnel-shaped entry wound. Amid the billowing smoke and infernal din from the exchange, Compans brought up four cannon on the right, hidden by the ranks of the 57th Regiment. They parted and canister was discharged at virtually point-blank range into the compact green ranks of the Russian infantry, who were shredded and dispersed by the blasts. The 57th then closed ranks and drove off the survivors at bayonet point as the 61st swept into the redoubt. Inside, Gourgaud discovered 'gunners, horses and every living thing had been destroyed by the fire of our *voltigeurs* [sharpshooters]'. It was 7 p.m. and starting to get dark when the redoubt was captured this second time. Three Russian guns were taken; the remaining nine on the slopes managed to escape. The 57th lost one of its battalion commanders and about 200 men killed and wounded gaining entry. Another, the 2nd, had sixteen killed and 168 wounded in the final charge.

The darkness, accentuated by thick smoke and fleetingly illuminated by blazing villages, luridly presaged yet another major Russian counter-attack. The Sibirski and Malorossiikii grenadier regiments were sent on their way, blessed by priests, scattering holy water as they attacked. That these were Siberian troops was not lost on the soldiers of the 32nd (Siberian) Division investigating the memorial obelisks in 1941. Two huge infantry columns came up the slope as the assault was expanded to include the 2nd Grenadier Division and four more battalions from the 2nd Combined Grenadier Division. Russian cavalry also joined the action, which was fast becoming a general battle between the two opposing southern wings of both armies. Friant's division was approaching from the north, having crossed the Kolocha river, and Poniatowski's Poles were coming up from the south. The Russian commander Gorchakov later admitted he 'wanted nothing better than for the darkest night to fall and bring an end to the battle'. A fierce hand-to-hand fight resumed around the redoubt mound in the encroaching dusk. It is thought the redoubt could well have exchanged hands three times, with a complete battalion of the 61st annihilated inside, before Gorchakov received the order to withdraw at about 11 p.m.[18]

Unlike 1941, planned attacks and actions by night were rare, and invariably resulted in confusion. There were no radio communications, mathematically calculated concentrations of artillery or even accurate time pieces to plan and co-ordinate such actions, unlike the *SS* division infantry attack during the night of 13–14 October. Instead there was the drum, bugle and word of mouth, shouted or delivered by mounted dispatches, to initiate commands. One of the very reasons Napoleon decided not to turn the vulnerable Russian left flank with a daring night march was the difficulty of ensuring mass control across unknown ground at night. One French regiment, the 111th, moving in the dark north of Shevardino, was suddenly charged by Russian cavalry, picked out by the flickering light of the burning village. Despite trying to form a square, the impetus of the Russian charge pierced it and inflicted heavy casualties. Louis Gardier, with the regiment, explained the Russian Cuirassiers looked like their own Saxon Cuirassiers in the dark:

> Assuming that they arrived to charge the enemy, we allowed them to pass nearby. But they rallied behind us and charged, killing anyone who came under their blows. We rushed as fast as we could to the orchard that was behind us and in front of the burning village.[19]

Having lost about 300 men and five guns, the 111th was then mistakenly engaged by another French regiment nearby as it retreated. It was not even clear which side was holding the redoubt when Gorchakov finally began his retreat near midnight. The Russians also found themselves isolated prey for marauding French cavalry. It was so dark Gorchakov was relying upon sounds, and it was clear a substantial body of horsemen was bearing down on his force. Thinking quickly, he ordered his Odessa regiment to beat their drums and yell 'Hurrah!' as if reinforcements had just arrived. This was sufficient to check the French cavalry approach and Gorchakov's infantry was able to melt away in the dark.

The battle was finally over, leaving the redoubt almost completely destroyed, with the general area strewn with the corpses of men and horses. The villages of Doronino and Shevardino either side were gutted, the smouldering, glowing embers from dying flames reflecting an ambient, desolate light. Casualties on both sides had been enormous. Dutheillet de Lamothe, with the 6th Battalion of the 57th, spent a gloomy night inside the wrecked emplacement, surrounded by some 500 dead, and writhing and whimpering dying from his regiment. They kept him awake all night. Major Eugène Labaume remembered soldiers 'lay down amidst bushes and slept profoundly, despite the vehement wind and excessively cold rain'. Intermittent pistol or musket shots punctuated the dark area that delineated the uncertain line between the two armies. Labaume looked up at 'a vast amphitheatre [of] lighted innumerable fires' on the Russian side:

> The whole of their camp was one vast uninterrupted blaze of light, which, while it presented a grand and sublime appearance, formed a striking contrast with our bivouac, where the soldiers, unable to procure wood, reposed in utter darkness, and heard no sounds but the groans of the wounded.[20]

Camp fires on the French side were clustered along the new Smolensk road and the high ground around the Shevardino mound. The other accompanying assaulting regiments had all suffered dearly: the 111th lost eighty-six dead and 555 wounded, with thirty-three captured and 138 missing. The 61st had thirty killed, 238 wounded and seventeen captured. Overall the French lost perhaps 4,000 to 5,000 men; not a single Russian was captured, which was unexpected and sinisterly dismaying. General de Caulaincourt tried to explain to Napoleon that the Russians chose not to surrender because their former enemies, the Turks, always killed their prisoners. 'Are these Russians determined to win or die?' Napoleon asked. Nobody was convinced by this rationalisation.

The Russians left about 6,000 dead or mortally wounded around the mound. When Hubert-Charles Biot, General Pajol's aide, strolled up, he found the redoubt 'cluttered with dead and wounded':

> Our infantry were busy 'stripping' the Russian corpses of the bad brandy which they had in their water bottles; short of everything, they did not despise this frightful drink.

He sampled it, 'but the pepper and vitriol burnt one's mouth'. Wandering marauders sought food, alcohol and valuables, in that order.

There was some bitterness in the Russian camp about miscalculations that had pitted 18,000 of their men up against 35,000 French. General Bagration, nevertheless, penned a glowing report, claiming constantly arriving French reinforcements 'endeavoured to overwhelm our troops' but 'they were vanquished everywhere by the courage of the Russian troops'. The 27th Infantry Division at the heart of the action lost 3,000 troops from 6,000. Four thousand of them had been recent recruits, drafted in to replace the crippling losses they had endured at the Krasnji rearguard action that checked Napoleon's advance on Smolensk. Its soldiers were less sanguine about the outcome than Bagration. 'There was no order at Shevardino,' one 27th veteran later complained, castigating the Russian command:

> Before the cuirassiers arrived, we were badly mauled and our battalion head in a fit of anger, grumbled: 'What a sham! First they cannot properly make any arrangements and then give us this nonsense!'

Prince Kutuzov, disposed to patriotically gloss over the brutal realities of negative outcomes, admitted in a letter to his wife that 'yesterday we had an infernal battle on the left flank'.[21]

Both the opposing lines began to shift and coalesce in the darkness. During the fighting around the mound, Bagration's Second Western Army partially redeployed on the left. The strong right remained anchored on Maslovo to the north but the centre now ran along ridge lines from

Borodino to Semyonovskoe village in the centre, bolstered by the Raevsky redoubt. The left was protected by the Bagration *flèches* and the extreme left had now to be anchored on Utitsy village on the old Smolensk road. De Ségur saw the vague outline of this forming configuration in the dark. Russian campfires 'blazed in a vast semicircle, but on our side they burned with a faint irregular light in no particular order'.

The lull that developed continued into daylight on 6 September. The Russians had no desire to stampede the French into an attack before their own preparations were complete. Napoleon needed to decide his plan of action and await the arrival of the reserve artillery and Latour-Maubourg's IV Cavalry Corps, since being given a foretaste of Russian resistance potential. De Ségur remembered, 'Our troops arriving late and in a great haste on an unfamiliar terrain, with nothing prepared and wood very scarce especially in the centre and left flank' appreciated battle was unlikely to resume on the 6th. The new arrivals were certainly aware what was now at stake:

> This incoherent sluggish, shifting war in which our best efforts had been fruitless and in which we seemed to be hopelessly, endlessly sinking, was at last centred in one spot. Here we touched bottom, here was the end, here everything would be decided![22]

This was not ground of Napoleon's choosing, neither was it arguably that of the Russians'. Colonel Karl Toll's choice of the site for the Russian army elicited as many questions as problems resolved. Kutuzov's scheme to hold along the line of the Kolocha river and counter-attack with Tuchkov's III Corps from an ambush on the left had been compromised by Napoleon immediately switching his main effort in that direction. The Russian line had had to swing back along its length to face directly west, to block the main enemy approach. All the previous Russian prevarication about the suitability of the site had come to naught, as the new stance conferred no particular advantage to either side.

Napoleon rode a number of mounted reconnaissances but was unable to glean an accurate picture of the Russian front, obscured by mist, thick brushwood, Cossacks and sharpshooter activity. He was not at his physical best, suffering from a severe cold and a painful bladder complaint.

He could not see whether there was a gap between the southernmost Bagration *flèches* and the right extent of Tuchkov's III Corps. He missed the outline of the northernmost *flèche* entirely. He also misinterpreted the course of the river and stream lines ahead of Semyonovskoe village in the centre. Misled by an inaccurate map, he thought the Raevsky redoubt and the Bagration *flèches* stood on the same ridge. His decision was to assault both, simultaneously.

Kutuzov only reluctantly agreed the advice of his army commanders to switch more resources to his vulnerable left during the fighting for the Shevardino redoubt. A total of 8,000 men from Tuchkov's III Corps was dispatched with 1,500 Cossacks and 7,000 Moscow *opolchenie* militia to cover the old Smolensk road around Utitsy village. The permanent mound or *kurgan* located there was not fortified, rather the newly dispatched troops took cover in the woods around, to initiate a giant ambush. The intention was to fall on Napoleon's flank and rear once they had exhausted themselves against the main Russian position. The ageing and noticeably overweight Kutuzov was not renowned for his tactical dexterity, rather his innate awareness of the capabilities of the Russian soldier, whom he was able to inspire, and his political cunning. He did not possess a flexible mind and was obstinately minded to stick broadly to his original scheme. Napoleon was clearly, by shifting to the left, not going to oblige.

Napoleon rejected Marshal Davout's ambitious suggestion to combine his I Corps with that of Poniatowski's V and try a daring outflanking manoeuvre to the left. This would take him up the old Smolensk road and into the Russian flank and rear. The former creatively energetic and inspiring leader at Austerlitz seven years before might well have done so. Instead, Napoleon opted for a linear struggle, with his main effort aimed at the centre of an established semi-entrenched Russian line, with only a feint at both ends. The confused fighting in the darkness after the fall of the Shevardino redoubt alerted him to the perils of risky large-scale manoeuvres at night across unknown terrain. He felt the *Grande Armée* was not strong enough to get itself out of trouble if the ruse came to grief. Ironically, the Soviet Left in 1941 along the Moscow highway bordering the old Smolensk road presented similar Russian vulnerabilities. Napoleon in a sense accepted battle on traditional Russian linear terms – a conundrum that generations of military historians have wrestled with since.

Poniatowski's corps was relegated to a tactical outflanking feint with 8 per cent of the army's manpower, some 10,000 troops, and fifty guns, or 11 per cent of the artillery. The main blow was to fall on the left wing of the Russian army along a 1½-mile sector stretching from the Bagration *flèches* ahead of Semyonovskoe village north to the Raevsky redoubt. Here Napoleon would strike with 85,000 men or two-thirds of his force. Overall, Napoleon fielded 133,000 men and 587 cannon against 125,000 Russians with 640 guns. The Russians had more so-called 'bone-crusher' battery pieces than the lighter assorted French guns.

Why should Napoleon accept such a linear confrontation against an almost equal opponent, who was in better physical condition and with fresher mounts? Part of the answer lies in the colourful religious ceremony that was conducted fervently around the Russian lines during the late afternoon of 6 September and strengthened their morale. Gorgeously apparelled Orthodox popes and archimandrites processed through the Russian camps, holding aloft the icon of the Black Virgin rescued from Smolensk cathedral. Men made the sign of the cross as their regimental colours and shaven heads were sprayed with holy water. Some wept openly. Russian soldier Fedor Glinka described the emotion:

> Acting upon the call of its heart, the hundred thousand strong army fell to its knees and bowed its head to the ground, which it was ready to satiate with its blood.

'Each of us gained new strength,' recalled another soldier, 'the live fire in the eyes of all the men showed the conviction that with God's help we would vanquish the enemy.' Kutuzov harnessed this emotional theatre: he stood upright bare-headed and addressed his men. There were shouts: the 'eagle is soaring' above his head and the multitudes yelled 'Hurrah!' 'We listened to him, barely breathing,' remembered one soldier, 'not feeling the ground under our feet – what a man the lord has created!' They were all inspired: 'He knew well the road to the soldier's heart.'[23]

Acceptance of linear battle meant that the outcome would be dependent on will power. Napoleon and his soldiers had been physically and psychologically fatigued by the rigours of a campaign that since June had yet to produce tangible benefit. De Ségur, Napoleon's aide, saw he had a 'heavy cold, he was tormented by a high fever, a dry cough and a burning thirst'. His urinary complaint caused him at times to dismount and lean against his horse with pain. Napoleon was assessing the tenor of his army, the 133,000 men who were the survivors of the 450,000 that had crossed the Nieman three months before. Only 29,425 serviceable mounts were left in his cavalry force, which had shed 20,000 horses even before reaching Vilna. They were in effect Darwinian remnants: the fittest that had survived thus far in a brutally physical campaign. Napoleon confided to another aide, General Jean Rapp, that 'this poor army is sadly depleted, but what remains is good. And my Guard is intact.' Rapp expressed a truism not lost on his soldiers, pointing out, 'There is no doubt about it, Sire, we have used up all our resources, and have simply got to win.'

'This was the cloud hanging over our army,' de Ségur observed:

> For several days now he had been in the midst of the army, and he had found the troops strangely quiet – the kind of silence you associate with a state of great expectation or tension, like the atmosphere before a storm, or the feeling in a crowd of people who are suddenly plunged into a situation of great danger.

The Russians fought for home, God and the Tsar, 'borrowing strength from all the heavenly powers,' de Ségur recalled, whereas 'the French were seeking it within themselves'. The French were fighting to survive. Despite the fact Napoleon 'felt that the army urgently needed a rest', de Ségur appreciated, 'There was no rest in store for his troops save in death or victory':

> He had thrown in a position where it was so desperately urgent for them to conquer, that conquer they must at any cost.

Napoleon confided laconically to Rapp that the battle would be 'bloody', 'but I have eighty thousand men, I shall enter Moscow with sixty thousand'. His soldiers had few illusions about the precarious nature of their situation, deep inside the Russian heartland. Major le Roy, with the 85th Line, recalled the 'gloomy reflections' veterans had 'on the outcome of a battle fought 2,400 miles from France'. Although most were confident at its outcome, he asked 'about what would become of oneself if wounded', A practical consideration. 'As for death, we didn't give it a thought,' Major Jean-François Boulart, with the Imperial Guard artillery, observed. However, he appreciated instinctively they *must* win:

> What if we're beaten at 750 to 800 leagues from France? What terrible risks we'll run! Can even one of us hope to see his own country again?

Moreover, 'if we're the victors, will peace follow at once?' The bitterness of Russian resistance thus far suggested this was unlikely.[24] Napoleon calculated the will to survive would transcend any doubts. Nevertheless, the casualties inflicted on them at Shevardino and his own poor health were blunting his edge as a creative risk-taker. News of defeat at Salamanca in Spain and the arrival of the portrait of his newborn son added further emotional strain. A daring flank march, he decided, was less predictable in outcome than smothering the centre of the Russian line ahead with artillery and violent frontal column assaults.

French engineers were erecting five bridges across the Kolocha river, upstream from Borodino, to aid manoeuvre. Construction work was also under way to prepare three large battery parks, which would open the French bombardment the next day. 'Never was there a quieter day than the one before the great battle,' de Ségur recalled atmospherically many years later. 'It was like something agreed upon.' However, this observation was not totally accurate. Throughout the day there had been a lot of shouting and echoing calling along the opposing skirmish lines, as well as exchanges of musket fire. Fedor Glinka, sitting in the Borodino church tower, remembered:

> [French] Bands [of *tirailleurs*] skirmished with our *jägers* for almost the entire day, since our troops did not allow them to get drinking water from the Kolocha river.

Indeed, the 30th Line lost sixty-seven men killed that day and there was further skirmishing along the line of Utitsy with Polish sharpshooters.

Scarcity of food and firewood on the French side contrasted with relative plenty on the Russian. Glinka heard the quartermasters calling, 'Vodka is here, come whoever wants it! Come take a goblet!' There were few takers. Another Russian soldier remembered they 'abstained from excesses in food and drinking, which they had in abundance'. The dampening distraction was what lay ahead, while many 'prayed to the Lord to give them courage and strength and bless them for the desperate battle'.

'I was eager to take part in a great battle,' Russian officer Mitarevsky recalled:

> To experience all the feelings of being in one, and to be able to say afterwards that I had been in such a battle.

Captain Fritz (surname unknown), a Russian staff officer, sat by a great watch fire with grenadiers from the *Fanagoria* Regiment, and:

> Often joined in chorus to sing the monotonous, melancholy, dirge-like yet not unpleasant national songs which the Russian people are so fond of. This singing before the battle had a strange effect on me, and I listened to it for several hours until eventually I fell asleep, exhausted by my horse.

Officers and soldiers prepared parade uniforms, and even the militia changed into white shirts, held back for just such an occasion. Clean linen was thought to reduce the chances of infection when wounded. Glinka rhetorically asked the universal soldier query on the eve of battle, common to all armies: 'What will happen tomorrow?' Soldiers facing imminent death focus on simple everyday things in life, normally taken for granted. 'A few stars shine through the cloudy sky,' Glinka noticed.

'Look can you see that large star in the sky?' a pleasant-looking *sous-lieutenant* asked his tent mates. 'When I will be killed, I want my soul to settle there.' His contemporaries doubtless regarded the sky the following night, because he was killed the next day.[25]

Such theatrical accounts are less evident in French veteran accounts of the final evening preceding the battle. 'We dined on grilled corn and horsemeat,' recalled Lieutenant Heinrich von Brandt with the 2nd Vistula Regiment, 'during a night that was cold and rainy':

> Many officers and soldiers drenched through and perhaps depressed by sad presentiments, tried in vain to sleep. They got up and, like wandering shades, walked to and fro in front of the camp fires.

Westphalian Captain von Linsingen, also unable to rest, shared this prevailing mood. 'I could not escape the feeling that something huge and destructive was hanging over all of us,' he remembered:

> This mood led me to look at my men. There they were, sleeping around me on the cold, hard ground. I knew them all very well … and I was aware that many of these brave troops would not survive until tomorrow evening, but would be lying torn and bloody on the field of battle. For a moment it was all too easy to wish that the Russians would simply steal away again during the night, but then I remembered how we had suffered over the last few weeks. Better an horrific end than a horror without end!

He resolved 'our only salvation lay in battle and victory!' Napoleon made certain his Imperial Guard were well provided for, issuing three days' rations of biscuits and rice, from their own integral supply wagons. They might prove to be the key asset in any frontal bludgeoning contest involving willpower the next day. Sergeant Bourgogne, with the Guard, remembered:

> Some cleaned muskets and other weapons, others made bandages for the wounded, some made their wills, and others again, sang or slept in perfect indifference.[26]

They had never lost a battle.

Monday morning, 7 September dawned gloomy and cold with a thick low-lying mist enveloping stream valleys and low ground. The sun did not come up until about 6 a.m. Auguste Thiron de Metz, a Hamburger Lancer, had time to reflect on the incongruous nature of their situation. 'Two armies gradually turn up on a piece of ground,' he remembered, and 'place themselves symmetrically facing each other':

> All these preliminaries are carried out with calm barrack-square precision. From one army to the other we heard commanders' sonorous voices. In sombre silence you observe the mouths of the guns being turned on you, which are going to send you to death.

Lieutenant Dementii Bogdanov, observing from the Raevsky mound, recalled generals issuing sonorous instructions:

> When suddenly a flash was seen to our left and a cannon shot rang out; this was followed after a while by a second report and then a third. Ten minutes later a fourth shot boomed forth – this was one of ours, replying to the enemy.[27]

Within minutes an ear-splitting carronade of more than 400 guns rang out, firing in volleys. The *Grande Armée* advanced with an average density of 44,000 troops per square mile. Waiting to receive them were Russian troops occupying ground at an average density of 36,000 soldiers per square mile, across an arena of 4 square miles of conflict.

5

The Road by Artyomki, Utitsy and Borodino Railway Station

From 83 to 82 Miles to Moscow

The Stop–Start Advance, 14–15 October 1941

On the morning of 14 October, *Kriegsberichter* (war correspondent) Hugo Landgraf passed the wreckage of the Soviet retreat on the road to Yelnya. He set up his sound-recording equipment in the trees on the outskirts of the village, anticipating he was going to capture the sounds of another victory. 'Strongly built' Russian defences on the road held a 'narrow entry point', he recorded, 'left is a tributary stream of the Moskva and to the right a marsh area':

> In between is a narrow area of road, and it is here we have to break through. Since yesterday midday there has been extensive co-operation between our infantry and panzer forces to get the breakthrough going. We found a weak spot on our left, where the first assault was mounted.

'It started during the night,' he added, his dramatic recording punctuated by audible sounds of shouting and shellfire in the background. 'The artillery is shooting now, and again from both sides, intermittently,' he described, 'trying to shake up the enemy.' An *Obersturmführer* (lieutenant) company commander arrived to confer with his commander at the command post, where Landgraf was listening in. An animated quick-fire discussion followed about the ground, vulnerability to Russian fire and what they could see. Two more officers turned up to give reports. 'The panzers would have to climb a slope, that is wooded, but no longer occupied by the Russians,' one of them said, 'but the Russians can shoot on to it.' These urgent exchanges are an authentic sound snapshot of what occurred at Borodino eight decades ago. Artillery is due to fire 'very soon,' they heard. 'I couldn't get any further forward with my platoon,' the *Obersturmführer* reported, 'because the 1st battalion is shooting into the depression,' adding 'I've got men in the houses over there.'

As the detail of the co-ordination of supporting artillery was tersely tied up, an outbreak of small-arms fire sounded in the background. Another infantry assault against Yelnya was being pressed home. Landgraf heard the attack got in among the Russian positions. The division commander, either Bittrich or Hausser, turned up and Landgraf moved closer to hear what was happening. 'That is the *nebelwerfer* [rocket-firing mortar] battery – right?' a voice asked amid a hubbub of instructions being issued and fire control orders transmitted by radio. 'When is open fire?' somebody asked.

Hauptsturmführer (Captain) Windisch was attending the same head-quarters group and recalled, 'Suddenly, I heard the characteristic sound of the Russian rocket launchers, so-called "Stalin Organs".' He immediately scrambled for cover:

> That was certainly meant for us, for everyone suddenly vanished into foxholes. Since I had not dug one for myself, I could not vanish without a trace. So I simply dived behind a tree and experienced the horribly beautiful spectacle of the bursting rockets as they impacted. The smell of the powder smoke and the gloomy black-red-violet light from the tulip-shaped shell bursts were something I shall never forget.

Landgraf carried on recording and announced the arrival 'of Stukas in the air, come to shake up the Russians'. His transmission is both vivid and self-congratulatory, with 'very few losses on our side' he assured his audience because 'direction is decisive and quick'. Suddenly, an urgently raised voice breaks in with '*Los: Feur frei!* [Now: Open fire!]' The scratchy recording picks up multiple bangs of artillery firing in the distance, followed by an echoing howling rush, as shells pass overhead. Then a series of shrieks in rapid succession indicate the *werfer* (rocket projectile) battery is also firing overhead. Crackling small-arms fire breaks out in the distance as Landgraf records 'the powerful detonations of the barrage' that has passed by, observing 'black smoke from the strikes that steadily rise'.

Windisch described the same scene: 'The entire area, the whole atmosphere, was filled with the explosions of the impacting rounds,' he recalled. His dramatic account illustrated how confusing these sudden actions were for soldiers, who had very little idea of what was going on:

Suddenly, all hell also broke loose behind us. I did not, in fact know what was happening and ran to my friend Mix, the division intelligence officer, who was under cover not far from me. He laughed and answered my question: 'our *nebelwerfer*'.

These 150mm rockets were fired in ripple salvos at two-second intervals, in multiples of six. Each 74lb missile delivered 22.5lb of explosive at each impact with devastating results. 'That ear-shattering racket had to be heard to be believed,' Windisch remembered. 'It whistled, thundered, hissed and roared.' The effect on the enemy was salutary. Windisch recalled:

I interrogated prisoners. They were in a state of severe shock, distraught and happy to have come through it alive. In their opinion, the effect of our rocket launchers had a decisive influence on the outcome of the fighting.[1]

Landgraf spent a lot of commentary emphasising the historical significance of Borodino. The implication was not lost on his audience back home. This was where Napoleon finally broke Russian resistance before entering Moscow, Landgraf explained. It had propaganda resonance; the *Wehrmacht* clearly intended to do it again in 1941.

The rapidity of information exchange in 1941 bore scant comparison to that of 1812. It took Napoleon one and a half months to learn about his defeat at Salamanca in Spain on 22 July 1812, which depressed him on the eve of Borodino. Communication was at the speed of horse-borne dispatch riders, who carried written or, less reliably, oral information.

Napoleon was often distracted by political intrigue occurring behind his back at Paris, as the Russian campaign continued to mount casualties with no discernible result. Landgraf's sound recording took about two weeks to process for universal wireless transmission throughout the *Reich*. He also shot film and sound for the *Wochenschau*, a weekly *Pathé News* equivalent, shown in cinemas throughout Germany in a similar timeframe. The movie camera he carried was powered by a clockwork mechanism, which he cranked each time to produce a few minutes' film footage. Sound could be recorded concurrently or added later in a film room. Negatives were processed and developed by machine and edited and cut in a studio before being copied and pasted for release. Landgraf was a pioneering correspondent because he uniquely developed a style of providing spoken commentary over his film footage. This gave his reports an immediacy that was not to be matched until TV news broadcasts later in the century. Secret *SS* home-front reports briefed to Himmler and senior Nazi officials in November 1941 remarked on the 'strong reaction' Landgraf's reportage evinced from that week's *Wochenschau* cinema audiences.[2]

'The tanks are ready waiting behind us, left and right of the road,' Landgraf reported from the Moscow highway on 14 October:

> Ready to frontally attack any break in point and pursue any Russian rearguards, and not allow any time to draw breath until they reach Moscow. We are about 120 kilometres [75 miles] from the centre of Moscow and hardly 100 kilometres from the outskirts. They should soon be able to manage this last 100 kilometres [60 miles].[3]

Both Landgraf and *XXXX Korps* were confident. *SS Oberführer* Bittrich, now commanding *Das Reich*, received his mission at 7.30 that night: 'The 10th Panzer Division is to cross the combat outpost line of *SS* Reich Division as early as possible on 15th October and advance past Mozhaisk to the south if possible.' His motorised infantry division was to mop up behind the panzer advance. Landgraf's 'on the spot' descriptions gave no inkling of the considerable casualties the *SS* endured, rather telling about hard-fought, precisely managed advances, tightly co-ordinated between the *SS* infantry and their supporting panzers. Operational high command was somewhat divorced from the reality of what was happening tactically on the ground. Landgraf exuberantly filmed columns of tanks and lorries inching slowly along the Moscow highway towards Yelnya. Exhaust fumes and clouds of condensation from tank commanders poking out of turrets provided an atmospheric snapshot of an apparently irresistible advance in winter conditions. What passed for progress was in fact film of a series of stop–start traffic jams. The 10th Panzer tanks were coming up, but without their accompanying infantry. Landgraf, blissfully unaware of all this, hitched a ride on a Mark IV heavy panzer, with the 4th Company, 7th Regiment, intent on filming the victorious panzer advance.

Motorised *Schützen* (infantry) Regiment 69 was only relieved at Vyazma by the slower foot-marching infantry columns with the 78th Division that morning. Just the day before the 69th had been fighting off repeated desperate Russian attacks to escape the dying Vyazma pocket. Relief in the line is a complex operation and the transition from fully committed static defence to resuming a mechanised advance was not easy. They did not begin moving until 9.30 that evening and were immediately caught up in the dense traffic on the Moscow highway. Their sister regiment, *Schützen* Regiment 86, had been waiting to drive forward since 6 that same morning. They waited and waited and froze. At 4 p.m. they finally received the signal to move on to the highway, only to be caught up in the same traffic delays. By midnight its II Battalion was obliged to pull off the road and camp beside the highway west of a crossroad near Gzhatsk. Regiment 69, jam-packed on the roads, was not able to find shelter until the following morning. The 10th Panzer was in effect bereft of its normal accompanying motorised infantry contingent. Panzer Regiment 7 operated forward on its own with the SS. By dawn on 15 October there was a realisation that the anticipated 'pursuit' order was not going to happen. 'Reports received in the morning negated that decision,' noted the 10th Panzer official history, 'even before a single unit moved out.' It was not only traffic jams, 'the Russians quite obviously had moved in significant reinforcements'.[4]

The village of Yelnya was overrun by the SS infantry, but the next village, Artyomki, 2½ miles further on, was found to be strongly defended, with two well-constructed field positions. This depth position linked with the village of Utitsy to the north, lying astride the old Smolensk road. 'In our trenches silence was the order,' recalled Major Vasily Chevgus, commanding 154 Artillery Regiment. 'Do not light any fires; the troops talked in whispers, we were not yet in battle.' The Germans were clearly closing:

> The cold autumn wind sprang up, bringing rain clouds from the west and the noise of artillery and mortar fire.

His men were determined and well aware that 'there were no troops to the east until Moscow itself'. They knew they would have to stand in the eye of an approaching storm. Chevgus's vivid account, typical of many others, is punctuated by the expressions of patriotism that bonded them together:

> They had to prevent the Germans from entering the capital, to carry out the order of the nation: 'Fight to the death! Do not take a step backwards! Moscow behind us!'[5]

Artyomki became the new linchpin for the Soviet defence barring the Moscow highway to German tanks. It was, nevertheless, an ad hoc block. Sapper company commander Alexander Kolmakov had fallen back from Yelnya, 'having held the advance defence line'. His men were committed to assisting units arriving from 32nd Division to unload and deploy around the village. N.A. Ivasenko, a company commander with the 17th Regiment, recalled the urgency of their situation. 'Parts of the 3rd battalion had not arrived in Artyomki yet,' he recalled when he met the acting regimental commander. 'I don't remember his name,' he added, and was accompanied by his aide de camp:

> Straight way he reprimanded me for having been on the road for too long. Then he ordered me to attack the village of Utitsy [1½ miles to the north] captured by the Germans. I had no idea of the number of Germans in it and neither did he.[6]

The problem of Artyomki for the Germans was that terrain limitations prevented it from being approached directly, nor could the panzers outflank it without their integral infantry. General Fischer, commanding

10th Panzer, pointed out the ground between Yelnya and Artyomki was intersected by numerous north–south watercourses, poorly suited to any attack by armour. Napoleon in 1812 had also not been able to deduce the extent of these gullies, which his infantry would have to cross in columns, to frontally assault the Russian line. Fischer was at least aided by over-flying *Luftwaffe* photographic reconnaissance aircraft to identify approaching physical obstacles.

Warfare in 1812 was fought across one dimension at ground level. By 1941 *Blitzkrieg* could be conducted across two dimensions: ground and from the air to the ground. Aircraft could not only fly across obstacles, they could also deliver munitions as a form of flying artillery, if mechanised or motorised units outran the bulk of their supporting artillery. In addition to self-propelled and vehicle-towing guns, the Germans could therefore call upon the equivalent of 'sky artillery', the *Luftwaffe*, a decisive force multiplier in the 1941 campaign. The Russians had been wrong-footed by a dominant *Luftwaffe* from the very onset of this campaign. Chevgus and the defenders of Artyomki needed no reminding how vulnerable they were to air attack. While waiting for the German attack 'aircraft with black crosses on their wings were heading for Moscow as a whole armada':

> They flew heavy and low with their cargo of death but, not for us now. We didn't have to wait for long. Other aircraft appeared with lethal loads. This load would be for us.

This dimension did not exist at Borodino in 1812, but since the Montgolfier brothers had first flown them in 1783, hot-air balloons had occasionally been used for French military air reconnaissance. A young German inventor, Franz Leppich, tantalisingly offered the Russian government an offer to develop just such a balloon with wings. Tsar Alexander was intrigued to receive a letter offering a machine 'shaped somewhat like a whale' that could lift '40 men with 12,000 rounds of explosives' to bombard enemy positions and could sail to London from Stuttgart in an astonishing 13 hours'. The Tsar approved the project in April 1812, and Leppich, working under the alias of 'Schmidt', began employing hundreds of labourers, who worked in seventeen-hour shifts in a village near Moscow after the French invasion had started. The Tsar visited the workshop on 15 July, when he saw a large gondola, 15m long and 8m wide, with attached wings. By then his government had spent a staggering 120,000 roubles on the project and the deadline for completion in August was missed. It was not ready for the battle of Borodino and 'Schmidt's' bogus workshop had to be loaded on to 130 wagons and transported to Novgorod, to avoid Napoleon's advance.

The whole scheme was unmasked as a scam when Leppich's first prototype balloon collapsed as it was wheeled out of its hangar at the Oranienbaum observatory. Napoleon's aide, de Ségur, only found out about the project after the war. 'This aerial machine was to fly over the French army,' he claimed, 'single out its leader, and crush him with a rain of fire and steel!' It never managed to get over 40ft from the ground, by which time Leppich had spent 250,000 roubles of the Tsar's money. He hurriedly departed Russia in 1814, having been exposed by the investigating Russian General Arakcheyev as a 'complete charlatan', who knew nothing about 'mechanics or even the principles of levers'.[7]

For Soviet artillery commander Vasily Chevgus, the German air dimension at Borodino in October 1941 was as lethal a threat as tanks approaching on the ground. 'German bombers began to lambast the forward area of our defence extending just under two miles from the [break-in points] from Rogachyovo to Yelnya.' Most Soviet veteran accounts remember swarms of *Stuka* dive-bombers constantly hanging over their positions:

> Columns of smoke and flames broke out all around. After dropping their bombs, the Nazi aircraft flew off, but soon others appeared. And again the ground shook with explosions.[8]

The Junkers Ju 87 *Stuka* dive-bomber was the most effective and accurate aircraft at the time for close ground support. Its distinctive gull-wing appearance was often distinguished loitering above the battlefield in search of targets. The howling scream produced by the on-board siren and air brakes during the dive unnerved Russian defenders. Field Marshal Albert Kesselring commanding *Luftflotte 2* explained:

Shocking flying weather hampered air support; it snowed and rained and the roads already pitted with craters, were further churned up by the heaviest fully tracked vehicles.

Dispersed airstrips, located in fields, soon transitioned to rutted runways that caused losses of men and machines on landing and take-off. The Soviets had the advantage of operating from hardened runways in and around Moscow. 'Attempts to move single aircraft by means of flak tractors ended with the snapping of tow ropes or tracks,' Kesselring remembered. *Oberleutnant* (Lieutenant) Hans Ulrich Rudel, with the II *Stuka Geschwader Immelmann*, explained, 'The fall in temperature gives me, as squadron engineer officer, all kinds of technical problems, for suddenly we begin to have trouble with our aircraft, which is only caused by the cold.' The mix of warmer air currents in cold temperatures that occur in early October produced lower cloud ceilings, a serious impediment for low-level air support missions. Rudel, on the Moscow front, described the deteriorating conditions as 'the weather goes from bad to worse plus a heavy fall of snow'.[9]

Sleet and snow impeded resupply and impacted on flying, while shortages, and the need to fly around squalls, often resulted in fighter escorts failing to turn up on time or at all. Navigation across the snowy white expanses that appeared was only possible following rail lines that converged on Moscow, burning villages on the approaches to Borodino, or the stark scars of roads across a landscape, scoured by tanks and trucks, that had turned into wide water-logged tracks. 'The filthy weather had completely reversed all the conditions that had previously been in our favour,' Kesselring complained. Flying constant operations since September 1939 had taxed the *Luftwaffe*'s machines and especially crews. 'The aggravation of nervous tension' became increasingly apparent, 'and the vagaries of the weather in the Russian autumn, rain, fog and cold did the rest'. Cloud ceilings were reduced at the very time that increased numbers of T-34 tanks were entering the battlefields, and these 'could move even in the worst ground conditions'. Low-level flying became increasingly dangerous, and Kesselring recalled that 'imposed a terrific strain on our ground-strafer pilots', who had to fly recklessly over forests, trees and villages to deal with them. *Hauptmann* (Captain) Helmut Mahlke, flying with the III Squadron of *Stuka Geschwader I* earlier in the Russian campaign, had been shot down and badly burned prior to Borodino. He nevertheless provided an invaluable insight into the demands close air support made on crews assisting the German ground advance. He recalled the damage inflicted on their machines as a consequence of constant low-level shuttle missions:

> Unlike many of our previous opponents, Russian troops tended to stand firm when under air attack. Rather than dive for cover, most would blaze away at us with whatever weapons they had to hand. And as infantry weapons did not use tracer bullets, we were unaware of the volume of enemy fire that was being directed against us.

Only when they landed with wings and fuselage riddled with bullet holes was it appreciated 'just how much lead we had been flying through'.[10]

'Prepare to dive,' Mahlke would warn his observer tail gunner sitting to the rear of the cockpit, during a typical mission. He would respond, having scanned the skies, 'All clear behind.' The attack dive was generally at an angle of 70° to 80°, 'impossibly steep' Mahlke thought at first during training. The pilot picked out an object – such as a tank – on the ground, as his aiming point, and would continue the dive until the last possible moment. 'What I found much more difficult was estimating the correct height at which to release the bomb,' he remembered:

> The altimeter couldn't unwind fast enough when the Stuka was in a near vertical dive and always lagged a little behind the machine's actual height. The pilot therefore had to rely mainly on his own judgement as to his altitude – or lack thereof!

There was a line etched on the canopy to judge the angle of dive and a window in the floor to spot the target. Rudel, with the *Geschwader Immelman*, remembered typical bomb loads of two 50kg (110lb) bombs under each wing and a 250kg (550lb) bomb slung beneath the fuselage centre. This enabled more than one pass, and the Dinart 'asparagus' bomb (named after its inventor) could be set to explode a metre above ground to maximise surface blast. Afterwards the aircraft would make strafing runs with its two wing-mounted 7.9mm machine guns. Mahlke described such a dive:

> Our chosen victim, a medium tank, slid slowly into the centre of my sights. I let go the first bomb – recovered – watched for the result – missed! Ten metres away from the target – oh sh … ame! That won't do at all. Have another go. While the following aircraft were still dropping their first bombs, we had climbed high enough to make a second attempt. The same target – and this time a direct hit! The Soviet tank slewed sideways and began to brew up.

The high-angled dive occasionally caused a build-up of painful pressure inside the ears, which could be popped by repeated dry swallowing. 'It was to a large extent very much in the pilot's own hands to make sure he didn't pull the aircraft out of its dive any more sharply than was humanly bearable,' Mahlke remembered. Cockpit film of *Stuka* pilot facial contortions in the descent bear witness to the physical strains imposed. Crews were pressed down into their seats by as much as three to five times their own bodyweight and some were known to have had momentary blackouts.

After the bombing runs 'it was the turn of the trucks' and 'we each made several strafing runs until the road was littered with their burning wreckage'. The difficulty was always to distinguish the extent of advance by friendly troops down below. These sent up Very flares or threw smoke grenades to mark the outline of the forward edge of the battlefield. Flying low level at treetop height over the Borodino battlefield was dangerous, as Mahlke previously experienced on a former mission. 'Bang! An ear split-ting crack,' as 'a bright tongue of flame lanced out of the engine cowling'. He was shot down on more than one occasion. 'Windscreen covered in oil,' he recalled, as he hauled back the cockpit canopy to discover they were too low to jump out. 'I tramped hard on the rudder pedals, lining the aircraft up' and, levelling out, he looked for a clearing so as to attempt a landing. He shouted to his gunner:

> Tighten harness! Open canopy! Prepare for emergency landing! Get ready in case we somersault!

Quick thinking was needed: flames 'were licking into the cockpit' and 'the intense heat was becoming unbearable'. Pilots would slam their machines down as hard as possible to snap off their fixed undercarriage legs and wheels because 'there would be less chance of the machine cartwheeling'. Both crew members had then to hang on beneath an opened cockpit as the machine careered across the broken stumps of a forest clearing, prepared to vacate at the first sign of the aircraft pitching over. Once on the ground, if they were on the wrong side of the line, there would be vengeful Soviet troops out looking for them.[11]

By 11 a.m. on 14 October the Soviet line at Borodino was under severe pressure. Resistance at Yelnya had been broken, elements of the *SS Deutschland* had reached Utitsy and *SS Der Führer* were attacking Artyomki. *Der Führer* had also crossed the Moscow highway to the south and were rolling up Soviet positions in the area of Yudinki on the other side of the road, where they clashed with fanatical resistance from teenage cadets from the Lenin military–political academy. The 32nd Division operations diary noted, 'The 5th rifle company, which held the defence to the north-east of Yudinki, was almost completely wiped out by enemy mortar and artillery fire.'

Captain Mikhail Kazmirov's 17th Regiment battalion had pulled back eastwards, having crossed the Moscow highway in darkness the night before. 'The Minsk–Moscow highway was on fire,' he recalled. 'It was burning with German tanks.' Pressure was increasing south of the highway as *Der Führer* captured Yudinki and began to press against the village of Fomino. Kazmirov was ordered to establish a blocking position on the western edge of Borisovka, to prevent a German approach on Mozhaisk, 8km away, from the south. They came across evidence of fierce fighting. 'Around the village,' he recalled, 'destroyed German tanks were smoking and there were burnt-out motorbikes lying around as well as dead German bodies.' Black smoke came out of the church and the weaving factory. In the distance they could hear the sounds of 'bitter fighting raging in the area of Dorokhovo' to their north. There was a scare when a light tank suddenly rattled along the road towards them, but they refrained from firing; being a lone vehicle, it was probably Russian. To their surprise, General Lelyushenko, the commander of the Fifth Army, clambered out 'with a bandaged hand', Kazmirov remembered, 'in tank uniform, wearing a black triangular sling'. He was on his way to hospital and 'warned us that the enemy in the area of Mozhaisk were concentrating heavy tank forces and to be on the alert'. Within twenty-four hours both the supreme German and Russian commanders at Borodino had been wounded at a critical moment in the battle, near the Moscow highway.[12]

Fighting for Artyomki village developed rapidly into a battle within the main battle. German artillery and mortar fire methodically probed and bracketed its defences before the *SS* infantry assault. 'Fires were starting in the villages,' Major Chevgus recalled, and 'from the burning homes came old people with women and children'. Civilians were at last evacuating under unremitting fire 'with cries and tears in their eyes' and 'those saved from death moved into the woods'. The bulk of the Soviet positions occupied the slightly higher and therefore dry ground to the north of the village, linking in with the trench network south of Utitsy. 'Our trenches collapsed as a result of ammunition explosions and mines blowing,' Chevgus remembered. 'Pillbox beams and dugouts were scattered and the dust and powder from the explosions made it difficult to breathe.'

Chevgus's batteries were behind and south-east of Artyomki and subjected the highway and its forest border to heavy fire 'virtually without let up'. The barrage, according to the 10th Panzer official history, was 'inflicting heavy casualties on the *Waffen SS*'. The heavy and largely unexpected resistance had negated the so-called 'pursuit' plan envisaged for 15 October. Artyomki would have to be reduced before the full combat potential of the 10th Panzer could move north of the Moscow highway to break into the depth and rear of the Soviet Mozhaisk line. 'The Nazis anticipated an easy victory,' Chevgus remembered:

> It was clear from this because their tanks were moving two at a time with open hatches. Dense masses of infantry set off on the slopes of the hills, not just in lines but columns of companies. Through our binoculars we had a good view of unfastened collars on their dress uniforms, pulled up to the edge of their helmets, sweating from drinking schnapps, with sleeves rolled up to the elbows.

This somewhat picturesque description is borne out by an admission of heavy casualties on the German side. 'Everywhere commands rang out,'

Chevgus recalled dramatically, and 'the Nazis did not expect such accurate fire, nor the suddenness and power of it'.

Captain Nechaiev, however, with a 322 Regiment artillery battery, remembered the Germans managed to overrun the headquarters of the 3rd Howitzer Battalion of 154 Regiment. 'The artillerymen fought an epic fearless battle, killing more than 40 Nazis in hand-to-hand combat,' he recalled, but they were virtually wiped out. Chevgus saw one of the first German penetrations overwhelmed and destroyed, in bloody fighting at the anti-tank ditch in front of the battery. He knew small groups of SS had reached as far as Borodino railway station and had penetrated Utitsy village.[13]

Borodino railway station, opened in 1869 on the Brest–Moscow line, was like many Russian stations of the period, constructed with fine brickwork, limestone trim and picturesque cladding. In 1903 it had housed the first Borodino battlefield museum, set up by stationmaster P.P. Bogdanovich in one of the waiting rooms. He exhibited his own personal Napoleonic finds alongside old engravings, books, weapons and awards. The collection was moved to its present site in time for the 1912 dedication of the hundredth anniversary of the battle by Tsar Nicholas. Borodino station was the favoured drop-off point for Muscovite weekend picnickers during the inter-war years. Already severely battered by the *Luftwaffe*, the station appeared to have been reached by the Germans. Ivan Barchuk, with the 1st Battalion, 322 Regiment, was dispatched with a reconnaissance patrol to find out.

Barchuk's account is one of the very few, apart from Chevgus, in Artyomki, that records civilians were still living in the villages in and around Borodino, despite its incorporation inside the restricted Mozhaisk defence zone. 'Find any resident,' they were told, and, 'in case there are enemy – how are they deployed, in what numbers and with what weapons?'

'When we went past the station,' Barchuk remembered, 'we noticed two or three buildings where the railway workers lived': a nineteenth-century feature, because 'it was rare to see individual family houses' in socialist Russia. They combed through the station building and found 'not a soul', but 'then we noticed the cellar'. 'Who's there in the cellar?' they demanded. 'Come out!':

We listened for voices, hearing male and female. 'We live in the station. We are Russian.' We were suspicious of everything, suddenly there might be Germans hiding among the residents in the cellar.

Wary about civilian fraternisation amid the barely contained German advance, 'We asked whether the Germans had been there, and when'. They had just missed them by thirty to forty minutes, they were informed – infantry, armed with rifles and sub-machine guns. After quickly passing on the report, they watched as other Russian units occupied the area around the station, 'riflemen, artillerymen, anti-tank guns, battalion mortars, signallers and transport with ammunition'. The assembling body of troops 'were gathering forces for battle' and pushed forward another kilometre toward Utitsy village and the Moscow highway. 'We were ordered to occupy previously dug trenches and foxholes,' Barchuk remembered, 'to prepare them for defence and await further orders.'

Russian Colonel Victor Polosukhin was conducting an aggressive defence with the 32nd Division, which had been bloodied against the Japanese at Lake Khasan two years earlier. Although taken aback at the strength and effectiveness of German air power, they were holding their own in conditions of parity. Ivasenko's 8th Company, with 17th Regiment, took Utitsy in the subsequent counter-attack 'despite losses', but 'soon the enemy regrouped and kicked us out of the village'. They attacked again.[14]

An alarm sounded at the *SS Deutschland*'s main dressing station near the Moscow highway, where both *SS* regiments were making only partial headway in bitter see-saw fighting raging up and down the dirt-covered streets of Artyomki village. 'The Russians have broken through!' came an urgent cry, transmitted by word of mouth. Mortar bombs burst among the helpless casualties laid out on the ground awaiting treatment at the aid post. Everyone who was able moved on foot to the *Der Führer* dressing station located further back along the highway. Severely wounded patients were hastily pushed aboard any available transport as vehicles speedily drove off in a snowstorm. They were chased by incoming Russian fire all the way to the main road, where they continued rearward to the *SS* hospital now set up at Gzhatsk.

Rolling down the highway from the east were tanks and armoured cars from the 32nd Division's 12th Reconnaissance Battalion, which had

precipitated this retreat. Polosukhin committed his final available reserves
just at the point when it seemed the Russian position was about to
collapse. This hastily assembled ad hoc force was reinforced by T–34 tanks
from the 20th Tank Brigade, a company of motorcyclists from the 36th
Regiment and a heavy artillery battalion taken from the reserve and were
led by Polosukhin's operations officer, Lieutenant Colonel P.I. Vorbiev.
Startled *SS* infantry, caught in the open on the main road and at the
vulnerable regimental boundary between the *Deutschland* and *Der Führer*,
fell back in haste. They could not deal with this number of armoured
vehicles. 'The small village of Artyomki drowned in a welter of explosions,'
Major Chevgus recalled, 'it was shrouded in smoke and dust':

> After this, our infantry and tanks went into the advance. The Germans
> did not stand up to this sudden attack, and withdrew in panic to the
> anti-tank ditch, leaving many dead and wounded Nazis in Artyomki.
> But our troops did not succeed in reaching Yelnya.[15]

The *Luftwaffe* had passed on no warnings that an attack might be impending. Kesselring, commanding *Luftflotte 2*, later remembered that 'after the
battle of the Bryansk–Vyazma pocket enemy movements in a formed
body were only exceptionally observed'.

'It is still a puzzle to me,' he recalled later, that 'although reporting lively
movement on the roads,' they invariably missed the strategic concentrations
gathering north and east of Moscow. 'The concentrations of the picked
Siberian divisions were not spotted, or at any rate, were not appreciated
as such.' The reason for this was not simply poor weather. Many of the
attacking units were Moscow-based militia reinforced by specialist heavy
weapons, anti-tank and artillery units drawn from the Moscow Control
Zone, the city's inner defence. The startling German achievements of
14 October had been unexpectedly reversed. *SS Deutschland* was further
checked by a Russian counter-attack by 322 Regiment near Shevardino,
compromising its open flank. There was still a considerable Russian
presence blocking the Moscow highway at Artyomki. Far from the 'pursuit'
plan envisaged for 15 October, the process of securing the jumping-off
point for the panzer advance on Mozhaisk had been transformed into a
precipitate retreat.[16]

The Battle of the Giants, 7 September 1812

6 a.m. to 11.30 a.m.

Pooff! – Suddenly a round compact ball of smoke flew up, turning from violet to grey to a milky white, and 'boom!' followed the report a second later.

'Pooff-pooff!' – and two clouds rose up, pushing one another and merging together; and 'boom-boom!' came the sounds confirming what the eye had seen.

Leo Tolstoy's atmospheric description of fictional Pierre Bezukhov's first glimpse of the opening salvos of the 1812 Battle of Borodino in *War and Peace* coincide with that from Russian engineer Lieutenant Dementii Bogdanov, who saw it from the Raevsky redoubt.

Tolstoy spent two days wandering the site in the summer of 1867, as the railway was being constructed. He interviewed veterans, elderly friends and some politicians, for whom the events were still part of living memory. Active military service at the siege of Sevastopol in 1855–56 was a similar experience, because little had changed in terms of military technology and tactics since 1812. He wrote the epic novel at Yasnaya Polyona, not so far away, which in 1941 was in the path of General Guderian's *Panzergruppe 2* advance on Tula, on the outskirts of Moscow.

Borodino village was 5 miles north-west of Artyomki, on the Moscow highway, defended stubbornly by the Soviets in October 1941. Those 5 miles of road linking the two villages broadly corresponded to the Russian line of defence in 1812, and would see the heaviest fighting. Borodino's church of the Smolensk Icon of the Virgin stood in front of the Russian right flank. Its two-storey structure with an octagonal-shaped bell tower and a large, raised octahedron had twin onion domes that seemed almost to survey the Russian line. Russian militia soldier Fedor Glinka had watched Napoleon's army surge to the left of the Russian forward defence from here, and his vantage point was later to be hit and damaged by French artillery. Fire gutted the interior, which was later restored, but by the 1930s it was being used as a workshop. The Soviet 1937 commission saw little justification in restoring it to its former glory.

At dawn on 7 September 1812, Russian eyes were focused on the vulnerable left of the line, whereas the initial French blow fell on the right. The lookouts in the church tower did not see it coming. Borodino village jutted out as a salient into the French side of the Kolocha river and was held by a crack division of *jägers* from the Russian Imperial Guard. Only a narrow plank bridge on wooden supports linked it to the main Russian force. Russian outposts peering through early morning mist and ground fog eventually identified two enemy columns, probably 8,000 men strong, bearing down on the right western side of the village. Delzon's IV Corps division, led by the 106th Line in platoon columns trotting to the attack 'with unbelievable speed', approached undetected to within 200 yd, which in effect made defence of the salient untenable. Russian officer Nikolai Mitarevsky, standing at the eastern bank of the Kolocha, watched the little cloudlets of musket smoke, which 'soon covered the village'. The sound was different from the 'pooff-boom' reports of artillery. Tolstoy described musket fire as 'little echoes in just the same way':

> Trak-ta-ta-tak! crackled the musketry, but it sounded thin and irregular in comparison with the roar of artillery.[17]

The noises emanating from Borodino did not bode well, Mitarevsky recalled:

> A confused fighting occurred on the way out of Borodino, near the bridge; although it was in front of us, and so close that some bullets whizzed by us, we could not see what was happening there because of smoke, dust and fog.

Everyone's attention focused on the village. General Barclay de Tolly had 'insisted it was dangerous and futile to defend this village and suggested recalling the *jägers* at once', according to his Chief of Staff's adjutant Pavel Grabbe. He believed the force should have been long withdrawn and the bridge burned; now it was too late. The 106th Line crashed through the village at the point of the bayonet, brushing aside local *jäger* company attacks by sheer weight of numbers. General Yermolov, the Chief of Staff, suspected the Russian infantry had been caught napping:

There was such widespread carelessness on the outposts of this battalion that many ranks were asleep, having taken off their uniforms.

The initial Russian response was disorganised. Engineer Lieutenant Ivan Liprandi was particularly damning, recalling the *jägers* had originally been:

> jubilant to find large bath houses in this opulent village and decided to use them that night. Thus when the French attacked, the entire battalion was still in the baths.

Thirty officers and half the men were lost in the desperate bayonet melee fought out in the streets. 'Many, leaping out from the bath houses, barely had time to dress and, grasping their muskets entered the fighting at once.'[18]

On turning up, Barclay de Tolly watched the tragedy unfold from the east bank. 'General Delzon's column moving on the main road, was already entering the village,' he recalled. They vastly outnumbered the retreating Russian *jägers*. 'It was marching quickly and with a drum beat.' He watched as the second French column reached the river bank and deployed a chain of skirmishers to fire on the Russians fleeing over the bridge. The 106th Line column caught them up, coming up the village street, and pressed hard, catching the retreating Russians in a 'very effective and deadly' crossfire. The bridge had been partly demolished, with many planks removed in the middle, and soon bodies were pitching into the river. 'We were so crammed,' de Tolly remembered, 'that not a single enemy shot missed its target.' Many were cut down in this maelstrom of fire before they could cross. 'Combat continued no longer than fifteen minutes,' de Tolly remembered; by 7.30 a.m. the village had been taken.'[19]

Flushed with success, the French pursued the fleeing Russians over the bridge. According to Colonel François Lejeune, General Berthier's aide, the 106th was 'carried away by its bravery', crossing the river and climbing the heights beyond. This was a mistake because it was a well-defended sector of the river bank. The regiment was scoured by canister and round shot, caught inside a crossfire of fifty-six Russian guns, fired from batteries sited on the far bank. Moreover, they were pitted against three Russian regiments. 'It was horrible to see as the extended line' of French infantry 'was ravaged and broken by enemy cannon balls,' one French eyewitness recalled. They were deluged by 'a devastating fire from the front and flanks', having launched themselves into a corridor of death.[20]

Impelled by the same reckless impetus, the 92nd Line crossed the bridge to rescue their comrades. Césare de Laugier, watching from the French bank, saw them 'listening only to the voice of the guns advancing at the double' to traverse the planks and hurl themselves against three hostile regiments. The outcome was predictable. Major Mikhail Petrov, commanding a Russian battalion in one of these regiments, fired 'an accurate close range salvo into the [French] ranks'. Then, 'while the smoke was still shrouding the enemy, which had become confused and disordered due to my regiment's volley', he remembered, 'our *jägers* charged with their bayonets'. The 92nd was shattered in a three-regiment-strong counter-attack. General Plauzonne, the French brigade commander, recognising his men were overextended, was killed on the bridge while trying to extricate them, as they beat a hasty retreat back across the river. This time French bodies were shot from the bridge, plunging into the water. Trapped between the enemy and trying to negotiate a narrow, partially destroyed structure of planks, the retreating French were blasted at point-blank range by Russian artillery wheeled forward to the river bank. When it was over, the French were left in control of Borodino village and the Russians burned the bridge.

Württemberger infantry Private Jakob Walter surveyed the devastating scene that resulted 'on account of the congestion before and during the burning' of the bridge:

> The banks on both sides of the bridge were filled with dead piled three and four deep. Particularly the wounded who could still move, hurried to the river to quench their thirst or to wash their wounds; but the suffering brothers had no help, no hope of rescue: hunger, thirst and fire were their death.[21]

For over an hour now, 'continuous artillery fire', Mikhail Petrov remembered:

> Produced a deafening rumble and enormous columns of smoke, which completely overwhelmed and obscured the musket fire, the groans and distress of hand-to-hand combat. Cannonballs, shells, incendiaries

and canister raged with menacing hissing and howling in the air and ploughed the ground with fierce determination, bouncing over it and mauling everything encountered on their way.[22]

With up to 100 cannon pieces booming out each minute, one of the enduring veteran memories of this battle was the sheer intensity of noise. Artillery officer Lieutenant Ilya Radozhitsky claimed 'rounds were so frequent that there were no intervals between them', which Johann von Dreyling, one of Kutuzov's orderlies, recalled, 'combined into one continuous rumble'. The cumulative impact was that 'one's consciousness faded away and all feelings became numbed'. It was 'as if you are not feeling any more', he recalled, to the extent one had to ask 'are you still alive?' Kutuzov's forward headquarters was about 1,500yd from the Borodino village confrontation. Unable to see anything, he had to rely on the sounds of the rise and fall of battle and what his aides could tell him. The fight at the Borodino bridge suggested his original assessment that Napoleon would force the line of the Kolocha to his right was correct, borne out by the impetuous rush of the 106th Line across the river. He was not to know this happened without orders, and the action distracted him from more obvious developments to the left, as he watched for follow-on activity to his right.[23]

Napoleon had set up his headquarters on the Shevardino mound, observing the fighting from a camp chair erected to the right and slightly in front of the remains of the redoubt. He was to spend the day sitting or pacing around, with his imposing entourage of Imperial Guards, resplendent with black bearskin shakos, situated just behind. He also saw little, again having to interpret noise and receive dispatch rider reports about activity unfolding ¾ mile away. By 6.30 a.m. he sensed the feint attack at Borodino village 1½ miles away to the left was in full swing and that Poniatowski must have begun his outflanking move along the old Smolensk road to the right. He now launched most of I Corps against the southernmost part of the Bagration *flèches*, the first part of his main assault left centre of the Russian line. There was a northern and southern *flèche*, or arrow-shaped dug earthen emplacement, and a third one at the rear. However, only the southern and rear fortifications had been picked out by the French. Built on sinking ground and lacking tools, the dirt walls were not particularly robust, and the outer ditch at the northernmost *flèche* was too shallow. One Russian officer described them as 'rubbish, and it is even shameful to call them *shantsy* [*flèches*]'. The gun enclosures were at ground level, 'which made it easy to scale', he recalled, 'and every soldier inside could be seen' through them.

Napoleon had massed 60,000 infantry and 20,000 cavalry around Shevardino, and 297 guns. Davout's corps spearheaded the attack with 22,000 men in three divisions, supported by seventy guns. They were up against 25,000 of Bagration's Russian infantry with 2,500 cavalry, deployed in and around the three emplacements. Baron François Lejeune remembered Compans's division setting off as 'the peaceful plain and silent slopes erupt in swirls of fire and smoke'. Artillery paved the way with 'countless explosions and the howling of cannon shot ripping through the air in every direction'. As he watched, he saw the heads of the columns 'have disappeared into a cloud of dust infused by a reddish glow by the radiant sun'. Firing 'with a sound that seemed like a distant echo' came from Borodino village to the left, 'and from beyond the woods to our right,' where Poniatowski's Polish V Corps moved on Utitsy village.[24]

In 1941, tactics were characterised by manoeuvre and stealth, attempting whenever possible to achieve indirect approaches, unsuspected by the enemy. The modern battlefield was a lonely place, where everyone sought cover from sight, to avoid the lethality of hi-tech weapons. Few weapon systems and men could actually be seen. By contrast, Davout's I Corps advanced in parade-ground formation in the open, three to six columns of sixty men abreast, muskets shouldered or at the present with bayonets, aiming to converge on a single objective. Up to 3,600 men might advance on a 500yd frontage some 30yd deep. Shock action in the *Blitzkrieg* era across the same area of ground at Borodino would be two panzer companies wide, about a dozen tanks visible up front. Combat power came from a combination of medium quick-firing artillery and *Luftwaffe* air support, creating momentum for the tanks. In 1812 shock was applied through massed cannon blasting an entry point, followed by human battering rams of marching infantry in compact columns. Maybe in concert with cavalry, they would force an entry into the Russian defences more often at the point of the bayonet, after firing a few preparatory volleys of musket fire. The assault on the *flèche* emplacements was quite literally French blood and flesh versus Russian blood and iron, formed from cannon and bayonet-wielding infantry, with an earth bank in between.

Davout and Poniatowski's divisions advanced across the same irregular ground covered by the *SS Deutschland* and *Der Führer* infantry regiments, when they attacked Artyomki and Utitsy villages in the area north of the Minsk to Moscow railway line in October 1941. French infantry in 1812 were impeded by the line of the Kamenka and Semyonovskoe north–south running streams, the same obstacles that General Fischer's commanding 10th Panzer Division felt he had to bypass and avoid in 1941. The railway line built across the Borodino battlefield park in the 1860s bisected the area between the (Mozhaisk) new Smolensk road in 1812 and the present Moscow highway. It broadly marked the boundary of the First and Second Russian Army sectors in Napoleon's time, although the Bagration *flèches* lie just to the north of the rail line.

For most of the day the *Grande Armée* was to attack into the teeth of concentrated Russian artillery and musket fire. General Compans, the victor of Shevardino, led his already bloodied division in two groups of columns, one to the left aiming at the southern *flèche* and another to the right, to clear Russian *jäger* infantry from woods peppering their flanks with effective fire. General Dessaix's division came up behind, now with 102 guns in support.

The French infantry marched forward at about seventy-five paces to the minute, tightly bunched in three-rank company lines, one after the other, almost treading on the heels of the battalion 5yd ahead. Such formations were clumsy and difficult to hold in formation, ploughing through muddy stream bottoms and scaling steep slippery slopes beyond, through a backdrop of noise, as Lejeune recalled:

> The guns roar and thunder, the crashing and crackling of musketry the whining and soughing of round shot large and small, the screams of the wounded and dying, oaths in every language.

Such compact formations were especially vulnerable to round shot and canister artillery fire. Only the front three ranks had peripheral vision out to the flanks and only objectives high up, such as the top of the earth-walled *flèches*, could be made out by the rest of the column, over heads through the smoke. 'It was often only from the rows of flashing flames one could make out the enemy regiment's positions,' Lejeune recalled, 'or their batteries as they came riding up.' Battle was physically felt rather than seen. Howling artillery strikes would suddenly sweep away a dozen or more men in the ranks in a welter of screams and flying limbs before the ranks would close and they would proceed. 'The impression of all this went through the marrow of one's bones,' Lejeune remembered. 'Anyone who claims to go into enemy fire without an oppressive feeling is a poltroon.' Advancing by column was, in essence, leading by herd mentality. Men were physically up close, bonding through this collective effort by the reassurance of touch and voiced encouragement. Direction came by sound: drum, bugle or the shouted word, barely audible above the maelstrom of noise that accompanied incoming fire. 'The struggle which developed was one of the murderous I have ever seen,' recalled Louis Planat de la Faye:

> The cannon balls and shells rained down like hail, and the smoke was so thick that only at rare intervals could one make out the enemy masses.

Napoleon could barely follow the action from his vantage point ¾ mile from the *flèches*; smoke and ground mist blotted out that part of the plain. Dessaix's division soldiers at the rear were visible only when they began to descend the Kamenka stream ravine, separating them from the earthworks ahead. Smoke from cannon and musketry at the *flèches* was so dense it curtained off the approach slope, so that only the occasional black silhouette of a struggling man or the glint of a bayonet shone through. It was impossible to distinguish what was going on; shouts and cheers might mean success or failure for both sides. Württemberger infantryman Jakob Walter recalled 'the earth was trembling because of the cannon fire':

> and the rain of cannonballs crossed confusedly. Several entrenchments were stormed and taken with terrible sacrifices, but the enemy did not move from their place.[25]

The preponderance of less-well-trained conscripts in the ranks meant the flexibility to deploy from column into extended line to neutralise the defence with musket fire before charging with the bayonet was less of an option. Napoleon's more professional force at Austerlitz in 1805 had benefitted from intense training conducted at Boulogne on the coast waiting for the anticipated invasion of England. Now the tactic was to bludgeon and force entry into the emplacement in column, like so many human battering rams. Lejeune saw the 57th Line enter the southern *flèche* at the *pas de charge*. 'To our left we'd a redoubt [*flèche*] which was firing murderously at us,' recalled *Sous Lieutenant* Aubin Dutheillet. Being the nearest and on the regiment's left, 'I began shouting "at the redoubt, let's march against the redoubt!"' and together with 'two or three hundred men I flung myself against it'. They forced an entry and pursued the Russians 'more than 200 paces beyond our conquest'. Major Liègre, also with the 57th, came up to order them back inside the emplacement, having seen large numbers of Russian cavalry massing in the ravines. The regiment repeatedly beat back numerous Russian attacks:

> A brave [Russian] officer, seeing his men about to fall back, placed himself across the entrance to the redoubt and did everything he could to prevent them leaving it, but he was shot through the body.

Dutheillet admired the man's courage but was unable to save him as his men rushed forward with the bayonet. Compans, previously wounded in the left arm at Shevardino, was struck again in the shoulder by a musket ball, so Dessaix took command of both divisions. 'We got there just as the first redoubts had been taken by storm,' his aide de camp Captain Girod de l'Ain remembered:

> They were nothing but redans – i.e., chevron-shaped works not closed at their throat in such a way that the enemy's second line swept their interior with the sharpest musketry and grape. So it was a lot harder to gain a foothold and stay there than to have stormed them.

General Jean Rapp took over from the wounded Compans, whose division was now a ruin, and the Russian 7th Combined Grenadier Division ejected it at the point of the bayonet. 'Within the space of an hour I was hit four times,' Rapp recalled, 'first quite slightly by two shots, then by a bullet in my left arm', which 'took away the sleeve of my coat and my shirt down to the skin'. He was in front of the 61st Line and 'cannon balls and shells rained down all round me'. The 5th Division had taken the brunt of the first attacks on the *flèches* and was now scattered about in ditches and folds in the ground.

Command and control was exceptionally difficult in the thick of these parade-ground-like mass engagements. Compact formations sent in by their commanders came back as mobs after a bayonet melee. Messages sent back by horse or on foot were out of date before they arrived. Napoleon was informed Compans had been wounded and then, shockingly, Davout killed. Then he heard he was concussed, but had survived. 'Soon after-wards,' Rapp remembered, 'I received a fourth wound, when grapeshot hit me on the left thigh and threw me off my horse.' This time he had to quit the battlefield, being 'my twenty-second wound'. On the way back he saw and alerted Marshal Ney, commanding III Corps, that his troops were mixing up with his own I Corps. General Dessaix took his place again 'but a moment later he had an arm broken'. General Friant, the 2nd Division commander in I Corps, was also hit.

'So it's your turn again,' Napoleon commented to Rapp as his wounds were dressed. 'How are things?'

'Sire,' Rapp replied, 'I think you will be forced to send in your Guard.' The battle had degenerated into an indecipherable choking smoke: a crowd of small battles occasionally broken by a massed attack or a sudden withdrawal.[20]

Four regiments from Ney's III Corps were given the responsibility to reduce what appeared from the French side as the northernmost of the Bagration *flèches*. They had still not detected there was a *third* fortification to their right rear. Returning mobs of French survivors were reorganised and sent in again. Increasing numbers of Russian troops were mean-while transiting from the right of their line but had yet to arrive in force. General Vorontsov's 7th Combined Grenadier Division was swallowed up yet again in the maw of determined French attacks. 'Resistance could not be long,' he later explained, because 'it only came to an end, so to speak, with the existence of my division'. 'It is frightful to advance on an enemy who does not shoot!' Russian soldier Fedor Glinka acknowledged, as they came closer into accurate range. 'The French advanced' and 'the Russian lines splashed them with a whiff of bullets and canister!' he recalled, but their progress was remorseless:

Bleeding, the French refused to stop. Like madmen, they charged into the gaps between the redans and captured the second of the three!

Some 3,700 of Vorontsov's men fell in two hours, leaving just three officers and some 300 men. Bagration remarked to his adjutant, 'Even a coward could not find a safe place here.' Taking the *flèches*, however, proved a hollow victory. Unenclosed rears created deadly traps, because hemmed in by waves of counter-attacking Russian infantry, the French were forced into a funnel, which had a narrowing wall to their backs.[27]

At 7 a.m., barely an hour into the battle, Kutuzov transferred three Guard regiments, three Cuirassier regiments, eight battalions of grenadiers and thirty-six guns from the reserve to bolster Bagration's Second Army on the left. At 8 a.m. a brigade of infantry and another 100 guns followed and, sixty minutes later, an infantry and a cavalry corps. The 18,000 Russians in this sector rose to more than 30,000 supported by 300 guns. The French responded, raising 40,000 more attackers while 200 additional guns were brought to bear. The fighting was taking on an unprecedented bitter character. Outmanoeuvred units did not fight to the death in Napoleonic warfare, as was happening here. Accounts differ, but it is thought the *flèche* earthworks were stormed and recaptured as many as seven times.

At the extreme right of the French army, Poniatowski's V Corps of some 10,000 men had a fitful start, moving at daybreak. Cutting through dense and marshy Utitsa forest to reach the old Smolensk road was not a viable option. Artillery caissons needed a road move and marauding Russian *jägers* could have severely delayed progress through the trees. Poniatowski decided, therefore, to backtrack the force via the settlement at Yelnya, before turning eastward along the old Smolensk road. In 1941 this was the axis of advance for the *SS Deutschland* and *Der Führer* regiments, seeking to advance on the same objective, the Utitsy and Artyomki villages, although the latter was not a settlement in 1812. It was the weakest spot in the Russian line and vulnerable on both occasions.

The delayed start meant the first shots were not exchanged with the Russians west of Utitsy village until about 8 a.m., when the massive attack on the Bagration *flèches* was already under way, to Poniatowski's left. General Nikolai Tuchkov was blocking the advance with about

23,000 men, half of whom were Moscow and Smolensk *opolchenye* or militia, armed mainly with picks and axes. He had already weakened his corps by sending four regiments from his 3rd Division to bolster the desperate defence of the *flèches*. Poniatowski, likewise, received reinforcements from part of Junot's VIII Corps, dispatched by Napoleon to clear Russian *jägers* peppering the southern flanks of the advance on the *flèches* with intense musket fire. Tuchkov's corps was reduced to just 4,000 men and thirty-six guns. His 1st Grenadier Division clashed with the advancing Poles and was forced back on Utitsy village, which was set on fire and then abandoned. The old soldiers stood their ground impassively as French cannon balls could be seen howling through the air, and splattering mud in all directions at each bounce on the ground, as they came toward them. Militia attempts to dodge these incoming projectiles were laughed at; veteran wisdom insisted there was no point, as each missile already had somebody's name on it. They were alerted, however, to the danger of attempting to block those running out of momentum with their feet, as there was invariably sufficient kinetic energy remaining in the harmless rolling balls to take off a limb.

Poniatowski's men were able to use the open ground in front of Utitsy village to gain momentum. The Russians retreated to a *kurgan* or hill just under a mile beyond the village, and retreating grenadiers kept up a desultory fire, obscured by smoke from burning houses. Emerging from the woods, Poniatowski saw 'a strong column of infantry near the village'. Appreciating he was likely to encounter a resolute defence, he also noticed the ground ahead was 'full of woods and thickets', he recalled, 'from the small wood to the top of a knoll, which dominated the whole plain and which was strongly occupied by the enemy'. As he closed to engage the knoll with artillery, time was lost in wood skirmishing and hesitant actions to line up his forces for an effective assault. An intense action followed. 'Both sides maintained such a petrifying fire that salvos of guns arranged in line resembled battalion volleys of infantry,' Russian General Akim Karpov recalled, 'while the artillery thunder suppressed any other sounds.' The Poles launched an attack and seized the *kurgan* in bitter hand-to-hand fighting. Russian reinforcements were, however, on the way.[28]

By late morning the whole Russian army would have been in grave danger if Poniatowski had been able to continue his fitful advances. Kutuzov, Barclay de Tolly and Colonel Toll, his staff officer, finally appreciated they were facing a crisis on the left wing. Lieutenant General Baggovut, commanding the Russian II Corps, until now uselessly strung out along the Kolocha river to the right of the line, was ordered to dispatch his 17th Division to the left; then his 4th Division as well. Soon the entire II Corps, less its six *jäger* regiments, was streaming to the south, across some of the hottest fighting of the day, just behind the main army line. 'How are things going over there?' Baggovut asked a staff officer. 'They could hardly be worse,' was the response:

> We are finished if you don't hurry up. Bagration's army has been pounded into the ground, and it's a miracle that Tuchkov is still hanging on.[29]

Napoleon, meanwhile, was informed by his aide, Lejeune:

> The unpleasant news that Prince Poniatowski, manoeuvring on his right in the very dense and swampy woods, had run into obstacles which were preventing him from bringing the Polish corps on to the Russian rear and doing enough harm to make a powerful diversion in favour of I Corps.

I Corps was still battling against the Bagration *flèches*. Poniatowski had dispatched his aide, Lieutenant Rostworowski, to tell Napoleon Utitsy had been captured, but one of his arms was shattered by a musket ball en route. He arrived 'pale and with his coat covered in blood'. Roman Soltyk, another Polish officer, saw 'he could hardly keep his horse' and fainted by the ambulance from blood loss. Napoleon did not get the news for another two hours.[30]

The Raevsky redoubt was a linchpin of the Russian defence, dominating the right centre ground of the Russian line. The capture of Borodino village could not be further exploited to generate an assault against the redoubt. As fighting around the village ended between 7.30 and 8 a.m., the French Prince Eugène made some adjustments to his IV Corps of 33,000 men and 7,000 cavalry massed in the area. It was decided to commit 24,000 of his infantry and cavalry for an attack on the redoubt, which would be supported by over 135 guns. They would face an 8ft-high palisade, stepped at 6½ft for the defenders, which was open at the rear. It completely commanded the open ground that gradually fell away from its front, and was supported by the Russian-occupied village of Semyonovskoe forward to its left. There were twelve guns positioned inside the palisades manned by the 26th Battery Company with a six further guns of the 47th Light Battery nearby. The gently sloping front bisected by the Semyonovsky stream ravine lent itself to the bouncing 'graze' effect much prized by artillerymen. Units from the 12th and 26th Divisions were deployed in line at its flanks and rear. The fortification lay in the centre of a web of crossing fire that came from 110 Russian guns covering along the new Smolensk road, to the right of the redoubt. The strong point anchored the right of the Russian line with about 26,000 infantry and 8,500 cavalry deployed for its immediate defence. The methodical pounding it had received from the French guns since the beginning of the battle now increased in violence.

The Russian III Cavalry Corps standing left rear of the redoubt found itself deluged in shot and shell. A company of its horse artillery was annihilated and a replacement company sent forward was also wiped out. 'The horses and men were struck down,' one witness recalled, with 'the ammunition boxes blown up and the guns wrecked'.

Nine o'clock came and still the attack had not materialised, apart from a probe by General Broussier's 14th Division, which was lashed by withering fire from *jägers* hidden in the thick bush land to the redoubt's front. They pulled back into the protection offered by the Semyonovsky stream ravine. By now, alarming French pressure to their left was encouraging the Russian High Command to treat its right as a form of disposable reserve. Raevsky's overstretched VII Corps was obliged to hold the redoubt and a long stretch of ground further south to Semyonovskoe village. All the time he was hemorrhaging reinforcements to prop up Bagration's Second Army in the south. Two battalions were sent to support Tuchkov barely hanging on in Utitsy village. Next, the whole second line was removed, leaving just eight battalions from a former sixteen. Bagration's adjutant, Sergei Mayevsky, was sent by the general to assess what was happening around the redoubt. It was obvious that

Napoleon was gearing up to strike. 'Raevsky took me to the battery,' he recalled:

> which was to the battlefield what a belvedere is to a town. A hundred guns bombarded it. Raevsky, with an elated face told me, 'Now go back and tell the Prince what is going on here.'

Mayevsky had no need to embellish his report to Bagration, because on the ride back:

> I suffered a hit from a flying projectile and the impact was so severe that I could not regain the hearing in my ears or close my mouth for over two hours.[31]

His report was all the more convincing; Napoleon was ratcheting up the level of violence.

Morand's 1st Division, attached to Eugène's IV Corps, appeared suddenly at the lip of the Semyonovskoe ravine and came pouring out of the smoke. It advanced in a mixed formation of column and line known as 'linked brigades', with the 30th Regiment of the Line heading directly at the redoubt. Captain Charles François at the front recalled 'entire files and half platoons fell under the enemy fire, leaving great gaps'. The 30th was raked in line while the 13th and 17th Line Regiments similarly laboured through a hail of shot, with their heads down, as if weathering a storm. Russian officer Nikolai Mitarevsky remembered:

> Fire was maintained by the batteries to the left of us, as well as from the lunette itself, and from behind it; musket fire could not be heard at all since it was overpowered by the deafening cannonade.

'General Bonamy, who's at the head of the 30th, orders us to halt in the midst of the grapeshot,' François recalled, because the line was degenerating into a ragged mob. 'He rallies on we go, at the *pas de charge*.' Coming up against a line of Russian skirmishers, they were ordered enough 'to fire a regimental volley at 30 paces and pass over it'. Suddenly the redoubt embrasures loomed out of the smoke, spitting out flashes of musket and canister fire.

General Raevsky recognised 'this was the decisive moment':

> My guns began to thunder out when the enemy came within range and the smoke hid the French so completely that we could see nothing of their array or ascertain what progress they were making.

His orderly, standing to his left, outlined in the smoke of yet another volley crackling out, exclaimed abruptly, 'Your excellency, save yourself!' Raevsky turned, 'and fifteen yards away I saw French grenadiers pouring into my redoubt with fixed bayonets'. François climbed through one of the embrasures just as the gun poking out fired deafeningly. 'The Russian gunners received us with blows of their handspikes and ramrods,' he remembered. Bitter hand-to-hand fighting erupted throughout the redoubt as the 30th Line forced an entry. 'We fight them man to man and find them formidable adversaries,' François recalled:

> A great number of Frenchmen fall into the wolf pits pell-mell among Russians, who're in them already. Once inside the redoubt I defend myself against the gunners with my sabre and slash down more than one.[32]

With this forward surge, the entirety of the Russian line from Utitsy to Borodino village was now engulfed in conflict; it was now truly a titanic 'Battle of the Giants'. One idealistic young Italian officer, Césare de Laugier, waiting in reserve, had been 'still too young to have been present at one of these famous battles'. Until now he had witnessed local fights, numbering about 10,000 to 18,000 participants. What he now witnessed was entirely different. 'How often I have longed to be witness to and be an actor in so gigantic a conflict!' he recalled. He climbed the ridge from where the Italian Guard artillery was firing, to get a better view:

> Never in my life shall I forget the sublime impression yielded by this view of this long and vast carnage. At a glance we embrace the sinuosities of the terrain, the folds of the ground, the positions of the various arms, the actions engaged on all hands. A marvellous panorama!

In the distance he saw a thick wood from which 'out of it spurt at each instant great jets of flame accompanied by terrible detonations'. As he watched, the 30th Line grappled with the defenders at the edge of the redoubt. 'Under cover of these whirlwinds of fire and smoke', he could discern 'deep masses deploying to advance under cover of no less terrible a fire'. De Laugier, an idealist, was able to paint his epic panorama in words, sanitised from the visceral sights, smells and emotions that emanated from the vicious bayonet fighting. From the ridgeline perspective he saw how 'the sun flashes on the arms and cuirasses of infantry and cavalry marching to meet each other'. Down below, François was being 'crushed by grapeshot and by the fire of others taking us in the front' as they pressed on. 'I skip and jump about to let the iron balls go their way as they come rolling into our ranks,' he remembered. Whole files and half platoons were swept away in a welter of howling canister balls, rattling off shattered equipment and eviscerating flesh from bone, carving great gaps in their ranks. François and his men had 'overrun the redoubt by more than 50 paces' before they realised they were 'not being followed by our division's other regiments'. Only a battalion of the 13th Light was still with them.

The normally imperturbable Eugène, watching with cavalry from behind Borodino village, exclaimed excitedly, 'The battle is won!' The noise coming from the murk around the ravine and redoubt suggested a success. Colonel Lubin Griois, pausing with Grouchy's cavalry in a dip in the ground, recalled 'a grenadier who'd been wounded in the attack came back, covered in blood and drunk on glory, to confirm for us this happy success'. Griois appreciated that 'opening the enemy centre and separating his two wings, seemed to decide victory for us'.

General Barclay de Tolly, commanding the right wing, had also noticed the commotion around the redoubt, as had his Chief of Staff and several other senior Russian officers. The 12th and 26th Divisions either side of the redoubt were rallied and the Siberian and Irkutsk Dragoons were set in motion to pinch out the French salient from both flanks before it was established. Césare de Laugier saw it all unfold as 'a spectator might make out what's going on in the ring below him'. What he witnessed prompted 'indescribable anxiety'; it looked like the 30th was going to be wiped out. Several Russian columns were bearing down on the redoubt from four directions. 'This unhappy regiment which I've just been admiring,' he recalled, 'is letting itself be massacred.' His own position on the ridge top was likewise becoming perilous, because 'fresh Russian batteries have just been placed to reply to the Italian ones on the heights where I am'.[33]

The menacing Russian counter-attack came in as if on parade-ground review 'in astonishingly good order'. Prussian officer Ludwig Wolzogen admired the move from the Russian perspective:

> The various columns approached the foot of the hill in an even step to the time of the drum, and not a single cry arose from the troops. All this so intimidated the French that we could clearly see that many men were fleeing from the ranks and that the garrison of the redoubt was diminishing perceptibly.

'We're forced to retreat, recrossing the redoubt, the Russian line,' Captain François remembered, 'which has sprung to its feet again.' The 30th Regiment was pushed back out at bayonet point, fighting desperately through the embrasures as they retired. Russian soldiers who had previously feigned death were suddenly resurrected and joined the fight. 'Never had I found myself in such a bloody melee or up against such tenacious soldiers as the Russians,' he admitted. They were driven back down the slope and beyond the wolf pits. 'In this way our regiment is shattered,' François remembered. They rallied behind the redoubt and even attempted another charge, 'but not being supported, we're too few to succeed'. The 30th was virtually annihilated 'and with only 11 officers and 257 men we retire'. A mass of Russian cuirassiers charged their right, which Colonel Griois saw 'was causing a certain amount of disorder'.

'I was in a deplorable state,' François admitted. 'My shako had been carried away by grapeshot and the tails of my coat had remained in their hands.' His previous leg wound was 'hurting dreadfully' and 'I was bruised all over'. He passed out from loss of blood on the forward plateau, where the scattered regiment tried to rally. General Bonamy, their commander, was pierced fifteen times by bayonet thrusts inside the redoubt and only saved himself from being finally skewered by shouting out his insistence he was Murat, the king of Naples. Russian grenadiers proudly hauled him off to Prince Kutuzov, who took one look at his battered and reeling state at his headquarters before ordering him to be carried off to hospital.[34]

As the French attack on the Raevsky redoubt was pressed home, the battle for the Bagration *flèches* reached a climax on the vulnerable Russian left. The ebb and flow of attack and counter-attack had left thousands of lifeless bodies and wounded strewn about the emplacements and fields beyond. At about 10 a.m. the French captured all three *flèches*, causing General Bagration commanding Second Army to rally his troops for one more effort. This broke into the rearmost *flèche* once again, but a bullet smashed into his leg and lodged in the bone. Swaying in the saddle, he tried to conceal what had happened, but eventually slid from his horse in some agony, in sight of hundreds of his men. The moral effect on the soldiers was not unlike that felt by the *Das Reich* Division in 1941, when *SS* General Hausser's eye was pierced with shrapnel. It occurred about 4 miles from the spot where Bagration fell. This left the Russian left in considerable disarray in 1812. An hour or so later, the first major French assault on the Raevsky redoubt was finally broken, leaving about 3,000 French corpses strewn across the redoubt and its forward slope.

In the dying stages of the fighting around the *flèches*, General Alexander Tuchkov tried to rally the Revelskii Regiment for one final desperate effort. 'His soldiers, whose faces were lashed by a storm of lead, hesitated.' Fedor Glinka recalled him shouting: 'So are you going to stand here? Then I will attack alone.' Grasping the regimental colours, he rushed forward only to have his chest stove in with canister. His body was never recovered, because Glinka remembered:

Numerous cannon balls and shells resembling a boiling cloud fell on the very place where the dead General lay and ploughed the earth, burying the General's corpse.

His death devastated his wife, Margarita, who, distraught at never finding his remains, laid the foundation of a church near the spot with Tsar Alexander, who financially supported its construction. The Church of the Saviour, gracing the site where her husband was allegedly killed, was the first monument built in 1818 on the battlefield, and exists today. It became the Borodino Saviour Monastery in 1838, with Margarita Tuchkov appointed its first Mother Superior. She had barely recovered from her husband's death when she lost her son in 1826 and her brother was exiled for his involvement in the Decembrist uprising. Thereafter she lived a life of recluse. Over the next few decades the church was further developed, culminating in 1912 when Tsar Nicholas II and his family visited the site to unveil a monument to the 3rd Division. The Soviets closed the monastery in 1929 and it was used as a dressing station in 1941. Damaged during the fighting, it was later adapted as a hospital for the remainder of the war. It was not actively restored to the Russian Orthodox Church until 1992.

Alexander Tuchkov's brother Nikolai was hit in the chest and killed by a Polish bullet leading a charge on the Utitsy knoll, repelling Poniatowski's advance up the old Smolensk road. He was not aware his brother had already perished in the fighting for the *flèches* on the other side of the intervening woodland. Poniatowski had, meanwhile, gone over to the defensive in the face of further Russian reinforcements, which trickled in all the time. He was starting to appreciate that he had insufficient force to gain access to the Russian rear, left of their line. General Dessaix, arriving at Napoleon's headquarters on the Shevardino mound, confirmed this to fellow Polish officer Captain Heinrich von Brandt, stating:

> I have just come from the right and your Prince Poniatowski is not making any progress. The Emperor is not very pleased with him. Our losses are enormous; the Russians are fighting like madmen.[35]

Victory appeared to be eluding the *Grande Armée*.

Under the guise of an infantry advance, on a crowded battlefield at the climax of the action, Napoleon's cavalry unconventionally captures the Raevsky redoubt during the afternoon of 7 September 1812. (Painting by Louis-François Lejeune, courtesy of Wikimedia Commons)

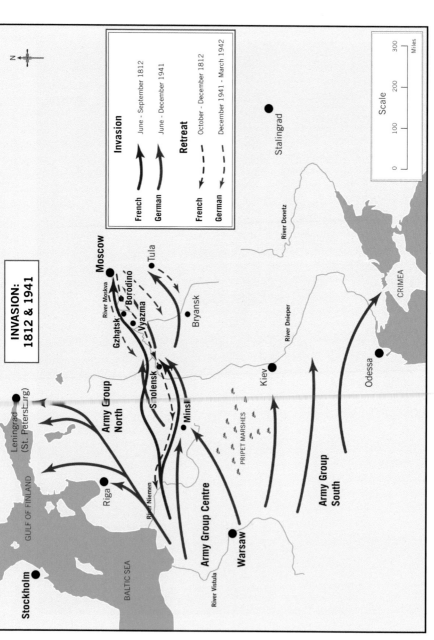

It took twelve weeks for Napoleon's *Grande Armée* to march and fight its way 570 miles to Gzhatsk, 31 miles from Borodino. Hitler's *Wehrmacht* took fourteen weeks to reach the same point, with Army Group Centre broadly following Napoleon's route. They were 114 miles from Moscow. Both armies were decimated by catastrophic winter retreats.

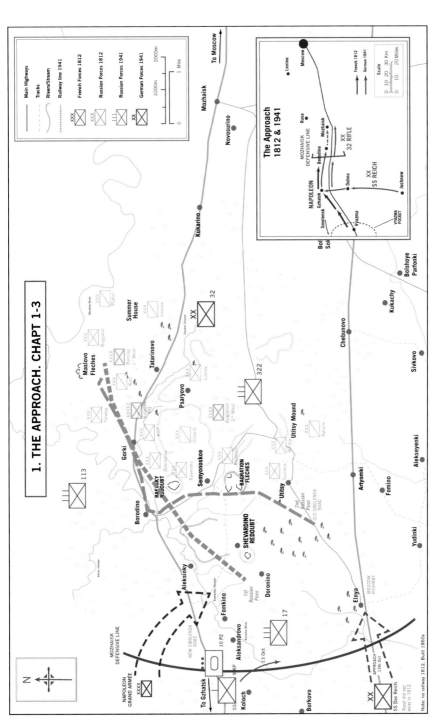

1. THE APPROACH. CHAPT 1-3

1812: Napoleon approaches from the north-west following the old Smolensk road and surprises the Russian army anchored on the Shevardino redoubt. The Russians are obliged to transition to the second position marked to receive the French attack coming in from the west.

1941: The *SS Division Das Reich* advances west to east from Gzhatsk along the Moscow highway. A joint SS and 10th Panzer reconnaissance discovers a likely entry point into the Soviet Mozhaisk defensive line at the Koloch railway halt near the village of Rogachyovo.

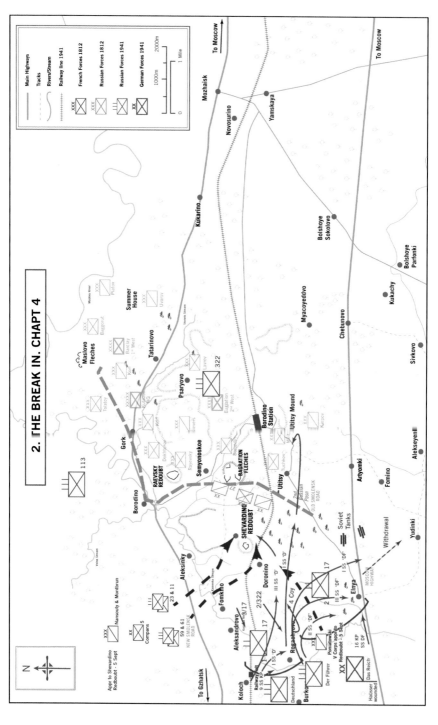

2. THE BREAK IN. CHAPT 4

1812: On 5 September the French infantry division under Compans crosses the Kolocha river and envelops the Shevardino redoubt with Nansouty and Montbrun's cavalry corps in support. The rest of Napoleon's *Grande Armée* follows on and fills in a line running north to south facing east.

1941: Both regiments of the *SS Das Reich* break into the Mozhaisk defensive line between Rogachyovo and Elnya on 13–14 October, with the 10th Panzer Division following up on the Moscow Highway.

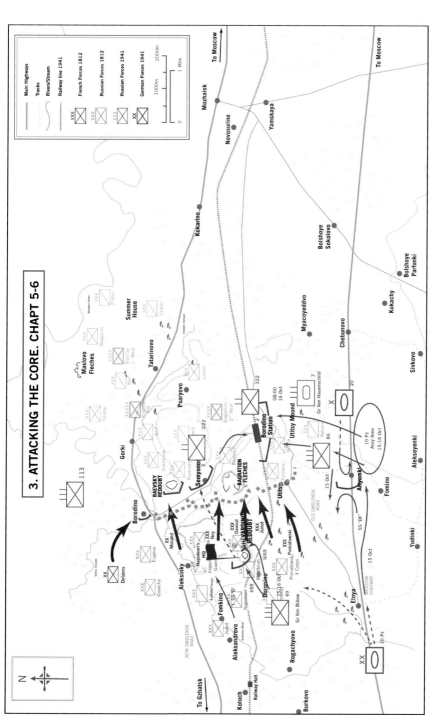

3. ATTACKING THE CORE. CHAPT 5-6

1812: On 7 September, Napoleon elects for frontal assaults across the entire front after a diversionary attack from the north flank against Borodino village.
1941: Soviet resistance at Artyomki blocks the Moscow highway to the 10th Panzer approach. Von Bülow's 69 Regiment *Kampfgruppe* attacks Shevardino while the bulk of the 10th Panzer armour and von Hauenschild's 86 Regiment *Kampfgruppe* bypass Artyomki to the south. They attack north to Borodino railway station, breaching the Russian southern flank and emerging into the rear of the Mozhaisk defence zone.

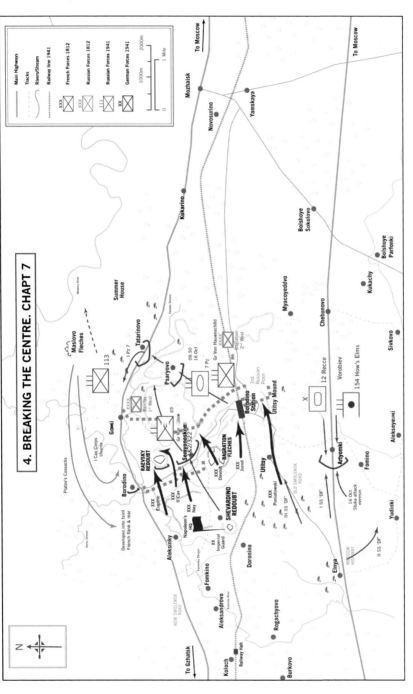

4. BREAKING THE CENTRE. CHAPT 7

N

To Moscow

Mozhaisk

Kukarino

Novosurino

Yamskaya

To Moscow

Bolshoye Sokolovo

Bolshoye Parfonki

Kukachy

Sivkovo

Chebunovo

Myacoyeldivo

Alekseyevki

Vorobiev

154 How's Elms

Fomino

Artyomki

16 Oct Stalla attack overrun

12 Recce

Yudinki

Elnya

MOSCOW HIGHWAY

II SS 'DF'

I SS 'DF'

Rogachyovo

Burkovo

Aleksandrovo

Koloch

Railway Halt

To Gzhatsk

Fomkino

NEW SMOLENSK ROAD

Doronino

Napoleon's HQ

XX Imperial Guard

Aleksinky

Borodino

SHEVARDINO REDOUBT

RAEVSKY REDOUBT

XXX Eugene

XXX II/Cav

XXX Ney

Gorki

I Cav Corps Uhuslov

Platov's Cossacks

Develops into faint French flank & rear

Vina Stream

Gr Von Chalov

69

XXXX Barclay 1st West

XXXX 62/322

Semyonoskoe

XXX Davout

BAGRATION FLECHES

XXX Junot

XXX Poniatowski

Utitsy

III SS 'DF'

OLD SMOLENSK ROAD

Utitsy Mound

Borodino Station

3rd Russian Posn

86 Gr Von Hauenschild XXXX 2nd West

7 Pz

09.50 16 Oct

Psaryovo

1 Pz 7

Tatarinovo

Summer House

113

Maslovo Fleches

Moskva River

Semka Stream

Kamenka River

Kolocha River

1812: After capturing the Bagration *flèches* at great cost to the south, Napoleon's main effort switches to frontal assaults against the Raevsky redoubt to the north. He is distracted by a Russian cavalry foray on his left flank, threatening the French rear.

1941: Gruppe von Bülow's 69 Regiment attacks through Semyonovskoe village after taking Shevardino. Gruppe von Hauenschild attacks through Psaryovo to Tatarinovo, linking with 69 Regiment. A panzer battalion is sent westward past Gorki to attack Soviet positions at Borodino and the Raevsky mound from the rear. Artyomki village is finally captured by the SS *Der Führer* Regiment on 16 October.

Legend

	Main Highways
	Tracks
	Rivers/Stream
	Railway line 1941
XXX	French Forces 1812
XXX	Russian Forces 1812
XX	Russian Forces 1941
XX	German Forces 1941

0   1000m   2000m

0   1 Mile

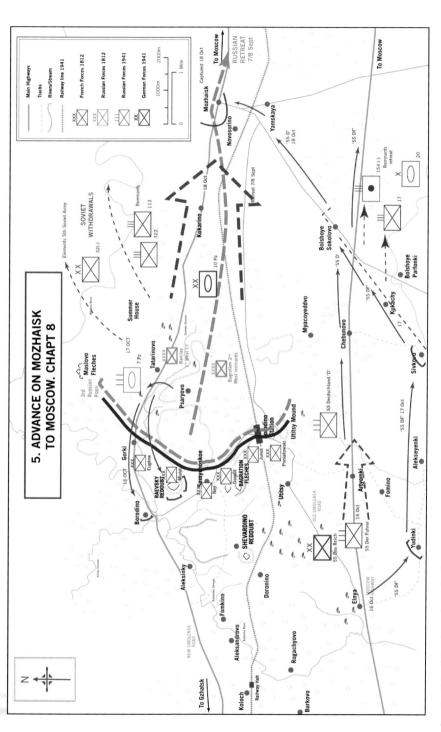

5. ADVANCE ON MOZHAISK TO MOSCOW. CHAPT 8

Main Highways
Tracks
River/Stream
Railway line 1941
French Forces 1812
Russian Forces 1812
Russian Forces 1941
German Forces 1941

0   1000m   2000m
0   1 Mile

N

1812: After the fall of the Raevsky redoubt to a surprise French cavalry attack, both armies stop, completely exhausted. The badly mauled Russian Army retreats toward Moscow on 8 September; Napoleon's battered army is slow to pursue.

1941: Having finally breached the Mozhaisk defence zone to the rear, *SS Das Reich* moves south of and along the Moscow highway linking with the 10th Panzer Division, which advances east to capture Mozhaisk on 18 October.

Desperate fighting among the ghostly obelisks and memorials of 1812 on this less crowded battlefield near Borodino village, captured by the German Panzer Regiment 7 in October 1941. (Painting by Fyodor Usypenko © Alarry)

6

The Road Through Borodino Field

83 Miles to Moscow

The Fight Among the Monuments, 15–16 October 1941

The planned German pursuit to Mozhaisk was completely disrupted by the sudden reverse at Artyomki on the Moscow highway. Some of the *SS Deutschland* units were pushed back to start lines where they had set off the previous day. Even the initial break-in point achieved at the Koloch railway halt and Rogachyovo village were far from secure. Meanwhile, more and more armoured vehicles from the 10th Panzer Division trundled down the Moscow highway in a stop–start traffic flow that spilled out into an assembly area in woods south of Utitsy village, where the forward outposts of *Der Führer* were located. *Kriegsberichter* Hugo Landgraf had stopped his sound recording near the *Reich* headquarters and moved to film this build-up of German infantry and lines of tanks moving across rough tracks and wooded clearings into the assembly area. The plan was for the *SS* infantry to retake Artyomki while the panzers would cross the highway and head north-east, to break into the rear of the Soviet defence works. This would take them into the heart of the old 1812 battlefield. They were then to turn oblique right and advance over Utitsy and Borodino railway station to Tatarinovo, the site of Kutuzov's main headquarters in 1812. After breaking through, the aim was to pursue to Mozhaisk, 10 miles further east. Landgraf's voiceover for his *Deutsche Wochenschau* newsreel, shown in German cinemas within two weeks, described how:

> We are approaching the positions which are being fiercely defended, with strong panzer forces. I am sitting at the radio operator's post inside a heavy [Panzer IV] tank and will be filming the attack from there.

The scene opens with him filming through the post-box-size forward vision slit of the tank. It atmospherically conveys claustrophobic crew conditions as the tank bumps along, flattening tall undergrowth rearing up ahead and following the parallel track marks of the leading panzers. Platoon and company files of heavily laden infantry can be seen hurriedly crossing open ground with a panzer company moving in *Keil* or wedge formation in front to secure the start line ahead.[1]

As this panzer build-up developed, elements of the Soviet 2nd Battalion, 322 Regiment, were stealthily approaching the outposts of the *SS Deutschland* at Rogachyovo village to their rear. Soviet Captain Sherbakov set up a battalion tactical command post inside a recently constructed pillbox at the edge of the shoe-shaped clearing just east of the settlement. He had mortars, artillery and two tanks in support and 45mm anti-tank guns. The plan was to rush the village at dawn with three companies, attacking one after the other. 'Open fire when the infantry breaks into the village,' he briefed his artillery observer, 'hit the concentration of the enemy at Koloch station, and the village of Burkovo', a likely staging point for reinforcements, a mile inside the German line to the west.

At dawn and in a light frost, the first company of infantry scrambled across 200yd of open ground from the forest track that converged in a junction at Rogachyovo. The silent rush burst into the village from two directions. One of the platoons commanded by Lieutenant Vasily Xomuch was immediately knocked down by a crossfire of automatic weapons that spat out from the north-east corner of the houses. 'Caught unawares at the extreme village huts, they were annihilated,' Sherbakov remembered. 'None of them managed to save themselves by escaping.' Tank, anti-tank, mortar and artillery fire scourged the village as German panzer and motorised reinforcements rolled up. Sherbakov called down three batteries' worth of fire from 133 Artillery Regiment and 'many Nazis caught by the sudden artillery fire did not escape from the vehicles, remaining dead inside'. Very soon 'eight vehicles burned like bonfires,' he remembered. The sudden Soviet attacks were reported by German radio, describing how a 500yd gap was levered open between I and II *Deutschland* Battalions. By 10 a.m. the III *SS* Battalion reported repelling Russian attacks coming out of the woods on both the north and south sides of Rogachyovo. This aura of crisis reigned on the radio net until 12.52 p.m., and even an hour later the *SS Deutschland* was urgently requesting reinforcements to hold on to the village.

Sherbakov's attacks bogged down. 'Despite their great losses, crack Nazi troops from the *SS Reich* Division stubbornly defended Rogachyovo,' he admitted. He watched from the pillbox as 'an enemy machine gun rattling away from the second row of standing sheds' took down many of his advancing troops. 'The tempo of the advance slowed down,' he remembered. Unable to drop artillery fire on to it, a 45mm anti-tank gun was manhandled forward to engage with direct fire. The first round splattered earth skyward just left of the embrasure. Having exposed his position, the gunner twirled the wheel of his siting mechanism 'with sweat pouring over his face and burning his eyes', having spotted a panzer creeping out of a nearby barn. Switching target, he hit and smashed one of its tracks. Even so, the Russian attack had petered out. Three more times the village exchanged hands until news came of apparent deep enemy penetrations along the Moscow highway to their left. Sherbakov's supporting units were drawn off to meet this new threat, so that by late afternoon on 15 October he had to pull back his battalion remnants around high ground to his rear. This was the preserved historic mound that had housed Napoleon's former headquarters at the Shevardino redoubt. The action, according to the 32nd Division operations log, cost his battalion 30 per cent of its men.[2]

Ivan Barchuk had reoccupied a position dug by another unit – since relocated – just forward of Borodino railway station. 'The defensive area was silent,' he recalled. They did not bother improving the trenches because 'everyone was waiting for the order to advance'. Nerves were taut and plummeting temperatures were starting to have a detrimental effect on the working parts of their automatic weapons and self-loading rifles. They were 'oiled with light oil but the oil thickened', Barchuk remembered. Veteran NCOs urged them to dry clean the moving parts, which with the rubbing warmed them up. Overhead, a menacing Italian double-fuselage aircraft, nicknamed 'the frame', was circling their position. 'We wanted to open fire,' he remembered, 'but were forbidden lest we reveal ourselves.' They had no idea they were sited within the proposed advance axis of the II *Abteilung* from Panzer Regiment 7. The aircraft loitered a while before flying off.

'An hour passed,' he remembered, 'and ahead we could hear the roar of tank engines revving up.' It was assumed these were their own tanks 'which would support our offensive'. The sinisterly 'growing clank of tank tracks' came closer, 'but no firing' occurred. Despite being on alert, neither the regimental commander nor platoon commander had given any indication of alarm. Tanks camouflaged with branches drew up and their platoon commander, the popular and respected Lieutenant Shamatov, left his command post to meet them. 'It was clear that the platoon commander took these tanks as ours,' Barchuk explained. When the panzer halted, the turret lid opened and Shamatov was beckoned forward. As he ran around the tank 'the German tankist shot Shamatov point blank, and he fell down straight away on the spot'. At the same time, the German tank commander was immediately hit by their sniper, Miroshinkevo, from the command post:

> Then suddenly Nazi tanks appeared in front of us, firing both main guns and machine guns. Behind the tanks came sub-machine gunners [infantry], who shouted *'Russians surrender!'*

Barchuk and his men counted more than thirty German tanks moving toward them and 'a tornado of fire swept away everything in its path'. The panzers rolled into their rear, shooting up ammunition trucks and the horse-drawn anti-tank guns – anything they could see. He recalled, 'it seemed that every living thing was going to die in this inferno.'

The panzer that shot down their platoon commander 'passed over our trenches firing both its gun and machine guns', heading for a circular-section trench behind them. It locked and then reversed tracks in a squealing skid that sought to crush the occupants. 'It twisted its tracks splattering us with mud,' Barchuk remembered, 'pouring in machine-gun fire, but we were in dead ground and he didn't notice us.' Panzer crews were trained to direct their main gun against opposing tanks. Only when machine-gun fire was inadequate to achieve a fire task would they switch armament because machine-gun belts were always more plentiful. They advanced in wide formation, to bring the maximum number of weapons to bear. 'Our trench was located in surrounding tall trees and that saved us,' Barchuk explained. Total confusion reigned:

> The grinding of tank tracks, explosions of shells and mines, the return fire of anti-tank guns, explosions on German tanks, the rattle of machineguns, whistling bullets, continuous fire and the moaning and crying from the wounded and neighing of horses. All this mass chaos and wild noises blended into one barrage of fire.

It was difficult to differentiate German from Russian. The III Battalion *SS Deutschland* provided the infantry support for this advance, and the fighting was pitiless. 'Among us were western Ukrainians, who had been conscripted in 1940,' Barchuk recalled, 'and many put up their hands and laid their weapons down.' Little distinction was made between Germans and these 'proper traitors' caught up between. 'A few of our men had had enough, stood up and began to walk towards the enemy,' he remembered, 'but we shot them down.' The Germans also 'used psychological tactics – taunting us through loud hailers, and playing the sound of weapon fire all around us through their speakers'. 'Several with weak nerves accepted the deception as reality.'

They managed to fight off the German infantry but at the cost of many of their key junior sub-unit commanders. Telephoned instructions ordered them to fall back across the railway line and form a new defensive line on the embankment at the other side, 'so we got on with it'. German tanks identified the crossing points and cut down many of the fugitives attempting to scramble over the railway tracks.

Freezing temperatures continued to take their toll on the efficient operation of automatic weapons. Even 'light grease hindered the mechanism, because it froze,' Barchuk explained. He was rubbing his breechblock clear even as they fought. Others, like his friend Rusanov, had not and started to panic. 'Instead of bursts, he was firing single shots,' Barchuk noticed and when he disappeared beneath his cape on the ground he kicked him, yelling, 'You vermin, why are you not firing?' The only response was an 'indistinct babbling'. Barchuk worked his breechblock for him until 'it managed to fire single shots, then short bursts, then long bursts'. Once the machine gun started to perform normally, Rusanov calmed down and began to accurately engage attacking Germans. 'In this way we repelled numerous attacks,' Barchuk remembered. Occupying the railway embankment briefly stabilised the line, but 'we were running out of ammunition for the automatic weapons' and 'we had suffered many dead and wounded soldiers'.[3]

The *I Abteilung* of Panzer Regiment 7 moved northward to Utitsy, bypassing Artyomki to its left, and came under fire from Soviet field emplacements. Hugo Landgraf filmed the bumpy advance from the hatch of his heavy tank, following behind medium Panzer IIIs advancing in loose arrowhead formation. There was 'extremely heavy fire on our approach,' he recalled. Artillery explosions can be seen bursting ahead on the newsreel, filmed through his vision slit. 'You can hear the clack-clack of artillery, mortar and machine gun fire on three sides.'

The second wave of panzers was moving with the *II Abteilung* to their right, edging toward the 1812 commemorative obelisks on the Utitsy mound. 'A monument to Napoleon stood there,' remembered Walter Straub with the 10th Panzer Division. Accompanying *SS* infantry mopped up the fortified positions overrun by the tanks. The *I Abteilung* was heading north-west of Borodino railway station, while the *II Abteilung* axis of advance went directly through the station buildings. The significance of the moment was not lost on the panzer crewmen. 'With that,' Straub recalled, 'the tanks of the Württemberg Regiment stood on historic ground':

> On 7 September 1812, other soldiers from Württemberg had fought and won a victory on that same ground for Napoleon.

About a mile ahead were the Bagration *flèches*, which Württemberg infantry soldier Jakob Walter had charged in 1812. The convent where they had stood was being used as a dressing station by both sides in 1941. Walter recalled the start of that day when 'like thunderbolts, the firing began both against and from the enemy'. His muttered prayer likely reflected the emotions of his fellow panzer crewmen in the advance, over the same ground, 129 years later:

> God, Thou canst save me; but if it is not Thy will, I hope that my sins will be forgiven because of my sufferings and pains, and that my soul will ascend to Thee.

With that, Walter recalled, 'I went on trustingly to meet my fate.'[4]

Landgraf's dramatic newsreel showed burning village houses and hay-ricks on fire, interspersed with momentary images of panzers rocking on their tracks from the recoil of the main tank gun firing. 'We remain in this position for hours,' he recalled, a veritable slugging match as 'armoured fighting vehicles and artillery are locked in bitter fighting'. The heavy Panzer IV company was firing in support of infantry, who can be seen in the film walking alongside, while lighter Panzer IIIs are jockeying in and out of their firing positions up ahead. 'Our barrels are becoming hot after continuously firing, with shot after shot roaring out,' Landgraf recorded, while, 'Our tank shakes with the mortars landing all around us.' The newsreel transitions to dusk, as he reported, 'As night draws in, we manage to advance several kilometres.' Glowing tracer lines spit out from his turret and gently arc into the distance, seeking out Soviet positions at the edge of shadowy wood lines.[5]

Private Jakob Walter, advancing against the Bagration *flèches* with his fellow Württembergers in 1812, would have regarded the shock action of the Panzer Regiment 7 attack from Utitsy on their right with some incredulity. No fighting machines capable of operating cross-country had existed since ancient chariots and war elephants two centuries before Christ. The chariot had a driver and javelin thrower, the war elephant, maybe a saddled crew compartment. Panzers drove faster than a running infantryman and could fire high-velocity projectiles on the move. Tanks to the Napoleonic soldier would be as comprehensible as *Star Wars* laser guns to modern soldiers.

Shock action for Napoleonic infantry was about bludgeoning the opposite line with columns of musket-firing, bayonet-wielding infantry, supported by smooth-bore cannon. *Blitzkrieg* concentrated tanks, guns and motorised infantry in concert with a new dimension – air power –

to achieve a breakthrough, in a fraction of the time. The tank company Landgraf filmed would typically advance on a frontage of 250yd, with ten to fourteen armoured fighting vehicles. When Walter's Württemberg infantry advanced, they did so in gorgeously attired uniforms maybe 180 to 200 men across on a front of three battalions, maybe even six across. A 500yd Napoleonic frontage (nine ranks deep) would number about 3,000 men, which was the equivalent of two panzer companies, motoring in arrowhead formation, manned by crews wearing black loose-fitting overalls like factory workmen. The contrasts could not be greater.

The fight along the line of the railway offered some stability to the hastily reorganised Soviet defence. It was readily recognisable in the confused conditions of a retreat under fire and offered value as an obstacle. Embankments and cuttings tended to channel advancing panzers towards crossings negotiable by tank track, between Koloch and the village of Doronino, thereby predictable. Silver birch woods grew in profusion across the area because the water table was high, also providing cover in higher dryer areas, the only possible areas to dig in.

For both sides, but particularly the attackers, the need for soldiers to fling themselves on to saturated muddy ground, or into water-filled ditches for cover, was physically and emotionally draining. Mud impregnated soaking greatcoats, which would double in weight, as did boots and footwear. Wet clothes, moreover, froze at night. SS infantry, unlike their Russian counterparts, rarely enjoyed the benefit of hot food being brought forward in containers. There was also scant opportunity to dry clothes in alternately freezing then thaw conditions. Days of wading through mud, slush and rain 'dissolved' the men's socks, the *Reich* unit history noted, and no supplies apart from ammunition made it forward. When temperatures dropped to -15° Centigrade a few weeks later, SS soldiers were fighting barefoot in their boots, reliant on wrapping their feet in newspaper or plundered bed linen.

Otto Kumm, commanding the *SS Der Führer* Regiment, was seriously concerned that, despite their achieving objectives, this was 'at the cost of unspeakable pains and strain'. Infantry companies were gradually being whittled down by the weather and enemy action from start states of 185 men to average fighting strengths of thirty-five. Companies had to be reorganised into just two platoons containing two small squads of about seven or more soldiers, which with sleep interrupting guard duties, and normal fatigues, was hardly sustainable. The cumulative outcome of all this was the disbandment of the third *Reich* regiment, the 11th *SS*, six days later, to enable the fighting strengths of the *Deutschland* and *Der Führer* to be brought up to workable levels. 'The forces have been attacking without let up since the 6th October 1941,' the main *SS* office in Berlin was informed:

> Great successes have been attained in spite of terrible road conditions and the worst weather imaginable, (snowstorms, snow glare, ice, thaws) and oftentimes without opportunity to bring vehicles, particularly field kitchens forward.

The overall impact of this was, the report read:

> The forces are now at the end of their capabilities: officers, men and vehicles. Intestinal diseases, stomach diseases, frostbite and a general condition of weakness are setting in. Uniforms and equipment must be repaired and maintained.[6]

'Snow fell overnight,' recalled Landgraf on the morning of 16 October, when he saw 'the infantry have dug themselves between our tanks'. He watched them trudge past wearing thin greatcoats, heavily laden shadowy figures silhouetted against a white snow vista, raising clouds of condensation from their wet uniforms as they struggled by. 'The battle went on,' his film commentary recorded, 'the infantry advance against the enemy,' toward Borodino station and the Minsk–Moscow railway line.

Ivan Barchuk helped a machine gunner encumbered with his Maxim and two boxes of ammunition across the track. He agreed to remain and serve as the number 2 (loader) because 'the heavy machine gun is a formidable weapon'. They recovered a wounded junior artillery lieutenant, lying on the embankment, who appealed plaintively, 'Don't leave me here, I'm wounded in the foot, help me.' On the other side, Barchuk remembered, 'We discovered a ready-dug circular trench for the machine gun post.' Getting heavy weapons across the tracks was difficult. A soldier burdened with the base plate for a 1937 model 82mm mortar could well snap a cervical vertebrae if he stumbled and fell in the carry. As Barchuk and the other remnants from 322 Regiment began setting up this new defence line, German panzer and infantry attacks came in. The tank 'fired over our heads and we bent down and hid in the bottom of the trench,' he recalled. It then 'turned on the spot,' once again attempting to crush and bury them, but 'we stayed down and were alive, it just showered us with soil'. Once the panzer moved on, they popped up again, heaved the Maxim on to the parapet 'and cut down the infantry with our own machine gun when they were 60 to 70 metres from us'. The disjointed fighting was part of a 'new defence, conducted in a cutting in the wood, or a road, I've forgotten'.[7]

During the night the two motorised infantry regiments belonging to the 10th Panzer Division managed to close up, despite falling snow and atrocious road conditions. By the time Landgraf reported the continuation of the battle that morning, they had joined the two panzer groups, *Abteilung I* and *II*. By 8 a.m. the *Gruppe von Hauenschild* from *Schützen* Regiment 86 had joined in the attack on Borodino railway station, with two howitzer battalions in support of the *II Abteilung*, which had struck Barchuk's section of the line. The *Gruppe von Bulow* with *Schützen* Regiment 69 and the panzers of *Abteilung I* reinforced by a motorcycle battalion, flak and anti-tank guns, emerged on to the historic 1812 battlefield to their left. They were fired on by a Russian howitzer battalion, after transiting through the village of Yelnya and attacking towards the village of Doronino, beneath the railway line just south of Shevardino. The *SS Deutschland* was to their left. *Der Führer* had been ordered to feint along the Moscow highway, while attacking the village of Artyomki yet again, from the south.

Landgraf took up the newsreel commentary, describing how 'rolling forward again we encounter an enemy wall of resistance, with thousands of gun barrels pointing straight at us'. Assaults were hotly contested, distinguishable by rising pillars of smoke coming from burning village houses ahead. 'Our tanks advance forward metre by metre,' Landgraf recalled. Barchuk remembered, 'the enemy attacked us from the air' in support. 'Hedge-hopping aircraft strafed us with cannon and machine guns.'

'To save ourselves being destroyed' amid bursting bombs, 'we took cover in a gully and a copse'. Landgraf filmed these low-flying aircraft flying right to left over their stationary tanks. 'Our comrades in the *Luftwaffe* attack the enemy positions in low-level runs,' he recorded. 'Hardly is a battery silenced that another opens up on us.'[8]

By 8 a.m. the *II Abteilung* with Regiment 86 had reached the station and changed direction to the north-east, rapidly bearing down on the village of Psaryovo. At last panzer momentum was making some headway, having broken through the defence crust on an attack width of some 1,200yd. Supporting panzers sought to dominate the attack axis by pausing and firing from high points on the rolling terrain. German tanks did not fire on the move: they fired and 'jockeyed' forwards and backwards into fresh positions, evident from Landgraf's film report. Attack widths were expanded to bring even more direct fire weapons to bear, attempting to neutralise Soviet blocking positions by firepower alone. Once momentum built up with succeeding fire and movement, panzers bypassed to strike the Soviet flanks and rear. Tanks surrounded woods and the infantry would comb through to mop up or flush out the opposition. Landgraf's Panzer IV Company, with its 75mm high-explosive rounds, were particularly effective against Soviet infantry ensconced in village houses. Thatched roofs were shot into flames by tracer, while the main gun would knock down walls to force entry or get the enemy out.

By 10 a.m. the panzers had fought through Psaryovo and reached the village of Tatarinovo, deep inside the Soviet position. This had some historical resonance, being the former site of Kutuzov's headquarters in 1812. 'When our commissars had told us we would inherit the strength of those who had defeated Napoleon,' Boris Baromykin with the 32nd Division recalled, 'something changed within us':

We began to think about Moscow, and about our responsibility to defend the Russian capital. It was our city – and we did not want the enemy to seize it. We resolved to make a stand.

Strong Soviet positions were encountered beyond Tatarinovo holding both sides of the road, and four German tanks were knocked out on the outskirts of the woods. 'Dusk falls again,' Landgraf recorded. 'We're standing in front of a forest, the main defence line of the Soviets.' The newsreel picks up the pulsating metallic rattle of the turret machine gun firing, with brass cases cascading on to the metal floor. Arcs of tracer reach out into the darkness, flashing and crackling along the edge of the dark wood lines to their front. They had brushed aside elements of the 322 and 320 Rifle Regiments sited in depth. 'Up to 35 enemy tanks and about a battalion of infantry, mounted on vehicles broke through along the road from Psaryovo and Tatarinovo,' the 32nd Division log noted, 'and engaged our units having reached the artillery positions of the 133rd.'

The Soviet situation was becoming untenable. If motivation was lacking, draconian discipline was applied. Infantry officer Fyodor Sverdlov admitted during one particularly intense action he personally shot one of his men. This was permissible under Stalin's declaration, later announced, of a state of siege on Moscow. 'It happened once during a successful attack,' he remembered:

> There was one soldier, I don't know what his name was, but because of his cowardice and because the combat was very severe he broke down, and he began to run, and I killed him without thinking twice. And it was a good lesson to all the rest.[9]

The *II Abteilung* were about to resume the advance when von Hauenschild was alerted to Soviet counter-attacks, coming in from the west, hitting von Bulow's 69th Regiment to their left. This indicated substantial enemy activity to their rear, which made von Hauenschild uneasy. He halted the *II Abteilung* and put out security outposts to protect his advance positions for the coming night.

Captain Sherbakov, with the 322 Regiment, had pulled back the remnants of his 2nd Battalion to high ground at Shevardino, after his failed counter-attack to retake Rogachyovo. An uncompromising interrogation of a captured German lieutenant, 'with a swollen lower lip hanging down chattering teeth', revealed a steady build-up of German force around the village. Shevardino was next, and the attack would be delivered by von Bulow's 69th Regiment *Gruppe*, approaching from Yelnya, after staging from the Moscow highway.

Russian accounts recall that on the morning of 16 October 'a clear bright sun came through' and snow the preceding night was 'covering the silver birches like a fluffy mantle'. Sherbakov had a breath-taking panoramic view beneath a 'sky blue horizon' of the historic villages of

Shevardino, Semyonovskoe and Borodino. He could see all the key points of the 1812 battlefield from the Shevardino mound and felt patriotically inspired by 'numerous monuments standing across Borodino field like sentries guarding the sacred ground of Borodino'. Lermontov's epic verse came to mind, 'Lads! Is Moscow behind us? Give your life for the sake of Moscow.' Many would, as with a warning shout of 'Air!' they scrambled for shelters on hearing 'a powerful continuous rumble on the enemy side out to the west'. They stared in the direction of the approaching sounds until the first aircraft appeared. At the same time, large numbers of tanks and infantry 'crawling like geese drawing in their feet' approached at ground level across the snow, 'so many, that nobody could count'. Three *Stukas* peeled off in a line and came howling down from the clear blue sky.

'Bombs exploded three at a time: crump, crump, crump,' remembered artillery battery commander Captain Petrovich Nechaiev. 'It seemed like the earth was on the point of cracking.' Tensions rose as 'the roar got closer, a scream, and again the grey Shevardino hill quivered'. The aircraft became obscured through all the smoke and mist until eventually 'the roar diminished and moved away'. They emerged from their shelters shaking off earth, rubbing eyes, and observed the other battery positions being similarly dive-bombed. Nechaiev could see 'fires were breaking out in the villages of Borodino and Gorki'. For several hours, rifle and mortar fire raged to and fro across the line of the railway embankment. Doronino was finally captured after costly fighting. German observers, peering over the fire-swept rail lines, could detect the outline of the memorial on the Shevardino mound, where Napoleon had watched the battle. It appeared tantalisingly close enough to touch.

Sherbakov, observing from the high ground, could see German battle formations assembling at the edges of the woods between Fomkino, near the Kolocha river, and Doronino. This was the very area where the French division commander Compans had formed up for his assault against the Shevardino redoubt, after crossing the river. Two substantial German *Kampfgruppen* (combat groups) were diverging. Von Bulow's 69th Regiment with elements of the *SS Deutschland* were heading towards him with about thirty panzers, while von Hauenschild's 86th Regiment was moving north-east of Borodino railway station, across the old battle-field, spearheaded by tanks. The Soviets deluged the advance with artillery and mortar fire, and tanks were engaged with anti-tank guns and artillery, firing over open sights. The II Battalion 69th Regiment before them was pinned down and pulled back, suffering heavy casualties. The *Luftwaffe* intervened but the next ground assault was also beaten back. Sherbakov's depleted battalion lost another ten killed and twenty-two wounded. 'They buried the dead in the anti-tank ditch,' he recalled bleakly. The wounded were carried off to the same museum where division commander Polosukhin had sworn to defend the battlefield in his written entry to the visitor's book. It now doubled up as a regimental aid post.

During the afternoon, Nechaiev recalled, 'After softening up by artillery the enemy began an attack on the front and left flank.' The I Battalion of Regiment 69 was brought forward after five hours' costly fighting and crossed the railway line to attack the Shevardino defenders from the east. As darkness fell, they broke into the village, at which point their sister II Battalion, pinned down, rose up and stormed the defences from the front. By about 8 p.m. its 7th Company was fighting among the emplacements on 'Monument Hill', the site of the bloodily contested redoubt in 1812. By now Captain Nechaiev could see that 'amongst the rank and file confusion was arising'. Ammunition was running out and bedlam ensued. 'They fired,' Nechaiev remembered, 'threw grenades, struck with rifle butts, moaned, cried, swore – everything mixed together!' Amid shouts of 'Russians surrender!' the Shevardino position was overrun. In so doing, von Bulow's men fought themselves to virtual exhaustion. They captured the mound and eastern end of Shevardino but could advance no further. It was at this stage that yet another Soviet counter-attack crashed in from the west. The situation was so serious that von Hauenschild's further advance with 86 Regiment beyond Tatarinovo to the east was placed on hold.[10]

The village of Semyonovskoe had been Bagration's forward headquarters in 1812, where he directed the epic defence of the *flèches* nearby. Colonel Polosukhin, likewise, established his 32nd Division tactical headquarters in the village. Semyonovskoe was the rallying point for all the disparate and fought-out elements of his division during the October 1941 battle. According to Ivan Barchuk, it was also a useful and welcome replenishment point. 'Finding the kitchen, we discovered a lot of food,' he recalled. 'The dishes smelt wonderful' and 'the concealment was thorough'. When Barchuk's platoon commander was killed, they were moved back to the village from the railway station. 'The Sergeant Major said take whatever you want,' he remembered, and 'they would give us 100 grams of vodka as a warmer.' No further encouragement was needed.

'Everyone received "the Minister's 100",' infantry officer Fyodor Sverdlov recalled, 100g of vodka routinely issued by the Ministry of Defence. His men often fought under the influence of alcohol:

> There's a Russian saying that a drunken man can cross the sea. Whenever a man gets drowned in the Moskva river, he would always be a drunk. A drunk thinks that everything is easy, and this makes it clear why Russian soldiers were given vodka.

Heavy casualties meant more was available for fewer survivors. Sverdlov admitted:

> I usually drank 200 grams of vodka at breakfast, 100 grams of vodka at lunch, and if there was no combat in the evening, I would drink another 200 gram glass sharing dinner with a company of friends.

It did not necessarily hamper fighting ability, 'quite the contrary' he claimed:

> When a person gets drunk, he feels more determined, more courageous. He doesn't think about being killed in a minute. He marches on, trying to kill the enemy.

'We crammed emergency rations into respirator sacks,' Ivan Barchuk recalled at Semyonovskoe. They were housed in a barn, offered rest, and an armourer checked over and serviced their weapons. 'A lot of soldiers gather with us,' he remembered, 'they gathered guys together returning from battle, and others, and formed them into sub units.' Captain Zlenko the commander of the 3rd Battalion, 322 Regiment, was put in charge and Barchuk saw they had a new platoon commander, Lieutenant Kuznetsov. The newly formed composite battalion was ordered to 'Fall in!' and Zlenko announced, 'We are going to Borodino station, in order to dislodge the Germans and rescue our soldiers, wounded or alive.' Without further ado they were ordered 'by companies, quick march!' Barchuk was reassured by the presence of additional 'battle-hardened commanders, who had taken part in the battles against the Japanese Samurais at [Lake] Khasan'. Looking around, the men 'were well seasoned, we were not afraid of the Nazis, we had acquired courage and resourcefulness'. They might yet succeed.[11]

The composite battalion departed Semyonovskoe in a column and headed down the road, moving south-east toward the railway station. They shook out into two attack groups, one commanded by Zlenko left of the road, and another to the right under Captain Portyankin. Barchuk, on the right, recalled their advance 'crossed hills and ditches downstream from Semyonovskoe'. They entered woods where 'the conditions for occupying a position were comparatively good', the shrubs and trees 'enabled our group, where I was, to camouflage ourselves better, with cover from the enemy's destructive fire'. Zlenko's group, however, was traversing completely open ground.

As they advanced, 'We noticed that there were German tanks dug in and around Borodino station'. Deep-throated engine noises betrayed their presence as they began to start up and move on to the Semyonovskoe road to confront them, with infantry following behind. Portyankin directed Barchuk's men to start shooting at the infantry to separate them from the tanks. 'For us it was easy to see the infantry rushing about the field seeking cover from our accurate fire, especially from the artillery.' The panzers 'with clanking tracks' converged on Zlenko's group in the open, and at about 200yd opened fire with 20mm cannon, hull machine guns and mortars. Barchuk saw that, as they moved up, 'the panzers stopped periodically to bring accurate fire down on to our positions' off to the flank, but the main weight of fire was directed at Zlenko's men caught in the open. 'The frozen ground did not enable rapid digging,' he recalled, 'and the men took heavy losses.' They looked on helplessly as 'foxholes, dug by hand by our soldiers, hardly proved sufficient against the destructive fire' and 'literally everyone' in Zlenko's unfortunate group 'was exposed to fire'. A poignant last-stand scene unfolded:

> The battle increased in intensity. We watched the explosions of shells and mines relentlessly destroy our infantry, who had no shelter and could not do anything about it. We were not able to destroy the tanks.

The battle waxed and waned, some panzers were set on fire and the *Luftwaffe* intervened with treetop-level strafing runs. Barchuk's group managed to survive by constantly changing position amid the trees when the tanks sought to destroy them. They learned some hard lessons:

> The battle of the 16th October showed that it was possible to fight the Germans and defeat them, if you set out your forces correctly, teach them drills, strengthen them with tanks and aviation and improve co-ordination between units, and organise good intelligence. You must provide uninterrupted communications. There was not enough of any of these at Borodino.

Zlenko's group was cut to pieces and, Barchuk remembered, 'acquitted themselves heroically'. 'I and the other soldiers who witnessed it, sympathised with them, we defended ourselves and suffered major losses – so we could not help them.' Zlenko was reported missing in action to 32nd Division headquarters.

By nightfall Barchuk's surviving men were running out of ammunition. They were hungry and squabbles at command level were occurring. Sherbakov's 2nd Battalion was facing a crisis at Shevardino, and Portyankin's survivors were withdrawn and relocated in the half light to reinforce his failing positions. Colonel Polosukhin's main 32nd Division headquarters at Kourakino just beyond the German thrust at Tatarinovo reported 'up to ten enemy tanks and infantry broke through our defence and reached the division HQ, where they were stopped'. A rifle company from the 113th Regiment supported by the division chemical defence unit held them off in a bitter struggle with Molotov cocktails, hand grenades and hastily laid mines. 'Our situation was getting worse,' Barchuk concluded.[12]

Likewise, German results at the end of the day had not realised dawn expectations. The *SS Deutschland* to the left of the 10th Panzer *Gruppe von Bulow* at the railway embankment and station managed to clear the woods east of Rogachyovo and attacked Fomkino, but had made little headway under heavy fire. *Der Führer* had made progress south of the Moscow highway at Yudinki and Fomino, to create the conditions necessary to wrest back the block at Artyomki from the Soviets. After a feint along the highway, they crashed into the village from the south only to be driven out again by Vorbiev's detachment, this time reinforced with T-34s from the 20th Tank Brigade. The village exchanged hands six times in a costly see-saw battle that left the Russians still in possession.

The *SS Das Reich* Division was seriously haemorrhaging combat power, so much so that, within a few days, its third 11th Regiment was to be disbanded completely, to bring the two sister regiments up to an appreciable fighting level. *SS Deutschland* reported to the division that, in addition to its heavy losses of dead and wounded, 'men were totally exhausted, and had been pushed to the extreme limits of their physical and psychological capabilities'. The replacements were not there yet. 'A period of several days' rest with the opportunity to bring the men into heated quarters is required to accomplish the minimal preparations for a continuation of the attack,' the medical report to the main *SS* office in Berlin recommended. Little could be done at this stage, in the middle of bitterly contested advances. *SS Kradschützen* (motorcycle) Battalion *Reich* was brought up during the day along the highway, to at least offer the regiments some breathing space, by pushing on through, to apply more pressure south of the highway.[13]

Neither had the 10th Panzer combat groups been able to achieve appreciable momentum, despite having broken into the depth of the Borodino Field Soviet position. Von Bulow's 69th Regiment *Kampfgruppe*, with the *I* Panzer *Abteilung* on its right, had fought itself to a virtual standstill at Shevardino, and was repelling counter-attacks. The *II Abteilung* with von Hauenschild's 86 Regiment *Kampfgruppe* had come up against strong Soviet field fortifications south and south-east of Novaya Derevnya. When they heard about strong and aggressive Soviet resistance to their rear, they withdrew back to Tatarinovo and formed an all-round hedgehog defence. Between Gzhatsk and Artyomki on the Moscow highway, a German traffic jam of between 2,000 and 3,000 vehicles was stuck fast, in churned-up mud, shell craters and potholes. Both sides were approaching the limits of endurance.

Generaloberst Hoepner, commanding *Panzergruppe 4*, had arrived at Borodino on 16 October to see conditions for himself and urge his men forward. He was taken aback at the intensity of the Soviet resistance they were encountering. 'For the first time in the war, the number of Russian deaths far exceeded the prisoners we were taking,' he remembered. He was convinced they were on the cusp of winning this campaign, but the defenders at Borodino were fighting and dying where they stood. The Germans were only too aware of the symbolism of Napoleon's pyrrhic victory in 1812; it was also the prerequisite in 1941 for any successful entry into Moscow. Hoepner was aware of reports of panic in the city:

> The approach of our panzers and infantry was bringing terror to the Russian capital. Its people were fleeing, its factory equipment was being destroyed. Looting had begun. The Soviet leadership was preparing to leave the city.

Clearly a tipping point had been reached. The next day would decide this battle. Hoepner looked around. 'Villages were burning,' he recalled, 'colouring the low clouds with a blood-red light.' A supreme effort was required.[14]

Indecision in the Centre, 7 September 1812

11.30 a.m. to 2 p.m.

The situation was analogous to that of a spring tide battering a sea wall. The French surge against the Russian line had lost power and momentum. Eddying and swirling into and over north–south-running ravine lines, it had failed to lap over the top and flow on to the Semyonovskoe plateau. Brief penetrations to the right of the Russian wall at Borodino village and left along the old Smolensk road had not weakened the line. It had taken a tremendous battering at the *flèches* at left centre, where the French tide gained entry, but not at the Raevsky mound to its right. The French tide there had forced its way in, swirled around in a melee of infantry and cavalry actions, and then flowed back out. By 11 a.m. a form of stalemate had coalesced. Choppy waters continued to lap against a seemingly impervious Russian wall, which was becoming porous in places. The line bent backwards on the left, presenting a concave front. The spring tide of the *Grande Armée*'s offensive had yet to rise enough to produce the mass and depth of a wave sufficient to tumble the Russian line. As for the Germans in 1941, a supreme effort was required by the attacking French to create these breakthrough conditions.

Immovable willpower on both sides had created this impasse. Over 30,000 men had fallen at some 6,500 casualties per hour. This was normally the point at which most Napoleonic contests were decided, with one of the protagonists actively seeking a way out. Thus far there had been no attempts at large-scale manoeuvre. The armies had embraced tightly and were seeking to crush each other to death. The outcome was dependent upon reserves, and these were the soldiers subjected to the greatest psychological and emotional pressure for the moment.

Leo Tolstoy portrayed their lot accurately, describing how 'each new explosion diminished the chances of life for the survivors'. Regiments waiting to go into action were drawn up in battalion columns about 300yd apart. The men stood arrayed in parade-ground order, unless given the order to 'rest', when they were permitted to sit in the ranks. Most were exposed by being located too far forward. When General Barclay de Tolly came across two Life Guard Regiments in Lavrov's V Corps awaiting the call forward, he found them 'calmly standing with a true military bearing':

> Enemy cannonballs already began to devastate their ranks but they remained steadfastly and silently with their muskets and quietly closed their ranks as soon as cannonballs hit their victims.

Tolstoy, a veteran of the Crimean War, had an instinctive understanding of the generally 'taciturn and morose' atmosphere that reigned in the ranks. Talking, during the rare intervals it could actually be heard, 'was hushed at each thud of a successful shot, followed by the cry, "Stretchers!"' Men sat on the ground and fiddled with the linings of shakos, loosening and tightening them. They absorbed themselves in mindless distracting activities:

> Another crumbling some dry clay in his hands, polished his bayonet; another fingered the strap and altered the buckle of his bandolier; while still another carefully smoothed and rewound his leg bands and pulled his boots on again. Some built little houses of the clods of the ploughed field, or plaited straws of stubble.

These distractions from the visceral action around them, intermittently obscured by the murky fog of war, were only momentary. They waited, no food appeared, nothing to do but endure 'in constant fear of death'. Tolstoy wrote how 'their pale haggard faces grew paler and more haggard'. The areas where assembled reserves were lined up began to resemble and smell like middens. Bodily functions had to occur where they stood. There was scant opportunity to leave the ranks. Quite often the final command 'Prepare to move' was sufficient to trigger bowel release, the soldiers having watched the constant procession of shattered and mutilated casualties making their painful progress to the rear in unending streams. Lieutenant Louis Planat de la Faye had been 'smitten with the diarrhoea' before arriving at Borodino and going 'through the worst sort of agony one can imagine', like many soldiers of the *Grande Armée*. He was unable 'to quit my post or dismount,' he recalled:

> I dare not describe just how I managed to dispose of what was tormenting me, but in the process I lost two handkerchiefs which I threw as discreetly as I could into the trench of the fortifications we passed. This was a serious loss in a country devoid of washerwomen, at least for us.[15]

Much of Murat's cavalry remained immobile for hours, forming the centre of the French battle line. It was subjected to ferocious cannon fire, particularly from the Raevsky redoubt, as their own infantry manoeuvred forward in the attack. French cavalry officer Antoine Fortuné de Brack, with the 'Red Lancers', taught how officers should ride the line, 'at a distance of four paces' to 'speak a few words to the officers and soldiers to cheer and encourage them and make an opportunity for calling the men by their names'. He extolled the need to instil confidence in the men, so 'as to cause the soldier to say in every situation, "He is there, that suffices."' How both sides were able to endure and stand with stoic acceptance in lines faced with certain death would be anathema to modern soldiers today. Captain Jean Bréaut des Marlots emulated de Brack's leadership style, riding the line to encourage his assembled cuirassier troopers to remain brave under fire. 'When I rode over to congratulate one gay officer, Monsieur de Gramont, on his good bearing, I witnessed some terrible things,' he wrote to his sister:

He told me that he had nothing to complain of and that all he wanted was a glass of water. He had barely finished speaking when a cannonball cut him in two. I turned to another officer and said how sorry I was about poor de Gramont. Before he could reply, his horse was struck dead by a cannonball. And a hundred other incidents of this kind. I gave my horse to a cuirassier to hold for half a minute and the man was killed. I was covered with earth thrown up by shells, yet I escaped without the slightest scratch.

Black humour was a common response to maintain emotional stability. Captain Franz Morgenstern, with the 2nd Westphalian Line, was invited by his senior sergeant, who had a wicked sense of humour, to look at 'three flankers next to me'. He had ordered them to stick out their tongues. Morgenstern 'was surprised to see that all their tongues were as white as their uniforms'. Others were told to do the same and 'theirs too were white'. His sergeant assured him, 'This was the case with all men who were going into action for the first time.' Dry-mouthed fear had this effect, as veterans today would vouch. Morgenstern invited his sergeant to display *his* tongue, which he saw 'was lobster red!' 'And yours Captain?' he was asked with a grin. 'We will just let that remain my secret,' he replied. 'The "tongue test" quickly spread to neighbouring companies,' Morgenstern remembered, 'and caused considerable hilarity as they were all white.'

Most soldiers, as in 1941 and today, drew reassurance from an unproven assumption that the 'other man' would always be hit first. 'It is a lottery whether you survive or not,' des Marlots insisted. 'One has to die some-time, would you rather live in dishonour or die with honour?' he asked rhetorically. Conduct on the field of battle influenced the social standing of any officer who survived to return home, and was supremely impor-tant. Soldiers in the ranks were likewise dependent on 'mate-ship' to survive on campaign and could not be seen to countenance fear. Once battle was joined, conflict was all-embracing. 'When one is brandishing one's sword,' des Marlots explained, 'the fire which tingles in one's veins wipes out all thought.' Even so, men consciously held fear and emo-tions in check. 'To see death as almost a certainty, or rather to wait for it, is often more than the human frame can stand,' he admitted, and the horrors he was exposed to were a constant reminder. 'To hold inactivity under fire must be one of the most unpleasant things cavalry can be called upon to do,' explained Lieutenant Roth von Schreckenstein, commanding the Saxon Life Guard Cuirassiers:

> There can scarcely have been a man whose neighbour didn't crash to earth with his horse or die from terrible wounds screaming for help.[16]

There was a lull in the intensity of fighting between 11 a.m. and midday, or more accurately an absence of large-scale movement, amid the countless small-scale actions going on. Men paused to take stock and look around. There was even commercial activity. François Dumonceau, serving with the Red Lancers of the Imperial Guard, had a connoisseur's eye for quality horseflesh. 'Every instant trophies captured from the enemy were being brought to us,' he recalled. 'A superb black courser was ceded to our commander Cotti, for a 20-franc piece,' he remembered. 'Then the cuirassier who'd brought it went resolutely back to the scrum.' Hundreds of corpses were strewn about the hotly contested locations. Russian artillery officer Nikolai Divov remembered passing the ravine forward of the Raevsky redoubt after its recapture. 'This ravine,' he recalled, 'was already filled in level with the ground, it was full of corpses.'[17]

Cavalry medical officer Major Heinrich von Roos occupied a first aid post further along the same ravine, or its offshoot, by the Kamenka stream between the villages of Shevardino and Semyonovskoe. It was 'a gully, through which flowed a small easily jumpable stream,' he recalled, 'thick with bushes and served as a standpoint for myself, my assistants and our horses.' He had set up forward, nearer the action, to recover wounded. 'But when a few balls of considerable calibre whistled close overhead, I took this as a warning to curb my curiosity.' He was near enough almost on top of the cavalry actions fought around the Raevsky redoubt and the *flèches*, and by the area where Murat's immobile cavalry were being pounded with Russian artillery. Wounded Frenchmen and their allies and Russians were constantly trickling in to the gully, and 'most of them were cavalrymen with severe wounds and broken limbs'. By noon, his section of the gully was crowded with wounded, a number 'remained as corpses', he remembered, and 'I could see myself being kept fully occupied until nightfall'.

Von Roos complained that, unlike previous campaigns, they were not shown the collection points for the wounded before the battle. Some came to the cover afforded by the ravine, others were transported to nearby villages and the monastery at Kolotsk. Medical instruments were washed in the stream, which became increasingly red with blood, while all the time artillery projectiles from the Russian redoubts howled overhead. 'Some of them,' von Roos recalled, 'bored into the reverse slope of the gully, others rolled down the forward slope.'[18]

Very little, apart from isolated letters, is known about the individual lot of the private soldier in this battle. Johann Wärnicke, serving with a Westphalian unit, wrote that the number of bodies on the field polluted wells and streams 'so that we could not drink water anymore'.

'God helped me out,' he wrote to his parents, and 'without harm, though the bullets hailed down pretty well, as if one were to take peas and throw them at someone. But none got me.' He passed on what he could glean about local men known to his parents:

> Stutz and Gutwasser went to the hospital as it was going to start soon. Fritz Bär is gone, Grosche from Jorenzen and the little Selter from Bentorff. I can't give any news of the others. Denckwitz is also supposed to be dead his sergeant told me. I can't write anything for sure, but he is not to be found at the regiment.

His letter, posted on 13 October 1812, might just as easily have been from a young Westphalian serving with the 10th Panzer Division in 1941.[19]

Most veteran accounts describe the most horrific experiences in an understated way. Pain there undoubtedly was physical and emotional but Napoleonic soldiers were far more robust and mentally resilient than their modern counterparts. Russian toughness and powers of endurance were remarked upon in both the 1812 and 1941 campaigns. Artillery Colonel Lubin Griois observed the Russian wounded were 'overcome by their sufferings' yet 'made no complaint':

> Indifferently they watched the passing troops, and tried as far as possible to avoid being kicked by the horses. This insensibility, which I believe stems from a stronger and less sensitive make up than our own,

was increased still further by their fervent devotion to their great Saint Nicholas.

Many a wounded Russian soldier lay impassively clutching a medallion or image of the saint, which they kissed to alleviate the pain. The secular French had no such comforts. To be hit in this battle so far from home, on the eve of winter, was tantamount to a death sentence. Cavalry Captain Jean des Marlots rationalised survival amid the carnage about by appealing to philosophy, 'which alone has the power to set us above these troubles by revealing to us the nothingness of our being'. Scant comfort.

Some Borodino accounts do, however, reflect the distraught sense of loss among men who had lived cheek by jowl with their comrades since crossing the Nieman river seventy-six days before. Sergeant François Bourgogne, serving with Napoleon's Imperial Guard, remembered a pleasant chance meeting with ten drummers from the 61st Line, whom he knew from his home district near Condé, during the pause at Vitebsk. Corporal Dumont, another local acquaintance with the 61st Voltigeurs, informed him they had been cut down by grapeshot, charging the *flèche* emplacements. Dumont, who was also wounded, was stopped by a pretty young Spanish *cantinière* named Florencia, to help look for them. She had travelled with the drummers, who were often recruited from young orphan boys and older soldiers past their prime. These young women made a living as sutlers selling provisions to the troops. They tended to mother the drummer boys and look to the older soldiers for protection. They might even do washing for the troops. There was undoubtedly an emotional bond that held this group together, because Dumont recalled:

When we got near the great redoubt and that field of carnage, she uttered heart-rending cries. But when she caught sight of all the broken drums of the regiment strewing the ground, she became like a mad-woman. 'Here my friend, here!' she cried; 'they are here!' and so they were, lying with broken limbs, their bodies mangled by shot. Mad with grief, she went from one to the other, speaking softly to them; but none of them heard. Some, however, still gave signs of life, one of them being the drum major, whom she called her father.[20]

Surprisingly, it was the Russians who would attempt to manoeuvre beyond the confines an evenly matched linear contest of attrition. The normally tactically adroit Napoleon seemed unable to think beyond the self-imposed box he had superimposed on this battle. At 11 a.m. large numbers of Russian horsemen began to diverge from the previously static and uneventful right of the line. Lieutenant General Uvarov's 2,500-strong regular cavalry corps and General Ivan Platov's 5,500 Don Cossacks began to ford the Kolocha river near Maloye Selo accompanied by thirty-six guns. Prince Kutuzov had almost absent-mindedly given assent to a deep raid into the French rear. After cautiously negotiating a potentially dangerous gap between Borodino village and the woods to the north, the mass of Russian cavalry began to bear down on Count Ornano's Italian and Bavarian cavalry, screening the far left of the *Grande Armée*. This completely unexpected development overwhelmed the thin screen with swarms of yellow-clad hussars, dark green dragoons and Platov's blue and red Cossacks. The Bavarian horse artillery made off in haste, losing two guns to Uvarov's hussars. Uvarov's regular cavalry was soon checked by the static infantry squares of Delzon's division, which formed to the north of Borodino village. These sheltered Ornano's fleeing cavalry and caused the hussars and dragoons to about face and wheel around to return, under steady volley fire.

Platov's Don Cossacks went on to cross the Voina stream further west on a wide front and they began to roam about, causing havoc in the French rear. Artillery officer Ilya Radozhitsky, looking on, was 'thrilled', he recalled, 'to see as our cavalry moved on the opposite river bank in long lines of red and blue hussars and Uhlans' driving the French cavalry beyond Borodino. Cossacks were generally more canny and better educated than much of the dull Russian soldiery, and less amenable to its mindless rigid discipline. Their practical, robust frontier attitude originated from their forebears – Russian and Ukrainian settlers who had policed the frontiers of old Russia. This produced a looser and more informal interface between officers, junior leaders and men. They were born raiders, merciless in the pursuit and particularly adept at sniffing out vulnerabilities and defence gaps. Russian soldier Fedor Glinka recalled, 'the entire valley suddenly flashed brightly with Don Cossacks,' who 'began making circles and flaunting their tricks'. The forward French patrols fled in a virtual 'hare-hunt', which caused quite a stir on the Russian right. Glinka recalled the enthusiastic response from the spectators:

> Look! Look! The Frenchies are making square: they are in trouble. We are winning! And many of them clapped and yelled 'Hurrah!'

French and German cavalry trying to fend off the surges with long swords were outreached by the Cossack lance and sought to escape. Glinka watched as Cossacks 'flew like arrows on their small horses, circled around, rushed forward and stung them with their lances like incensed wasps'.

Cossacks were unlike the unthinking Russian infantry, who were totally resolute in defence. By contrast they were perceptively observant and cautiously independent, with a keen sense of self-preservation. Dying in place was not considered a virtue if they could fight with advantage another day. Artillery officer Nikolai Mitarevsky reflected the prevailing slightly disdainful view of many Russian officers looking on, who thought the raid deeply disappointing. Generals Barclay de Tolly and Löwenstern thought Uvarov and Platov were disgracefully slow to advance and were quickly worsted in the subsequent fighting. Mitarevsky saw the Cossacks 'approach to a musket range' of the infantry squares, 'and then quickly turned back, without the squares even firing'. 'Did you see that?' one contemptuous staff officer remarked, 'and there goes their attack!' The irregular Cossack proclivity for precipitate retreat, and placing loot above duty, did not endear them to the more traditional regular cavalry. Uvarov returned to a chilly reception from Kutuzov, who simply said on hearing his report, 'I know, may God forgive you!' Yermolov, de Tolly's Chief of Staff, was equally dismissive:

> It is a general view that Cossacks are of little use in an open battle, and the same held true here, when they came back after encountering a few obstructions.[21]

Napoleon had lingered morosely about the camp chair set up on the Shevardino mound all morning. He had spotted nothing of planning consequence through his spyglass, which had picked out fleeting images amid the battlefield obscuration to his front. The battle had deteriorated into a linear wresting match. All the tactical ploys employed successfully in the past had come to naught: massed artillery, bludgeoning column attacks supported by cavalry, and variations of the same. Five hours of attack at maximum effort all morning had yielded nothing. He still shaped the battlefield and held the initiative, but a sore throat, bad cold, migraine and an agonising urinary infection were distracting him from his normal innate creativity. Onlookers found him preoccupied, walking to and fro. 'Not once did Napoleon mount his horse during the whole battle,' claimed Dr Flize, a medical officer with one of the Guard regiments. His aide, Lejeune, did not appreciate how unwell he was, recalling, 'We weren't very satisfied' and 'our judgements were severe'. This was not the great man, 'sitting in the same posture' all day, to which they were accustomed:

> We weren't so happy as to see him, as formerly, going to galvanise with his presence, the points where too vigorous a resistance made success doubtful. Each of us was astonished not to find the active man of Marengo and Austerlitz.[22]

Just as he was planning a new attack against the centre of the Russian line, Napoleon heard the disturbing news about what was happening to his left. This rocked his former complacency. Until now, his only creative solution to the impasse ahead was to increase the level of violence at the same point or nearby. Suddenly it was the *Russians* who were manoeuvring. Cossacks on the loose had produced understandable panic among the wounded at the Kolotsk Monastery. At his Shevardino headquarters, the Imperial Guard was bustling about, ready to receive cavalry attacks to its rear. Napoleon's dilemma whether to commit the Guard – his final reserve – to exploit a gap reportedly opening in the Russian line near Semyonovskoe was shelved. Seventeen cavalry regiments were immediately committed to the left bank of the Kolocha river to shore up the increasingly exposed flank. General Eugène even crossed the stream from Borodino to supervise measures in person. Napoleon mounted his horse at last and rode off to the left. He was not seen at the Shevardino mound again until 3 p.m.

The French brushed the diversionary Russian cavalry foray aside and the Russians expected as much. But for more than two hours, midday until after two in the afternoon, the surprise appearance of Russian horse-men effectively paralysed the French left and centre. During this period casualties continued to fall at the rate of 6,500 per hour. Murat's cavalry remained immobile beneath the guns of the Raevsky redoubt as Napoleon pondered his next moves, and suffered hideously in the process.

In 1941 the fighting at Borodino Field was only one sector of the immense German advance on Moscow, but it represented the shortest and most direct route to the capital. Operation *Typhoon* was running out of steam by 16 October, even with the capture of several prominent Russian cities to the north and south of the main Minsk–Moscow highway. Following the huge encirclement battles at Vyazma and Bryansk, Field Marshal von Bock, commanding Army Group Centre, had chosen to dis-perse his armour, pursuing multiple objectives. This was much the case at Kalinin, on the northern arm of two pincers set to encircle Moscow. It was captured at the start of the advance on to Borodino Field on 14 October and developed into a substantial diversion of German resources, becom-ing a battle within the battle for Moscow. The 1st Panzer Division lost sixty tanks and many of its vehicles, along with 750 casualties, attempting to batter its way further eastward. This coincided with the very moment Hausser's *Das Reich* was denied armour on the most direct route. General Guderian's *Panzergruppe 2* captured Mtensk on 10 October, the southern encircling arm of the pincer heading for Tula. General Zhukov was fight-ing for time at Borodino, Maloyaroslavets and Volkolamsk, north and south of the highway, so as to create a new 50km front to shield the capital. Like Napoleon, the Germans had remained complacent after the resounding success at Vyazma, retaining the initiative. But manoeuvre in increasingly impossible sleet and mud conditions became illusory. The German advance simply occupied the wider areas of front the Red Army had abandoned in favour of blocking the main arterial routes to Moscow. Both von Bock and Napoleon dissipated momentum by pursuing multiple objectives, without concentrating on the shortest and most direct route to success. Napoleon's Imperial Guard did not even have to relocate; it stood immobile directly opposite an opening gap in the Russian line at Semyonovskoe village.

The Russian line around Semyonovskoe in 1812 was improvised, made up from units hastily assembled from other parts of the field, primarily from the inactive right. Eight battalions of the 2nd Combined Grenadier

Division were positioned in front of the ruined village, and had been under artillery fire since early morning. French General Friant's 2nd Infantry Division from I Corps advanced directly at the village with powerful cavalry forces from Latour-Maubourg's IV Corps to its north and left and Nansouty's I Corps massed on the right. The wooden Semyonovskoe village had been dismantled by the Russians for defence materials and what remained resembled a collapsed theatre scenery lot, with much of the site marked simply with glowing logs. By 10 a.m. the French onslaught was well under way. Saxon Lieutenant von Meerheim, to the left of Friant's infantry, crested the low ridges in front of the Semyonovsky stream and saw the 'whole extent of the battle in the central sector'. He had a panoramic view, but 'all he could make out' in the dense clouds of smoke, he recalled, 'were the thick masses of our troops, who were swaying backwards and forwards in front of the enemy-held ridge'.

Controlling columns of half squadrons in such an attack 'is a pious hope', recalled Lieutenant Roth von Schreckenstein, advancing with the same corps. 'Men who are imbued with true cavalry courage pursue and attack the enemy for as long as they can.' Meerham remembered, 'the slope was so steep' to climb the Semyonovskoe plateau 'that some riders, who did not appreciate the advantage of climbing obliquely, tumbled over backwards and were trampled by the horses behind'. The cavalry onslaught flowed on to the plateau just as the 2nd Combined Division grenadiers were trying to form themselves into three squares. Latour-Maubourg's Germans rode down one of the blocks of infantry trying to assemble, and charged the other two squares without bothering to re-form.

Von Schreckenstein claimed:

> Anybody who imagines that one can invariably control and direct a cavalry regiment just as one pleases by means of one's voice or a trumpet, as if on peacetime manoeuvres, has never been in an action where all arms of the service co-operated.

They were lashed with musket fire. Once released, a cavalry charge can rarely be called back, amid a maelstrom of noise and lethal flying objects. 'My horse fell back,' von Schreckenstein recalled, 'pierced by several case-shot bullets, which had been fired from somewhere away to the left.' This left him riderless, amid marauding bayonet-wielding vengeful Russian infantrymen. 'I was on the point of moving off on foot, pistol in hand, without knowing which way to flee.' He was fearfully vulnerable: 'I could see enemies on all sides.' A riderless horse passed by, which he managed to grab, vault on to its back 'and escape with a swarm of horsemen who were withdrawing'. Having blundered into the rear of Semyonovskoe village, Latour-Maubourg's Corps, fighting the squares, was promptly attacked by the Russian IV Cavalry Corps. The Russians, in their turn, were overblown by the charge and were swept off the field when the compact masses of a Westphalian cuirassier brigade came up in support.[23]

South of Semyonovskoe, Nansouty's cuirassiers and light cavalry came up against the superbly disciplined Izmail, Litovsk and Finland *Jäger* Life Guards, who formed up in impenetrable squares. General Dimitry Konovitsyn had seen the French coming: 'The clouds of dust ascending from the ground to the heavens' marked their progress. He arranged his regiments into chess board squares, and 'the terrible crossfire from the lateral faces of the squares,' he recalled, 'sped thousands of men to their deaths'. The cavalry lapped so close about them 'that practically every bullet toppled over a horseman'. Colonel Timofeyev, commanding one of his squares with the Litovski Regiment, held fire until the last moment:

> I instructed my men to move their muskets from side to side, knowing from my own experience that horses would never charge sparkling bayonets; if any cuirassiers forced their horses close to the front, I ordered my men to thrust at the animal's faces.

The square conducted an aggressive defence, even charging with the bayonet when horsemen gathered for a charge thirty paces away. Militia soldier Fedor Glinka saw the 'enormous enemy cavalry spread out like a sea, while our squares floated like islands that were washed by the copper and steel waves of enemy cuirassiers'.[24]

In the middle of the action, the 2nd Combined Grenadier Regiments strove to form a ragged line just in front of the village. Despite being over-ridden by cavalry, they stood up again and fought on. Friant's division, dismayed by the enormous number of casualties already incurred, began to waver and were rallied at one point by cavalry commander Murat. The

48th Line colonel, on the point of withdrawing, was halted by Murat, who declared, 'I'm hanging on for one!' Stopped in his tracks, the colonel regarded Murat calmly and acknowledged, 'You are right. Soldiers face front! Let's go and get killed!' This renewed attack finally unhinged the desperate Russian defence, which caved. The 15th Light Regiment swept through the glowing embers that marked the village site, and with that created a sizeable breach in the Russian line at arguably its most vital sector. Standing directly opposite was the Imperial Guard. The excited Murat and Ney appealed to Napoleon, claiming they could 'see clearly as far as Mozhaisk'. Even parts of the Russian baggage train were observed moving off into the woods, but they had insufficient force, with the tattered units at their disposal, to forge ahead. Urgent requests for reinforcement were sent off to Napoleon.

These were not the first requests to release the Guard. Murat and Ney, left to their own devices to battle against the Russian centre and left, had on at least two occasions sensed the disintegration of the Bagration's Second Army and appealed to Napoleon to commit the Young Guard (from the Imperial Guard). Napoleon prevaricated, setting General Lobau's Young Guard in motion and then stopping it. When Lobau continued to shuffle forward on the pretext of realignment, he was ordered to halt. By the time Napoleon received the second urgent summons from Ney and Murat to reinforce at about midday, he heard the Russians were consolidating the wreckage of their shattered regiments behind Semyonovskoe. Total victory appeared to beckon as a frustrated Ney complained, 'What business has the Emperor in the rear of the army?'

'Let him return to the Tuilleries,' he exclaimed, 'and leave us to be generals for him!' Ney and Murat were well forward enough to see, sense and exploit the *decisive* result they craved. 'Are we come so far to be satisfied with a field of battle?' Ney insisted. Napoleon responded, insisting, 'Before I commit my reserves I must be able to see more clearly on my chess board.' With 1,200 miles separating him from the French frontier, he would be well advised to keep his last major formation intact, otherwise it might be 'checkmate'.[25]

The resulting indecision enabled Generals Dokhturov and Konovitsyn sufficient respite to begin drawing up the remnants of the badly mauled Second Army on the plateau, behind the smouldering remains of

Semyonovskoe village. Barclay de Tolly started the process of sealing off his increasingly exposed southern flank by moving Ostermann-Tolstoy's IV Corps down from a quiet position on the right to a blocking position north-east of Semyonovskoe. Napoleon, nervous at this stage, saw the movement as an advance and did commit sixty pieces of the Guard's Reserve Artillery to shore up Friant's tenuous grip on the village. As Tolstoy's infantry moved forward to block, it was enveloped by devastating canister fire.

'One might have thought that the French were about to split our army,' recalled Glinka, 'but only for a short while! The enemy did not celebrate for long!' Four Russian grenadier regiments, 'four [human] walls came nearer, carrying muskets horizontally out in front'.

There are no private Russian soldier accounts of Borodino, because the serfs from whom they were recruited could neither read nor write. It is difficult to disentangle the lot of those in the ranks, obscured somewhat by a plethora of strident patriotic accounts from those in command. Ensign Rafail Zotov was a formally educated noble who did serve in the ranks of the St Petersburg Militia at Polotsk in 1812 and gives some insight of what it was like to be in the Russian line during such a major battle in 1812. Napoleon's aide, de Ségur, had watched the approach of Tolstoy's corps 'by thick masses, in which our round shot ploughed wide deep holes'. Zotov described his own experience under fire, as 'one cannon ball whizzed over our heads and dug into the earth behind the column':

> All of us squatted down as if enchanted by a magic wand. What a strange feeling strangled my chest. A feverish shudder ran through my veins. We all looked at each other with distrust and felt privately ashamed of our weakness, and each wanted to encourage his comrades. Then another ball flew over and we flinched the same way. The Colonel began to urge us wholeheartedly that this bowing was both indecent and useless. I do not remember if we obeyed him through the bombardment, but everyone held a very terrible feeling in his heart nonetheless.

De Ségur remembered the Guard artillery 'redoubled their fire and crushed them by canister'. Zotov recalled what this could have been like:

When three batteries from only God knows where began to welcome us with solid shot and canister. For five minutes we still advanced with some drunken and numb perseverance but then all at once and without any source, I could know, the whole line could not stand, trembled, and fled backward.

According to de Ségur, 'entire platoons fell simultaneously, and we could see the soldiers trying to restore their ranks under this dreadful fire'. This to and fro amid such bloody carnage had been going on all morning and now continued into the afternoon. Se Ségur recalled the Russian reserve called forward into this blocking position remained 'immobile for two hours', during which 'the only movement was the stirring in the lines caused by falling bodies'. Zotov remembered his furious colonel 'cursing at us, striking soldiers with his sabre and shouting, "Stop! Dress!"' He described the rally:

Somehow we all regained our senses. Shame returned us to our duty. Everyone vied to be the first to encourage his comrades and again the line moved forward smoothly and decisively.

The next stage was to win the musket firefight exchange. 'I heard the music of Charles XII [i.e. the sound of battle].' 'Every minute soldiers and officers dropped out of the line, but many of them fell where they stood.' The enemy approached, closer and closer, dimly outlined through their fusillade, 'because our fire was not terribly lethal for them'. That was probably a factor of nerves and clumsy firing drills, because the militia only received four days' training. Then their colonel commanded abruptly:

Cease fire! Officers into line! Charge bayonets! Quick step. March-March! *Ura!*

'What a terrible and energising minute,' Zotov remembered. Instead of the quick step, as they strode forward they broke into a run. The enemy fled at this and they continued to advance. Zotov's descriptions are atmospheric, with snippets of often ironic detail, absent from the many patriotic exaggerations that emerged in many 1830s Russian accounts. He tells the anecdote of 'one glorious sergeant' who in loading his musket 'just in case' as he walked was:

> struck by a bullet straight in the forehead between his eyebrows, just as he bit open his cartridge and fell backward, still holding the cartridge paper between his lips.

Whereas previously he could become mournful over the suffering of a dead horse, 'I laughed at the sight of the cartridge sticking out of his mouth and all the soldiers and officers shared in my amusement.' Black humour was one way of surviving the day emotionally intact, and Zotov's human insights into what it was like to be in the line at Polotsk, later the same year, offer a perspective absent from many contemporary Russian accounts of Borodino.[26]

The *Grande Armée* had most certainly secured the advantage to the left of the Russian line, but Murat and Ney's tantalising glimpse of the gap opening in the centre had gradually slipped from view; the moment was gone. Napoleon had been distracted by the unexpected Russian cavalry manoeuvre to his left, and uncertainty over the progress of Poniatowski's outflanking movement to the French right on the old Smolensk road. They were not the preconditions to launch his sole remaining reserve formation, the Imperial Guard. In fact, apart from ordering the advance at daybreak, Napoleon had not taken a significant decision all day. Two negative decisions had occurred by default, deciding what not to do rather than so doing. He chose not to outflank the Russian left and not to commit the National Guard when a potential gap emerged in the centre of the Russian line. Both sides had exhausted their physical strength in all options, to no decisive result.

As in 1941, a supreme effort was required.

In Moscow roving NKVD sections checked all movement, sweeping up defeatists and deserters.

The 10th Panzer Division joined *Das Reich* on 11–12 October, clearing the woods between Gzhatsk and Borodino and ejecting Druzhinina's 18th Soviet Tank Brigade, which was blocking the Moscow highway.

General Fischer commanded the 10th Panzer Division.

The German propaganda magazine *Wehrmacht* shows the formidable layout of the defences that faced *Oberleutnant* Lohaus on the morning of 13 October 1941. Automatic flamethowers are shown top right. 'Can it be done?' is asked left of page – 'Accomplished!' is the answer on the right.

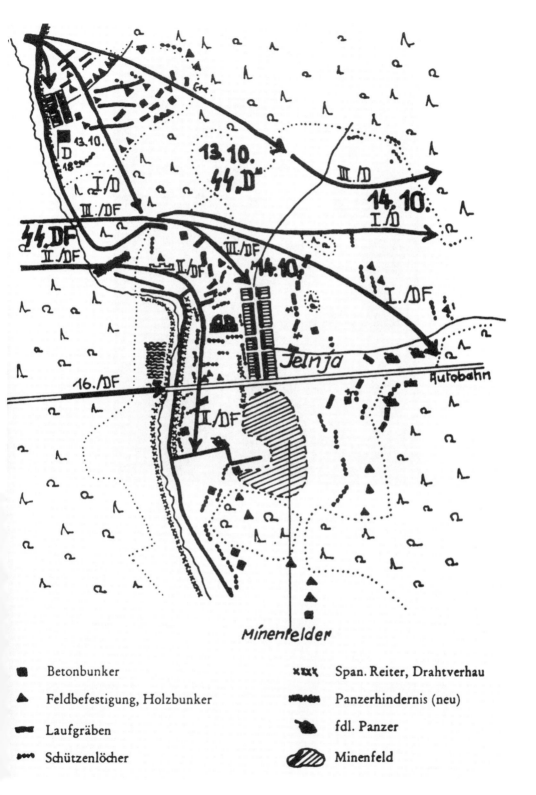

13.10.

44.D

13.10.
44.D

II./D

14.10.
I./D

44.DF

II./DF

I./DF

II./DF

III./DF

I./DF

14.10.

I./DF

Jelnja

Autobahn

16./DF

II./DF

Minenfelder

■	Betonbunker	
▲	Feldbefestigung, Holzbunker	
⚊	Laufgräben	
•••	Schützenlöcher	

xxx	Span. Reiter, Drahtverhau	
▬▬	Panzerhindernis (neu)	
🢂	fdl. Panzer	
▨	Minenfeld	

The *Reich* post-operation map charting the break-in battle by the *Deutschland* and *Der Führer* Regiments into the Mozhaisk defensive position at Elnya and Rogachyovo, north of the Moscow highway between 13 and 14 October 1941.

Artillery Captain Petrovich Nechaiev fought at Rogachyovo with the Soviet 322nd Rifle Regiment. Only 'Moscow is behind us, there's no falling back!' he announced.

Kriegsberichter Hugo Landgraf filmed the 10th Panzer attack at Borodino through the observation slits of his tank.

Landgraf films infantry following panzers off road from the panzer column on the Moscow autobahn, passing burning villages at dusk.

Landgraf captured these images of panzers passing the battlefield monuments at Borodino field with dead Soviet soldiers, the dark shadows, in the foreground.

Klingenberg Günther's CO (right) briefs the *SS Das Reich* Division commander, Hausser (left). He recalled that his officers were 'sharp, tough cookies' who 'could summon the devil from out of hell'.

Major Vasiliy Chevgus, commanding 154 Artillery Regiment, recalled bitter fighting around the vital road block the Russians had established at Artyomki village on the Moscow highway.

Ivan Barchuk, photographed after the war, was with the 1st Battalion Infantry Regiment 322, fighting around Borodino railway station and Semyonovskoe village.

Conditions deteriorated with the arrival of snow. Panzer Regiment 7 has joined with *SS* motorcycle infantry for a further advance.

During the afternoon of 6 September 1812, the icon of the Black Virgin rescued from Smolensk cathedral was paraded before the Tsar's Army. 'Each of us gained new strength,' remembered one soldier. (P. Mineeva, Moscow

One of the *flèches* is overrun. (Borodino Panorama, Moscow)

Napoleon observed the battle with difficulty from the Shevardino Mound. (Museum of the Great Patriotic War, Moscow)

PART THREE

BEYOND BORODINO FIELD

7

The Road by Raevsky, Gorki and Tatarinovo

From 80 to 76 Miles to Moscow

Supreme Effort, 17 October 1941

On 17 October General Hoepner commanding *Panzergruppe 4* was look-ing for a supreme effort from the *SS Das Reich* and 10th Panzer Division to break through the Mozhaisk line at Borodino. 'The Russians no longer have a recognisable army,' he wrote, after their crushing defeat at Vyazma, 'so should not have the capacity to conduct a successful defence here.' The plan that morning was for 10th Panzer to mop up the area between Shevardino and Tatarinovo and then push on to Mozhaisk. *Das Reich* were to attack along the Moscow highway, concentrating their *schwerpunkt*, or main point of effort, south of the road, from Fomino and Sivkovo to a key road junction about 3½ miles south-west of Mozhaisk. Hoepner was beginning to grudgingly accept the difficulties:

> The formations opposing us – the Siberian 32 Rifle Brigade and some tank units – have proved remarkably effective.[1]

The cold and heavy casualties were having an insidious effect on the momentum of the advance. Operation *Typhoon* was at its last gasp. *SS Stürmmann* Helmut Günther had moved forward with the

SS Kradschützen (motorcycle) Battalion *Reich* to spearhead the *Der Führer* II Battalion thrust toward Sivkovo, south of the highway. 'We had long since ceased to be the same fellows who had crossed the Bug river on 26 June 1941 at Brest-Litovsk,' he remembered:

> The constant being on the go, and the exorable battle with mud, rain, snow and cold had burnt us out. We had become hard, hard towards others and ourselves.

Battle fatigue took a toll. Hope and 'faith was generally a thing of the past!' The future was regarded with cynical scepticism: 'Boys had become men who were extremely critical about all that was said and didn't let anyone pull the wool over their eyes.' Nevertheless, they still retained a determination 'to show Ivan that nothing, nothing at all could stop us in driving him back'. Many friends had been lost, including his close friend Hans, who was killed shortly before *Typhoon* launched – news that 'struck me a heavy blow, and I had to work hard to pull myself together'. He wrote to Hans's parents. He had been the youngest of three brothers; one was killed as a *Feldwebel* (sergeant) in France in 1940, the other was serving with the Navy.

The penetrating cold was remorseless. In Germany they had been used to comfortable, well-appointed stone barracks, many still in use by the modern *Bundeswehr* and NATO forces today. This was their first winter in the open in the *Wehrmacht*'s longest campaign yet. They had much to learn. 'We wore everything that we owned on our bodies,' Günther recalled. The need to constantly adjust and regulate clothing layers was not yet apparent. Clothing needed to be ventilated or shed during violent action, something tired soldiers neglected to do. When the sweat from exertion evaporated it chilled the body and often froze at night. Metal weapons became brittle in freezing temperatures, and then rapidly overheated during rapid firing, causing unexpected breakages and stoppages.

German front-line soldiers were badly fed. The lack of carbohydrates, fat and protein alongside the physical difficulty of bringing hot food forward to the troops reduced body resistance. Lethargy was the result, slowing reactions and compromising the personal disciplines required to stay healthy in inclement field conditions. One prevailing problem was lack of fluids, much of which was lost breathing in cold air. This had then to be heated to body temperature inside the lungs, which drew in large amounts of liquid from the body, repeatedly expelled through urine. Thirsty soldiers in snow did not appreciate they needed more fluid than normal and would scoop up handfuls of snow, relying on body temperature to break it down. Seventeen times the volume of snow is required to produce the equivalent amount of water, so they rarely got enough. This unhygienic practice often resulted in dysentery, increasing fluid loss, which might be catastrophic.

Soldiers were also becoming increasingly susceptible to frostbite and 'trench foot', the latter prevalent in cold, wet conditions just above freezing. Both states occurred when blood supply to the extremities was inhibited by dehydration and adrenalin flow in action and the cold. Socks tended to disintegrate when unchanged inside sodden leather boots. Standing or sitting with legs down for long periods in mud and water produced the extreme chilling that caused irreparable tissue damage, which in extreme cases could result in gangrene. German soldiers living in the open since the spring had been plagued by high incidences of intestinal and bowel complaints caused by insufficient nutritious food, while enduring harsh elementary living conditions. If not afflicted by diarrhoea, which affected body resistance, they might suffer from constipation, through lack of fluids and the difficulty and inconvenience of defecating in sub-zero conditions while under threat. Russian soldiers, often from rural communities, were more attuned to robust living conditions in the open and the vagaries of their own climate, unlike their more comfortable-minded, barrack-living *Wehrmacht* counterparts. 'Deep inside, each one of us had something that prevented us from losing our minds,' revealed Helmut Günther:

> Each of us coped with everything in his own way. The only thing that was important was that you managed to cope with it somehow![2]

The human cost of the war in the East was becoming increasingly apparent to the families of serving German soldiers back home in the *Reich. Todesanzeigen* death notices were producing rashes of black crosses across newspaper pages announcing the *Heldentodt* (heroes' death) of family members who had 'fallen for the Führer and Fatherland'. Some

114,000 fell that October alone, which was only 31,000 less than the total
for the entire six-week French *Blitzkrieg* campaign of 1940. German press
accounts had trumpeted final victory in the East after the encirclement
battle at Vyazma, but continuing determined Russian resistance was suggesting otherwise. *SS Home Front* reports noted the public could not
understand, except 'with a certain scepticism', how it could be that, after
260 of the best-equipped Soviet divisions had been destroyed, the advance
before Moscow was slowing.[3]

The same reports picked up depression back home at the first mention
of snow on the Eastern Front. Soldiers wrote home asking for warmer
underwear, earmuffs, gloves and scarves to be sent to the front, while
casualties mounted inexorably. 'Being a postman suddenly became an
unpleasant occupation,' remembered housewife Hildegard Gratz:

> He became the bringer of bad news. There were terrible scenes of grief.
> The postman came to dread his round if ever there was one of those
> black-edged letters to be delivered. The official line was that women
> were bearing their news 'with proud grief' but many of the women in
> their despair screamed out curses on this 'damned war'. This was a risky
> business, such people were supposed to be reported.

One crass poignant case was noted in the *SS Home Front* survey of an
unfortunate mother handed tragic news at a tram stop with her children.
The unsuspecting postman continued on his round while, behind him, the
woman screamed and fainted in the street. News from Borodino sparked
momentary interest and optimism, with its memories of Napoleon's historic success. It was needed, because the war was sucking the very vitality
out of normal life back home. 'Three young women went around our village in black that autumn of 1941,' Frau Gratz remembered. 'I had danced
at their weddings, and they at mine.'[4]

The I and II Battalions from 10th Panzer's 69 Regiment had penetrated Shevardino village during the hours of darkness the night before,
approaching from the south and east. It was a confusing situation. The
Russians picked up the main passage of German groups penetrating the
village by the glow from burning buildings on its east side. A suicidal
Russian counter-attack checked the Germans, who decided to wait until

dawn before mopping up. Wooden houses blazed all night, leaving only forlorn brick chimney stacks and fireplaces in the morning. During the night, the 10th Panzer Division Headquarters at Chabrowa, south-west of Yelnya, shelved the intended mop-up plan when yet another Soviet attack materialised from the north, deep in 10th Panzer's rear, emerging from the forest of Golovino. The mission was now to pacify the areas the tanks had already occupied, before any further eastward advances towards Mozhaisk could be contemplated.

Ivan Barchuk's unit, much depleted by the abortive attack on Borodino railway station, emerged near Shevardino, having marched all night through the woods with map and compass. They were attached to Sherbakov's 2nd Battalion to make up its strength. By dawn on 17 October they were combing a clearing in the wood housing their regimental headquarters when they suddenly came under fire from machine guns and automatic weapons. A group of Germans had infiltrated the line and surrounded the HQ. After a brisk firefight, the Germans fled and Barchuk's section took a 'lanky' German prisoner. He was wrestled to the ground and disarmed by five of them. After the casualties of the previous day and the desperate situation around them, they were in no mood to compromise:

> In broken German we said 'look bastard, you want Russian soil? Hitler is kaputt!' To which the German replied, 'Never, Hitler ist good – Stalin ist kaputt!'

'Everyone shouted, there's no point in bothering with him,' Barchuk remembered. 'Shoot the rat!' The German was executed in the clearing and they moved on. Despite relative confidence, Barchuk insisted 'the skill of the soldiers grew by the hour', they were beginning to accept 'that for us, overcoming the enemy would not be simple'. With Germans closing in on Shevardino from two directions 'we realised that we were being surrounded, and were ordered to withdraw under covering fire further east, to a new line'. They sought to break out, across the Moscow highway to the south, before the ring closed. There was still fighting raging around the villages of Utitsy and Artyomki, bordering the road.[5]

When the Germans occupied 'monument hill' at Shevardino, Napoleon's former lookout point, it became clear why Russian artillery fire had been so devastatingly accurate. German artillery units immediately set up their own observation posts. Von Bulow's 69th Regiment *Kampfgruppe* began its advance eastward at 9 a.m. and became bogged down in costly fighting for Semyonovskoe village, an impasse that remained until 1 p.m. When the panzers from the *I Abteilung* Regiment 7 arrived and punched a way through, the advance was resumed to Tatarinovo, on the plateau beyond. There, they linked with von Hauenschild's 86th Regiment *Kampfgruppe*. Because of continuing Russian resistance in their rear around the Raevsky mound and Borodino village, the *I Abteilung* was redirected to turn about and head back west. At Gorki village, Russian forces attempting to withdraw northward were shot up, and soon the *I Abteilung* tanks were battling amid the monuments at Borodino field.

The *Das Reich* Division was, meanwhile, staging for its forthcoming attack in the woods east of Yelnya. It was to attack down the highway, but with its *schwerpunkt* coming up from south of the road. The tenacious Soviet defence blocking the highway at Artyomki was a real thorn in the side of a concerted German advance, and needed to be dislodged. As the Germans formed up, a Russian *Katyusha* rocket attack fired out of Artyomki caught 'a large group of infantry vehicles in Utitsy Wood'. Major Vasily Chevgus, commanding 154 Artillery Regiment, recalled:

> For several minutes howitzer and rocket rounds flashed by, penetrating the air. Utitsy wood was deluged in the thunder and flames of explosions. The wood burned, enveloped in black smoke, while the air above it trembled, as if in a powerful storm. Silence descended after the noise of the explosions died down. The only sounds to be heard were frenzied cries from the Nazis and shouts of 'That was bang on!' from our own trenches. This was the first time in this battle that the troops had heard the melodious drum roll of our legendary Katyushas.[6]

These truck-mounted multiple rocket launchers were nicknamed 'Stalin's Organ' by German soldiers unnerved by the sudden saturation bombardments that descended. Launched from a folding frame raised at an angle for firing, some fourteen to forty-eight rockets (depending on type) with an 11lb warhead could be fired in salvos lasting seven to ten seconds. They were an area weapon, pointed at the target, but devastating if they hit. Lucky escapes were occasionally possible, because the charge mounted at the tip of the rocket propelled a cone-shaped fragmentation effect upwards, unlike conventional artillery rounds that sprayed shrapnel along the ground. 'Ricochet' rockets that bounced up into the air before exploding were the most dangerous of all, alongside detonations in the upper branches in woods.

The *Deutschland* advance was also delayed when all three battalions were hit by Soviet spoiling attacks when they began their eastward advance. Gradually, they approached Artyomki. Then, at 3.25 p.m., an ammunition truck exploded spectacularly and burned after the woods and wood line was strafed and bombed by low-flying Shturmovik aircraft. This Soviet fighter-bomber mounted rockets and 23mm cannon, and was nicknamed the *Fleicher* or 'butcher' by German soldiers from grim experience. If they attacked from the side, as in this instance, damage was minimal, but far more pronounced if the strafing run followed the line of the road.

Der Führer spearheaded by the *Reich* motorcycle battalion launched its attack at 7.30 a.m. to the south-east of the highway. Fired in by two artillery battalions, the motorcycle troops were accompanied by the self-propelled *Sturmgeschütz III* gun *Ziethen* as well as an anti-aircraft and anti-tank platoon. They soon made good progress.

Young Kendzerski Iulianovich's T-27 militia tank company was deployed in the area of the Moscow highway, and was caught up in the *Deutschland* advance. His light 1½-ton vehicle looked more like an agricultural tractor with a square turret on top mounting a DT (Degtiarev-Tokarev) 7.62mm machine gun. Iulianovich, the driver, thought his tankette was 'rather a true plaything' with weak armour and an underpowered engine. He shared its claustrophobic confines with gunner Yurka Sharf, who had only three magazines for his machine gun. The tankette was hit on 17 October. 'I remember this date,' he recalled, 'it was my nineteenth birthday.'

It was a direct hit from Yurka's side and a shell fragment ripped open his belly and his bowels tumbled onto the engine. Another fragment brushed my head just on the rebound and flowing blood covered my eyes. At first I thought that I was killed but in a moment everything had been changed. I rubbed my eyes and I saw Yurka dying.

He started to raise the turret lid and 'through the open space between the roof and the hatch cover, I saw I was at rifle point'. 'Rus, surrender,' a voice said. He was unarmed except for two grenades at his feet and appreciated that if he stooped, he would be shot. There was nothing he could do:

> I was in a stalemate position! I still pray for this German ... why did he not fire? I lifted the hatch up and scrambled out of the tankette.

He was gathered up with fifteen other soldiers and marched off. Each of them was given a can of stewed meat and five packs of Belomar cigarettes, all looted from the Russians. 'No brutality, no killing prisoners,' he recalled, 'I have no complaints about how they treated us.' He was fortunate. 'I feel only gratitude to those who took me prisoner,' he remembered in an interview long after the war. 'That German needed only to press the trigger.'[7]

Helmut Güther's motorcycle battalion was soon under fire in the woods near Sivkovo. Soldiers leapt from their machines amid shouted orders. 'There was wild machine-gun fire everywhere,' he remembered, 'detonating hand grenades, and the breaking of tree limbs.' Riders raced away with empty motorcycle sidecars as riflemen advanced along both sides of the road, to re-establish contact with those engaging the enemy at the point of the advance. 'Men cried for medics and for fresh machine gun belts,' he recalled. It was not long before he saw sidecar machines winding their way down the road from up front, with the first wounded. 'I hunkered down by myself in a roadside ditch' as the action continued:

> The company's motorcycles had also been brought backward to the rear by the motorcycle section leaders. The sounds of fighting grew ever wilder. It banged, snarled and roared from all sides. I was alternately hot and cold, but it did not seem like a good idea for me to stand up just then.

Up ahead was a forest fight where the road dipped down into a valley, rising up on the far side over 400yd away. A Soviet self-propelled gun poked its barrel over the ridgeline and announced its presence with an 'Iiiiiuuu ... boom!' sound, as shells detonated to their rear. Their own supporting *Sturmgeschütz* assault gun *Ziethen* came 'chugging' up and engaged in a 'cat and mouse' duel with its opposite number, with Günther lying helplessly overexposed nearby. 'At first, you only saw the long barrel,' he recalled, watching the Russian, 'then the superstructure,' which was the signal to get down:

> Then the discharge from the main gun of the *Sturmgeschütz* nearly broke my eardrums. In addition, the gun on the other side was at it again. That's just what I was afraid of! Once again that loathsome hissing in the air and then a bang that took my breath away.

He opened his mouth in anticipation, to relieve the pressure in his ears, just as they fired. Two multiple reports rang out, indicating they had fired at the same time. 'While the *Sturmgeschütz* only rocked a bit, a giant shot of flame leaped up from Ivan on the other side.'[8]

The *Der Führer* Regiment advance continued through the wooded area to the south-east, overrunning the 154 Regiment battery areas positioned behind Artyomki. By nightfall the regiment and motorcycle battalion had captured Sivkova. The *Ziethen* fired on a retreating enemy column but heavy fire from ground role Soviet anti-aircraft guns signalled a halt to any further advances.

The *Deutschland* advance on Artyomki, scheduled to begin at 10 a.m., was held up by the Soviet spoiling attacks and it took another two hours before it could get going. The II Battalion had to drop off to occupy a flank screen to face the railway line, where Soviet positions were still entrenched behind Semyonovskoe village. Reduced to two weak battalions, the remainder of the regiment approached Artyomki stealthily, led by the III Battalion *Deutschland* with I Battalion following up behind in echelon. At 5 p.m. they were on the western outskirts of the village with 400yd to go and still undetected. At that moment, and completely unexpected by the closing *SS* infantry, a flight of nine *Stukas* peeled off in a howling approach from the sky, and dive-bombed the village houses. Orange smoke was released as an emergency measure by the forward troops and marker flares shot up into the sky to warn the diving *Stukas* about the extent of their approach. This devastating supporting attack was an uncalled-for bonus. Such attacks could, however, be a two-edged weapon, because there had been painful losses to such friendly fire at the Desna river during the Ukraine attack towards Kiev.

Major Chevgus, with Soviet Artillery Regiment 154, remembered, 'They swooped on to the woods like birds of prey, close to the positions where the horses of the 17th Rifle Regiment were located.' Few survived: 'they were brutally killed, depriving the whole regiment of transport means for rations and ammunition.' Each aircraft could deliver up to 660lb of high explosive in two passes. Tanks and identified emplacements were attacked with pinpoint accuracy as the village was subjected to eighteen separate bombing and strafing runs. Just as the shocked Soviet defenders emerged amid the clouds of disorientating smoke and dust, amid blazing wooden houses, the two *SS* battalions attacked, achieving complete surprise.[9]

Inside the village, the 2nd Battalion, 17th Regiment, and the battalion of cadets from the VI Lenin Political Military Academy were squeezed into a semicircle defence that broke into two segments. The *Deutschland* did not declare complete control of the village for a further three hours, after methodical house clearing and mopping up. Two hundred prisoners were set to work to clear the dead, most from the air assault. Two Soviet tanks were knocked out and three anti-aircraft guns and numerous machine guns captured; a further forty prisoners were winkled out of the houses. The Moscow highway had now been fought clear, and the traffic jam stretching as far back as Gzhatsk could at last get moving.

Stragglers emerged constantly on to the highway, after fleeing through the woods. Master Sergeant Loktionov, an artillery battery reconnaissance officer, struggled through the trees carrying the battery second-in-command slung across his shoulders, supported by two rifles hung around his neck. Captain Babikov had been severely injured in the legs and spine by an explosion. Dragging and at times crawling through bushes and trees, they were suddenly accosted by two German soldiers who shouted, 'halt!' The startled sergeant's instinctive reaction was to reach for a grenade in his waist belt, but to his surprise Babikov slipped from his back and shot both Germans with his pistol. Both were physically at breaking point when they finally broke cover, slithering into a ditch by the highway. Here they were snapped out of a fatigued stupor by a voice, this time in Russian, demanding, 'Who goes there?' It was the division commissar Matrinova, who loaded the wounded captain on to his vehicle.[10]

Meanwhile, a few hours before, the two 10th Panzer *Kampfgruppen* von Bulow and von Hauenschild had linked up at Tatarinovo, having covered the undulating ground north-east of Borodino railway station to Psaryovo and crossed the Stonets stream. At this point the *I Abteilung* from Panzer Regiment 7 was dispatched to the west, rearward, to clear the Mozhaisk road they were on, back to Borodino village. The panzers approached the main bunker defence line around the Raevsky mound, dominating the road, from behind. Major Chevgus recalled the historical significance of the ensuing action 'where in 1812 there was a Raevsky battery, but now there was the 2nd Battalion of the 154th Artillery Regiment, led by Lieutenant Oseana'.

SS Kriegsberichter (war correspondent) Hugo Landgraf filmed the advance from the side hatch of his Panzer IV with the 4th Heavy Company. 'Tracers fly overhead without pause,' he recalled and 'rockets are continually fired in our direction'. Tanks were lined up, pouring fire into the objective ahead. 'The camouflage covering the Soviet bunkers, made up of wood and straw from the houses, has caught fire,' he recorded on his commentary. His film account shows two huge pyramids of bright fire, belching up clouds of black smoke, vertically into the sky. 'On the third day of the battle, the final moment has come,' he announced, 'with the support of heavy artillery to assist in the final decisive blow.' The next few scenes show an 88mm dismounted flak gun, worked feverishly by its crew, each recoil dislodging heavy snow from the piece and whipping up a snow haze every time it fired. 'Flak artillery supports us,' he relates, and the camera switches to artillery fire controllers observing distinctive black puff-balls, air bursts, exploding over the wooded area to their front. The advance continued and Landgraf's film dwells on a scene of two Soviet corpses, the soldiers shot from his side hatch, sprawled in the snow with a Napoleonic monument silhouetted behind. Chevgus remembered how:

> Nazi tanks crept among the memorials to the heroes of Borodino. They passed by the obelisk in honour of the soldiers of the Ismailov Life Guards Regiment and came close to the command post of the division commander.[11]

Colonel Polosukhin's tactical headquarters was in Semyonovskoe village and he could see the panzers advancing on a wide front to his rear. 'The division commander carefully followed the movement the enemy took,' Chevgus recalled, 'which suddenly increased speed and drove directly towards him.' The panzers 'surmounted the high ground, from where they had a view of several hundred metres' and Chevgus anticipated 'catastrophe was inevitable'. At which point they were bracketed by intense artillery fire from the flank, directed by Lieutenant Lezgovko's 6th Howitzer Battery. Several panzers were hit, 'steel armour flew off like a shell', Chevgus recalled, knocking out four tanks. During the subsequent duel several direct armour-piercing shells holed the defending howitzer gun shields and dented the guns, which caused abnormal recoils. One group of panzers outflanked the battery and attacked it from the rear, coming under fire from Chevgus's 5th Battery, commanded by Lieutenant Golavachev. The Germans swung around and charged the battery from the front, and as Chevgus recalled, 'succeeded in breaking through to the fire position and put the gun tractors out of commission'.

Landgraf remembered the advance, 'breaking through over a wide front'. Smiling panzer crewmen were filmed cheerily cupping their ears for warmth, clouds of breath and perspiration rising into the cold air. 'We move in from the flank,' he states, 'to attack the middle of the Soviet defence line and wipe them out in bloody individual battles.' Infantry are filmed stumbling rapidly by at the crouch, utilising the protection afforded by advancing Panzer III medium tanks. 'In the distance, over there, you can see the Bolsheviks come out of their dugouts,' Landgraf comments, fleeting figures barely visible on the film frames. His commentary takes on a triumphant tenor. This is precisely what cinema audiences back in the *Reich* want to see, overpowering panzer advances, like in the previous summer. 'We have successfully broken through the enemy defence lines,' the commentary crows. His film report ends with a diagrammatic description of what was achieved:

> Here you see the defence position a few days after it was captured … the enormous tank ditch, the 'hedgehog' obstacles made of welded cast iron railway track. Behind them you can see the heavy-duty bunkers from which an enormous area could be dominated.

The newsreel ends looking through one of the bunker observation slits on the Raevsky mound overlooking the Mozhaisk road. Dead horses are harnessed to wrecked carts. The camera dwells on clumps of dead Russian infantry collapsed in and around field positions and shows 'last but not least' wrecked anti-aircraft batteries. 'But all this was all in vain,' the film report claims, because 'German soldiers still managed to eject the Soviets from their defence position'.[12]

The Mozhaisk defence line was crumbling visibly, but the cost to the Germans had been high. The *Deutschland*'s twelve companies were reduced to units numbering between twenty-seven and ninety-eight soldiers from a start state of 180 men. Of these companies, only two could field one weak platoon of thirty-seven men, and two others only two of three established platoons. Helmut Günther, with the regiment, had a surprising encounter with an old teenage friend, Willi, from *Reichsarbeitsdienst* (Labour Service) days before conscription. Willi was a *Leutnant* now with the 10th Panzer. There was little time for an animated discussion about old friends. 'We merely exchanged a few words,' he recalled, 'and promised to visit each other as soon as conditions allowed.'

'Take care, old man,' they agreed on parting.

> That very evening I learned from a tanker man that Willi had been killed. A well-concealed anti-tank gun had knocked out his tank with a direct hit! It was enough to drive you crazy. One after another my friends were taking the great journey!

Major Vasily Chevgus did succeed in withdrawing the surviving remnants of the 154 Artillery Regiment. He remembered surveying the aftermath of the fighting that left 'the field of military glory forever steeped in human blood'. Landgraf's film report concluded with the devastation around the Raevsky mound. The present-day Borodino museum is situated at the foot of this mound, and many of the gun slits of the surviving bunkers, sited to cover the crossing point of the Kolocha river, bear telltale gouge marks of high-velocity tank rounds and shrapnel scars. The scene on 17 October was bleak; Chevgus described ground:

Pitted with craters from shells, mines and bombs, scarred all over by tank tracks. Dead bodies lay there, horses, knocked out vehicles, guns, mortars, destroyed tanks and burning armoured vehicles. Thousands of tons of metal fragments had been absorbed into the earth at Borodino. The wood, previously green, was now covered with black wounds, transformed by fallen trees everywhere.[13]

'A Volcano Crowned with Vapours', The Raevsky Redoubt, 7 September 1812

2 p.m. to 6.30 p.m.

Following the failed French attack of the morning of 7 September 1812 on the Raevsky redoubt, debris and appalling human detritus covered the mound and its environs on an even greater scale than in October 1941. 'Here the corpses lay piled higher and ever higher around a position that had changed hands again and again,' recalled Lieutenant Heinrich Vossler. 'The ditches were filled to the brim with bodies,' and 'I found bodies in Württemburg uniform by the hundreds'. Topographically little had changed in 1941; Vossler claimed in 1812 that 'the top of these fortifications provided a comprehensive view of almost the entire field of battle'. Bodies of French infantry were strewn all over the gentler slope to the west front of the *kurgan* mound, which was 688ft high. Many had been tipped into the ditch forward of the two redoubt shoulders, or were sprawled over the earthen flank walls. Parapets had been half beaten down by pounding artillery, reduced to shallow mounds, and the embrasures had collapsed. Russian guns still fired out between these piles and continued to punish Murat's cavalry drawn up below, forming the centre of the French battle line. Eighteen heavy pieces raked the assembled ranks with a murderous fire. 'Cannon balls hit us and ricocheted through our ranks, as we stood at attention with our sabres raised to our epaulettes,' remembered Lieutenant Julien Combe, with the 8th *Chasseurs à Cheval*. 'We remained in this terrible position for six hours.'

Cavalryman Thiron de Metz stood opposite the Russian cannon: 'We could see them being loaded with the projectiles which they would direct at us,' he remembered. With horrid fascination, 'We could distinguish the eye of the gunner who was aiming at us, and it required a great dose of composure to remain still.

'The regiment of Württemberg cuirassiers near me seemed to have been singled out as a special target,' observed artillery Colonel Griois. After each detonation 'shattered helmets and cuirasses flew in splinters through the whole formation'. 'My turn came,' recalled chasseur Captain Pierre Aubry. 'I was hit by a ricocheting cannon ball or by an exploding shell fragment on the flat of my spur':

> The blow was so violent that my boot burst open like a sheet of paper torn up by children for their amusement. All that was left was the lining. Fortunately the projectile passed on the side of my instep instead of by the heel – if it hadn't, my leg would have been carried away. I got off with losing all my nails and the flesh of my toes.

Napoleon, galvanised for the first time in this battle by the Cossack raid to his left and rear, had returned to the Shevardino mound, and by early afternoon resolved to finally deal with the redoubt. Imperial Guard lancer Captain François Dumonceau, astride his horse nearby, thought the redoubt, about a mile away, looked like a 'volcano crowned with vapours, engaged in a violent artillery battle, while a compact mob swarms around its base'. The redoubt was almost indistinguishable at distance, having been pulverised methodically to half its height beneath the crossfire of 170 French guns firing from the villages of Borodino and Semyonovskoe. Marshal Bessières asked artillery officer Pion des Loches what he could see. 'I replied that I saw nothing,' he recalled, 'didn't even know where what he called the "Great Redoubt" lay.' Bessières, commanding the Guard cavalry, continued to mutter between clenched teeth that 'we're going to have a lot of trouble to take that big redoubt'.[14]

For once, Napoleon decided on a bold unconventional strike. Shortly after 2 p.m. the French were discerned massing for a general assault on the redoubt. Unlike the *flèches* taken that morning, the Raevsky redoubt was closed at the rear, by a wall of pointed stakes. Prince Eugène drew up three infantry divisions, 10,000 to 12,000 men, for the assault: Gérard, Broussier and Morand's from Ney's Corps. They were to be supported either side by two masses of heavy cavalry, 6,000 strong, with Grouchy's III Corps left and Latour-Maubourg's IV and the II under General Auguste de Caulaincourt (the diplomat's younger brother) right. Despite being closed to the rear, the redoubt had two open 'throats' at each end of the arrow-shaped earthwork, at the shoulders. The plan was that cavalry would feint an attack on the Russian infantry massed either side of the redoubt, but at the last moment they would change direction and lunge at these two open 'throats'. This was highly unconventional. Napoleonic cavalry was rarely committed against a fixed fortification. As the attack developed, the dense columns of forward-marching French infantry were quickly overtaken by the cavalry moving at the trot, on their flanks. Then they unexpectedly swept up against the left flank and rear of the mound.

The air above the redoubt was soon punctuated by the cracking reports of premature shell bursts, but a sufficient number were striking at ground level to further level the surviving emplacements to a shapeless earthen mass, filling the corpse-strewn ditches with sand. Lejeune, observing from Napoleon's headquarters, also likened the effect to that of a volcano, with its 'whirlwinds of dust and silvery smoke'. One shell set fire to a barrel of resin, used by Russian gun crews to grease gun axles, which produced 'purplish flames, coiling along the ground like the thrashings of an irritated snake' and 'rose to join the clouds, projecting broad zones of darkness across the sun'.

Griois watched the cavalry columns outstrip the infantry and saw them turn in, breaking into a gallop:

> Overthrowing everything in front of them, they turn the redoubt, entering it by the throat and by the place where the earth that had rolled down into the ditches, made it easier of access.

At the same time, the infantry closed in, struggling up the gentle slope in the teeth of a hail of Russian grapeshot. The gunners had completely focused on them, the greater threat. Sergeant Bertrand, with the 7th Light Regiment, on the rise saw 'a round shot took my captain's head off, killing or mortally wounding four men in the first rank'. At the base of the redoubt:

The lieutenant takes the captain's place, scarcely is he at his post than he's stricken by a piece of grape which shatters his thigh. In the same instant the sous-lieutenant's foot is shattered by another shell fragment. The officers *hors de combat*, the sergeant major absent, I, as senior Sergeant, take command of the company.[15]

Waithier's division of cuirassiers was the first to reach the rear palisade but were shredded by a devastating Russian infantry volley fired point-blank at 60yd. General de Caulaincourt, at the head of the 5th Cuirassiers, had almost cleared the northern gap in the palisade before being snatched violently from his horse by a musket ball, which pierced his torso just beneath the heart, killing him instantly.

The IV Cavalry Corps crashed into the southern flank of the redoubt, with the *Garde du Corps* heading for the battery breastwork left of it, unmasking the Zastrow Cuirassiers coming up behind. These piled into the sand- and corpse-filled ditch to the right. The best riders scrambled over the reduced breastwork, while others forced their horses through collapsed embrasures or worked their way around to the rear. 'The cramped interior space of the redoubt was filled with a frightful press of murderously intentioned cavalry and Russian infantry,' remembered Saxon officer Franz von Meerheim, 'thrown pell-mell together and doing their best to throttle and mangle one another.'

'The combat was frightful,' he remembered. When the Saxon cavalry urged their horses over the lip, they were confronted by Russian infantry in the ravine behind the redoubt, which produced a scrimmage. Leading horsemen toppled on to a phalanx of uplifted bayonets and many coming behind were shot out of the saddle by successive volleys of musket fire from the other side of the ravine. 'Men and horses hit by lethal lead, fell down the slope and thrashed around among the dead and dying foe,' von Meerheim remembered, 'each trying to kill the enemy with their weapons, their bare hands, or even their teeth.' Further ranks of cavalry charged in with wild cries 'trampling everything under the hooves of their horses and throwing themselves infuriatedly on the Russian masses behind'. While berserk cavalry rampaged around the redoubt, the French infantry flowed over the battered parapets and through gaps created by the ruined embrasures, at the point of the bayonet.

The enormous plume of smoke, dust and noise that rose up from the area of the redoubt attracted the attention of the whole Russian army to the bitter struggle that was going on there. A Russian officer observing from near Gorki remembered, 'The brilliant rays of the half-hidden sun were reflected from the sabres, swords, bayonets, helmets and cuirasses, making a dreadful yet sublime picture.' Before they realised what was going on, it was too late:

> Already the French were under the redoubt itself, and our cannon gave a final salvo – then fell silent. A dull cheering told us that the enemy had burst over the rampart and were going to work with the bayonet.[16]

Colonel Griois, watching with Grouchy's artillery in the rear, could hardly contain himself. Their cavalry appeared to flow over the area to the right of the redoubt: the helmets of cuirassiers could be seen slashing about inside, the sun catching the glint of sudden movements. 'Every one of us accompanied them with his wishes,' he recalled, 'and would have liked to give a helping hand to that cavalry, which we saw leaping over ditches and scrambling up ramparts under a hail of canister shot.' Cavalry attacking a major artillery battery set inside a redoubt was unprecedented. 'A roar of joy resounded on all sides as they became masters of the redoubt. Berthier, Napoleon's Chief of Staff, observing through his telescope on the Shevardino mound, declared excitedly, 'The redoubt is taken! The Saxons are inside!' Prince Eugène, watching from his vantage point, announced, 'The battle is won!' and his men all about broke into cheering. Napoleon took the telescope from Berthier, insisting they were 'my cuirassiers!' not Lorge's Saxons. 'They're wearing blue,' he insisted, and he was right, because both Saxons and Polish cuirassiers also wore blue. It mattered not: clearly the redoubt had been overwhelmed, a key development in the battle.[17]

Grouchy's cavalry swept over into the steep area behind the redoubt, followed by other French units, to discover General Barclay de Tolly had formed a second Russian line of defence, 800yd behind the mound. This was the 7th Division from Tolstoy's IV Corps, who waited in square. They had hastily formed a new southern flank to secure the salient that the Raevsky redoubt had become, with the bending of the Russian line back to its left. All the French cavalry could do was rage up and down hedge-hog islands of infantry squares, slashing futilely with swords as successive Russian volleys emptied their saddles.

Six Russian guns were extricated tenaciously from the redoubt, two were abandoned at the northern entrance and a third heaved into the ditch. Despite the resounding success, almost no prisoners were taken. 'At most a few Russian cavalrymen during our various charges,' explained one Saxon cuirassier, 'but I don't recall seeing a single officer taken prisoner.' This appeared sinister, so much so that Napoleon sent aides to check, while remarking to Berthier:

> These Russians let themselves be killed like automata. There's no taking them alive. This doesn't help us at all. These citadels must be demolished by cannon.[18]

It was now late afternoon and for the next two hours successive Russian and French cavalry regiments fought each other to the rear of the redoubt. They were inextricably mixed up in desperate slashing charges and counter-attacks amid smoke and flame jetting out from the Russian infantry squares. Hordes of riderless horses shrieking from terror ran amok, trampling the dead and the wounded. A frustrated Barclay de Tolly ordered up his cavalry reserve to salvage the front, only to discover that Kutuzov had already dispatched it elsewhere without telling him. He at least managed to muster sufficient men to mount a concerted counter-charge. The French drew back to the line of the redoubt, unable to venture forward again because of the density of Russian artillery raking the area in front. Very soon the rear palisade of the redoubt was swept away 'like a breach' amid the furious artillery duel that broke out, ploughing over the same ground around the redoubt again. The battle was losing impetus, but still Napoleon chose not to deliver a *coup de grâce* with his Imperial Guard.

Death became an all-encompassing spectre, seemingly enfolding them all in a hideous embrace. Sergeant Major Auguste Thiron was accosted by one of his cuirassier conscripts begging leave to retire; surrounded by corpses, he was convinced he would die. Thiron was attempting to steady the ranks: 'I try to reassure him by placing myself close to him, and more or less succeed,' he recalled. Thiron was hungry and exhausted, not having eaten since the previous day, and he asked for a piece of bread from someone nearby. As it was passed across, 'a round shot takes off my young cuirassier's head'. He thought the howling shot had taken off his elbow, but it was bruised severely by a segment of the unfortunate man's helmet. More to the point, his piece of bread had fallen to the ground:

> Not wanting to lose my bit of bread, I picked it up on the point of my sword and, finding it soiled by a bit of the dead man's brains, had to remove the wet bit.

Thiron was philosophical about predictions of death from the ranks, but he had to hold them in the line. 'If it hadn't been my duty to keep the men in their ranks and encourage the young soldier,' he admitted, 'I'd have granted this poor man's prayer.'[19]

Prince Josef Poniatowski, on the right flank, was in the midst of an artillery duel. Junot's VIII Corps, diverted south to get Poniatowski's V Corps moving, had been bogged down by determined Russian resistance in the Utitsy woods. Russians, French and Poles were intermingled in dense forest and shrubbery. Officers found it difficult to oversee troops fighting in small isolated groups and the resulting confusion produced many instances of friendly fire. After hearing of the fall of the Raevsky redoubt, the Poles launched a two-pronged attack on Russian positions around the Utitsy mound. The northern prong was blocked but the diversion to its left was outstandingly successful and V Corps's main infantry and cavalry force closed in to the south of the hill. On the cusp of this success, they were checked by a counter-attack from the 1st Grenadier and 17th Infantry Divisions, supported by Cossacks. General Baggovut, placed in command after Tuchkov's death, was left in a dangerously exposed salient by the loss of the *flèches* and now the Raevsky redoubt. He therefore fell back some distance along the old Smolensk road, abandoning the Utitsa mound to the Poles. With that the Russians had been driven back from almost the entire length of the original line they had held that morning.

Carl von Clausewitz, serving with the Russian staff, had discerned around 6 p.m. that it was 'striking how the action gradually reflected the weariness and exhaustion of the armies':

The masses of infantry had melted away so drastically that perhaps less than one third of the original number was still in action: the rest of the troops were dead, wounded, engaged in carrying away the casualties or rallying in the rear. Everywhere there were wide gaps.

Artillery fire became desultory and 'sounded languid and muffled'. Barclay de Tolly, who had lost all but three adjutants, had been in the thick of the fighting, and had only just managed to shore up his line beyond the Raevsky redoubt. Snatching a scrap of bread and a glass of rum, he sat on his horse and studied the opposing line intently. He looked for any indication that Napoleon might throw in the Guard, his reserve, to finish the battle. Nearly all Russian reserves were already committed. 'Napoleon's Imperial Guard had not been seen in any attack,' remembered Colonel Ludwig von Wolzogen. It might appear in the centre to finish them off or come in from the French right along the old Smolensk road, which would bring them into the Russian rear and maybe bar the way to Moscow. 'Barclay could not understand why Napoleon did not exploit his victory,' von Wolzogen recalled, 'for he had in fact already gained possession of the principal points of the battlefield.' He observed, 'A general weariness had gripped the Russian army.' Von Clausewitz concurred, observing 'the cavalry had almost everywhere taken the place of the infantry and it moved up and down in a tired trot'.

It never happened. 'I will not have my Guard destroyed,' Napoleon insisted. 'When you are eight hundred leagues from France you do not wreck your last reserve.' Napoleon had already sensed this was a battle that would be neither lost nor won, which so far from his homeland, was a negative outcome.[20]

The sky became overcast and a cold drizzle began to fall; only the odd cannon fired sporadically. Major Mikhail Petrov remembered, 'Now and then, artillery guns, as if snorting off their exhaustion, covered the battlefield with the thunder of their fearsome sighs.' An irritated Captain Count Corner, well to the rear with Napoleon's baggage train, complained, 'Isn't this damnable battle ever going to end?' By 6.30 p.m. a kind of stunned stupor descended upon both armies. The Russians fell back some 1,500yd to their second line, straightening up a badly mauled first line. Only the right flank, on the Kolocha river line, remained unchanged; the centre and left were driven back, with the fall of the Raevsky redoubt, the Bagration *flèches*, Semyonovskoe village and Utitsy. Colonel von Wolzogen was dispatched by de Tolly to Kutuzov, 'who had not appeared in the battle line all day' to report on the situation and obtain further orders. 'Get his reply in writing,' de Tolly insisted, 'because one has to be careful with Kutuzov.'

He found him 'on the Moscow road about half an hour's ride behind the army,' he recalled. Von Wolzogen was unimpressed with the headquarters and its 'suite' of rich raffish Russian noblemen, 'who were so numerous that they looked to me like reinforcements'. It appeared during the battle they had 'indulged in all kinds of pleasures' having 'taken no part whatever in the terrible and earnest events of the day'. Kutuzov was told 'all important posts had been lost on the right wing and to the left of the high road' and that his 'regiments were all extremely tired and shattered'. Kutuzov's response was testy and aggressive:

> With which low bitch of a sutler have you been getting drunk, that you come giving me such an absurd report? I am in the best position to know how the battle went! The French attacks have been successfully repulsed everywhere, and tomorrow I shall put myself at the head of the army to drive the enemy without more ado from the sacred soil of Russia!

Kutuzov's entourage of young nobles predictably applauded enthusiastically. Von Wolzogen was no fool; Kutuzov knew his men and the value of propaganda. Napoleon's army was certainly badly damaged: 'he assumed correctly' von Wolzogen remembered, 'that Napoleon, as he had been unable to gain a decisive victory between six o'clock that morning and five in the afternoon, and had, rather broken off the action, would not renew the battle'. The Russians would therefore retain their sector of the battlefield overnight, and success in a Napoleonic battle was based on who occupied the field after the action. 'His associates will not realise the true state of the army,' von Wolzogen further appreciated, and announcing an intention to renew hostilities in the morning might indeed forestall a rout or at least prevent anyone anticipating a retreat. Units would, meanwhile, stay together and try to reorganise. Barclay de Tolly was directed in writing to bring the army into line between Gorki hill to its right and the woodland on the old Smolensk road on the left. 'Everything had to be prepared for the next morning, so that Kutuzov could attack the enemy.'[21]

Tsar Alexander was informed that the bravery and tenacity of his troops had inflicted heavy losses on the French and had not given up an inch of ground. A public bulletin announced French attacks had ben unsuccessful: 'repulsed at all points', it read, 'the enemy fell back at nightfall, and we remained masters of the battlefield'. The dispatch caused rejoicing in St Petersburg and the Tsar sent Kutuzov a gift of 100,000 roubles and announced his promotion to field marshal. As von Clausewitz commented wryly, 'This mountebankism of the old fox was more useful at this moment than Barclay's honesty.' Colonel Toll and Kutuzov's aide de camp, Aleksandr Galitzine, toured the army's depleted ranks in the gathering darkness and advised him that only 45,000 men could be mustered for battle at dawn.[22]

It had been a sobering experience for both sides. A sense of shock rather than elation pervaded the *Grand Armée*; this was not the decisive single victory they had sought. The bitterness and skill with which some of the Russian rearguards had fought now culminated in a sense of wonder at the prowess of the enemy, which still seemed to pervade the battlefield, even though they were largely out of sight. Only about 800 prisoners were taken. Carabinier Sergeant Vincent Bertrand, with the 7th Light, counted himself lucky to have got off with a light wound to his shoulder 'thanks to the buckle of my pack'. Then, even after the day's appalling losses, a musket ball suddenly shot out of the dark and knocked off his shako and killed 'a sergeant, my compatriot, dead'. They were being sniped at by Russian wounded or stragglers:

> We weren't slow to discover the assassins, hidden in a big hole in the middle of a little ravine. We did justice on them with two balls and our bayonets.

Saxon Life Guard Cuirassier Lieutenant Roth von Schreckenstein appreciated the Russians would have to leave many of their wounded on the battlefield, but admitted 'any other army would have left twice as many'. His unit only took a few prisoners, twelve guns from the redoubt and some others during the first charge. 'A very small number of stragglers had been rounded up,' but 'the enemy hadn't abandoned so much as a cart'.

The Russians had shown the utmost tenacity. Their ranks hadn't broken. Never had ground been attacked with greater fury or skill, or more stubbornly defended.[23]

One hundred and twenty-nine years later, German soldiers with the *SS Das Reich* Division shared a similar opinion. *Stürmann* (Lance Corporal) Helmut Günther, with the motorcycle battalion, remembered pinning down five Soviet soldiers in a bunker south of the Moscow highway. Despite being grenaded constantly and called upon to surrender, they refused. 'The rascals were now at our mercy, but they should get one last chance,' he remembered, but 'not a sign, the Ivans did not stir'. Reluctantly they dropped a succession of hand grenades down the bunker ventilation stove pipe until 'it was done!'

> I felt sorry for the guys, but why did they have to be so stubborn? That was a typical example of irrational Russian behaviour.

After repeated muted detonations, the bunker roof heaved and sank and a number of Russians came out to surrender. They had survived because when one of their number was killed by the first explosion, the 'quick-witted' survivors grabbed him and held him next to the end of the stovepipe. 'The poor bastard absorbed all the fragments, thereby saving his comrades.' This innate Russian ability to absorb punishment and still fight back, irrationally or unpredictably, was unnerving. 'That was what Russians were like,' Günther remarked, 'through and through.'[24]

Napoleon's equerry, General Armand de Caulaincourt, recalled, 'The Emperor came to a decision,' and 'he suspended the order to attack' after discussions with his cavalry commander Murat and Berthier, his Chief of Staff. He prevaricated; the advice was the Russians were pulling back, but they were doing so in good order 'and showing an inclination to dispute every inch of the ground, irrespective of how much our guns were wreaking havoc in their ranks'. Committing the Imperial Guard was considered fleetingly, but 'success at such a price', the two suggested, 'would really be a reverse that would counterbalance the entire success of the battle'. There was unease, because as de Ségur observed, 'the victory, so long and ardently sought, so dearly purchased, was incomplete'. Napoleon knew it, and inside his tent his aide could see 'he was overcome by painful dejection, mental as well as physical'. Darkness dampened down the fighting, in any case. De Caulaincourt recalled Napoleon hedged his bets by bringing some troops forward 'in case the enemy should attempt something fresh'. Looking across the devastated landscape, he saw 'both sides were so tired that in several places the firing ceased without any orders being given'. De Ségur remembered the battlefield encapsulated the prevailing mood:

> Everything conspired to lend the field a dreadful aspect: a leaden sky, a cold rain driven by a violent wind, the charred ruins of the houses, and the whole ploughed up plain which was strewn with the wreckage and debris and rimmed about with the gloomy and dark trees of these northern climes. Everywhere there were soldiers wandering among the corpses and rifling for food amid the knapsacks of their dead comrades.[25]

The appalling casualty rate had been harvested at an average rate of 100 cannon shots and 2,300 musket rounds fired each minute. Russian troops drawn up in depth, 100 paces apart, had been in range of the French guns all day. A fresh wall of troops always seemed to confront every potential breakthrough by the French, and they attacked all day. Defence was less demanding in terms of command and control. The French, unable to manoeuvre, simply bludgeoned more violently at every attempt to pierce a Russian line that melted, but did not give way. French reserves were also exposed needlessly. One of Prince Eugène's Württemberg brigades lost 289 men, or 10 per cent of its effective strength, within thirty minutes, standing at ease in reserve. One-third of the 11th *Chasseurs à Cheval*, standing beneath the guns of the Raevsky redoubt, fell in hours, without even participating in combat.

Assessments of Russian losses vary from 38,500 to as much as 58,000, with more recent estimates at about 45,000. The numbers suggest the Russian army lost half its fighting effectives, line regiments rather than militia or Cossacks. The figures include twenty-nine generals, of which six were killed. French casualties were lighter at about 28,000 to 30,000, with most units losing between 10 to 20 per cent of their fighting strengths and forty-eight generals – a considerable number – of which eleven died. In strategic terms, the character of the French army altered. Theoretically, fresh troops could come from France and senior officers be promoted, but Napoleon had all but destroyed his own cavalry. Nominally 14,500 strong, only 4,600 remained combat effective. What remained now was essentially an infantry-heavy force supported by artillery. Imperial Guard lancer Captain François Dumonceau noticed in particular the huge numbers of dead and dying horses as dusk fell, twitching and twisting and 'emitting dolorous death-rattles':

> One saw some which, though horribly disemboweled or mutilated, yet kept their legs, motionless, with hanging heads, drenching the ground with their blood, or else straying painfully about in search of some grazing, dragging beneath them strips of shattered harness, intestines or a broken limb.[26]

Albrecht Adam, with Eugène's staff, later painted a picture of a group of Italian Guards of Honour warming themselves around a fire, stoked from destroyed wagon parts, gazing reflectively into the flames. 'Our situation was cruel,' he remembered on the cold damp night that had followed fine weather that day. 'Neither man nor horse had anything to eat and the lack of firewood meant that we felt all the rigours of this cold, wet night.' They were hundreds of miles from home and surrounded by 'fallen brothers in arms' with 'bleak presentiments of what the future might hold'. 'We had never suffered such heavy losses,' recalled Colonel Raymond de Montesquiou, 'never had the army's morale been so damaged':

> I no longer found the soldier's old gaiety: a gloomy silence had replaced the songs and amusing stories which previously had helped them to forget the fatigue of long marches. Even the officers appeared anxious, and they continued serving only from a sense of duty and honour.

Major Eugène Labaume walked the battlefield, depressed at the sight of 'mounds of wounded' and debris, and cannon balls lying about 'as numerous as hailstones after a violent storm'. He was especially affected by ghastly ravine interiors, filled with crawling wounded, 'piled up on top of each other' desperate to avoid further exposure to flying projectiles, 'lacking all succour and swimming in their own blood, groaning terribly'. He felt helpless, 'There was nothing anyone could do for them,' he lamented. 'Begging to be allowed to die, they asked us to put term to their horrible sacrifice.' These awful snapshot memories would endure to the end of their days. Dumonceau remembered one ghoulish image of a Spanish or Portuguese sergeant who 'seemed to have been shot in the middle of an access of hilarity and his features still bore the impression of it'.

Later that night, Captain Jean Bréaut des Marlots spoke with a group of Russians for two hours under a flag of truce. 'We asked each other what we thought about the war,' he remembered. The Russians answered:

> We know as well as you do we're going to be beaten. All we're hoping for is salvation in the winter, which will amplify your troubles. Winter and hunger will be the arms against which your courage will give in. Believe me, I know my country's climate.

As an aside he added, 'I hope it won't have any malignant effect on you personally.'[27]

General Barclay de Tolly completed Kutuzov's command to straighten the line to the best of his ability. He finally managed to get some sleep in one of the few houses in Gorki that had not been destroyed. It was therefore easy to locate at 3 a.m. when one of Kutuzov's adjutants brought an order to begin sending the reserve artillery and baggage back immediately through Mozhaisk. When these had achieved some distance from the enemy, he was to follow with the rest of the army.

8

The Road to Mozhaisk

70 Miles to Moscow

The Capture of Mozhaisk, 18–19 October 1941

'They knew that we were the last defence force before Moscow,' explained infantry soldier Boris Baromykin with the Soviet 32nd Division. 'Their artillery was constantly shelling us, and their planes hovered overhead, bombing and machine gunning our retreating columns.' Favourable weather on the morning of 18 October enabled the *Luftwaffe* to harass the road intersection south-west of Mozhaisk as well as Soviet armour and artillery on the Mozhaisk road. To the north of Borodino Field, Colonel Polosukhin's division staff and remnants of the 322 and 113 Regiments fell back towards Mozhaisk and the Moskva river. Baromykin retreated along the Moscow highway with 'tanks hard on our heels':

> We resisted doggedly. We frequently turned our guns and fire back point-blank to beat off their pursuit. We counter-attacked against their infantry.

Further south, the 17th Regiment survivors with remnants from Major Vorbiev's Artyomki command, mixed in with armoured vehicles of the 18th and 20th Tank Brigades, were falling back steadily. The

17th Regiment co-ordinated the withdrawal, but as Captain Anton Pastushenko, assisting their Chief of Staff, remembered, 'telephone lines had stopped operating completely':

> There were no signallers left. Only one telephone operator remained in my command post. I had no communications with the regiment commander, and runners were not coming back.[1]

Unteroffizier Ludwig Horn, with 10th Panzer's Artillery Regiment 90, was a keen photographer. He took one shot of a *Stuka* dive-bomber skimming menacingly at low level over their artillery emplacement. The swastika flag clearly laid out on the ground in front was sufficient to indicate theirs was a 'friendly' position. 'Stubborn Russian resistance had stopped our advance,' Horn noted beneath the photograph. 'Stukas had to soften up the enemy positions.' Russian stragglers fleeing eastward were in evidence all around. 'The village in front of us burns,' Horn remembered:

> I see something dark in the snow. It is the Lieutenant. He is still warm, but I get no answer when I call his name. We have heard that the Russians concentrate their fire at officers, who can be recognised by their slender custom-made boots.

The boots were totally inadequate in freezing conditions and were exchanged for Russian at the first opportunity. Veteran artillery officer Lieutenant Wigand Wüster later explained:

> Experience showed artillerymen dreaded hostile infantry fire far more than artillery bombardment. For the infantry the exact opposite was true. Weapons which men handled themselves were feared far less than the unknown.[2]

After the two 10th Panzer *Kampfgruppen* (battle groups) had combined at the village of Tatarinovo, von Hauenschild's Regiment 86 continued the advance to the next village, Novaya Derevnya, 2 miles further to the north-east. The Moskva river lay to the north and the city of Mozhaisk was 3½ miles away. Patrols pushed forward from Novaya Derevnya discovered only weak enemy forces ahead. Von Stumme's *XXXX Korps* issued a single concise order that morning, just as *Schützen* Regiment 86's commander committed his I Battalion to assault a key hill feature at Point 211, just under 2 miles from Mozhaisk. The order read, '10th Panzer Division is to launch a tightly concentrated attack on Mozhaisk from the Tatarinovo area.' It was already under way; the division artillery had closed up in preparation for the assault. General Fischer appeared at the regimental command post, pleased to learn the advance had been set in motion on their own initiative. The II Battalion Regiment 69 was dispatched immediately to attack the Moskva river bridge near Ilinskoje, to provide support from the north-east. The 10th Panzer's tanks set off from Tatarinovo through Kukarino heading for the northern outskirts of Mozhaisk. As they advanced, the retreating elements of Polosukhin's 32nd Division were split in two. Coming up from the south-west was the second arm of the pincer, the *SS Das Reich* Division.

'The retreat was a living nightmare,' Boris Baromykin, struggling along the Moscow highway, remembered:

> Human guts hung from the trees, where soldiers' bodies had been blasted by the sheer force of the explosions. The snow around us was soaked red with blood. There was an all-pervasive pungent smell of unwashed male bodies, hardened encrusted blood and burning. To slow the German advance, we set light to everything, so that the enemy would not have it. We were determined not to let them through.

Ivan Barchuk recalled, 'On realising that we were being surrounded, we were ordered to withdraw east to a new line under covering fire.' This involved wading the Moskva river, the Ruza and Protva several times. German rings, lit by Very flares in the darkness, enveloped them constantly. Progress was tough.

> Then it got very cold. When we forced our way across water obstacles, we took off our puttees and boots, crossed the water, dried our bodies, emptied water from our boots and rewrapped our feet in puttees, saving ourselves from certain death and frostbite.

With the 10th Panzer advance gaining momentum, 'the Germans moved on in vehicles north of us, we were south of the Mozhaisk road'. At one point they were bracketed by incendiary artillery shellfire. 'The Germans killed our cart driver, set on fire by a white phosphorous round.' Amid the screams the horses panicked, 'taking fright in the flames', which badly burned other Red Army drivers. 'There was nothing more dreadful for us,' he recalled. 'We only wanted that nobody should be set alight by the flaming shells.' Barchuk's platoon was earmarked as rearguard to cover their passage across the Moskva river. German tanks were, meanwhile, moving in columns along the Mozhaisk road and they sensed 'the encirclement was tightening'. They managed to extricate across the river and then realised 'one unit did not manage to escape, and was left at the rear of the Germans'.[3]

Der Führer and the *SS* Motorcycle Battalion *Reich* had turned north-east after capturing Sivkovo, driving towards Mozhaisk. On reaching the Moscow highway, they linked with the *SS Deutschland* advance attacking west to east along the road. Helmut Günther described the haphazard nature of such a motorcycle infantry advance along forested roads. 'It looked as if the Mozhaisk intersection would be the end of our advance,' he remembered. 'Ivan had thrown down the gauntlet at this strategically important point to finally demonstrate that he was still to be reckoned with.' For a long time the attacking spearhead was held up by a few rifle-men in foxholes and snipers in the trees. 'He fought with all the fierceness and stubbornness that he was capable of,' Günther remembered. Snipers hidden in treetops were knocked down by spraying the fir crowns with machine-gun fire. Several squads from the 3rd Rifle Company enveloped the foxholes on the ground, which were fought over to the death.

'Riding point' in a motorcycle advance 'was a difficult assignment,' Günther explained, 'possibly even the hardest'. The first four motorcyclists went forward, dispersed widely and covering each other, with the first machine crew regarded as 'bait'. 'Can you imagine what that did to your nerves?' Günther asked. 'Not knowing whether the enemy sat with weapons at the ready behind the next curve, the next ridge or the next clump of brush?'

'There couldn't be any lengthy shilly-shallying around,' because a smooth operation at point affected the momentum of the entire battalion and in turn the division. Risks had to be accepted. If the road and terrain to left and right could be observed and covered from behind 'we opened the throttle and sped up'. When the situation looked doubtful, the lone machine-gun sidecar up front would advance at such a speed that enabled the rider to wrench the machine about immediately if he came under fire:

> It goes without saying that the machine gunner had his finger on the trigger and was ready to jump from the sidecar with half his butt hanging on the edge and that the man on the buddy seat of the solo machine had both legs swung out to the left.

'The riders had it worse when the first shots came.' Riflemen could dive quickly into a ditch or roll into cover. 'There were machine gunners who were already firing their guns as they were still falling.' It was up to the squad leader, if he survived, to make a quick estimate while riflemen provided covering fire. Riders had either to leap from the machine, which invariably damaged it, or have sufficient presence of mind to stay in the saddle and take evasive action by turning, accelerating into the next available cover or curve in the road. Riding point was a 'risky mission of honour'. Cunning NCOs 'had a nose for dangerous positions' and such *alte hasen* (veteran 'old hares') tended to be selected for point. This did not promote longevity, but was often a dispassionate command decision, to maintain the momentum of the advance, which likely saved casualties in the long term. But, as Günther commented, the advance on Mozhaisk 'had long since ceased to be a skirmish conducted by a leading element. Now the attack was being conducted according to all the rules of tactics.'[4]

The *SS* advance coming up from the south-west was starting to evolve into deliberate company-size attacks on key road intersections, often preceded by two *Sturmgeschütz III* self-propelled assault guns. By 3 p.m. the I Battalion *Deutschland* had reached Novosurino, just short of the southern suburbs of Mozhaisk. Bittrich, the new division commander, had established his command post at Sobolki, where he was joined by *Generaloberst* Hoepner, commanding *Panzergruppe 4*. Two hours later, General Stumme, the *XXXX Korps* leader, also turned up in anticipation of decisive progress at last.

Capturing Mozhaisk would provide a bridgehead across the Moskva river and could provide a final jumping-off point for a meaningful advance against Moscow, 70 miles away. The *Deutschland* Regiment, depleted by casualties to about half its strength, was nearing the end of its tether. Together with the assault guns, the I and III Battalions began to attack the highway road intersections, south and south-west of the city.

Earlier that afternoon, the tanks of the II *Abteilung* from Panzer Regiment 7 and von Hauenschild's *Schützen* Regiment 86 began their west–east thrust along the Mozhaisk road into the city, having traversed the woods to the west of Kukarino. The panzers bypassed an anti-tank ditch at spot height 211 to the north, evading any enemy contact, and reached the main road, entering the city from the north-west. At 4 p.m., Regiment 86's infantry broke through the crust of the Soviet defence on the western outskirts, enabling the panzers to drive through at some speed to secure the eastern suburbs of Tschertanovo inside thirty minutes. *Schützen* Regiment 69, preceded by its 6th Company mounted on armoured halftracks, attempted a *coup de main* attack on the Moskva river bridge at Ilinskoje, but it was blown in their faces by the retreating Soviets. Undeterred, the German infantry forded the river and established a bridgehead on the east bank. As 10th Panzer motored through the city, they finally learned that the *SS Reich* infantry were coming up through the southern suburbs. The 10th Panzer screened off the eastern edge of Tschertanovo and fought off a hastily mounted Soviet tank counter-attack, knocking out four from eight approaching tanks. By 6 p.m. Mozhaisk was in German hands.

The cost of the six-day battle, for only one part of the Mozhaisk line, but the most direct route to Moscow, had been high. *SS Reich* suffered 1,242 casualties, of which 270 had died. The 10th Panzer had 776 casualties, with 167 killed, and probably about fifty tanks destroyed and many damaged – about one-third of its start-state strength. This was the first time a panzer unit had tried to breach a defensive zone, with such a high density of Soviet anti-tank mines, covered by 57mm and the highly effective 76.2mm anti-tank guns. Colonel Polosukhin's 32nd Division and the 20th Soviet Tank Brigade was reduced by 60 per cent losses, rendering the best parts of the Soviet Fifth Army barring the direct approaches to Moscow largely combat ineffective. With the Germans 70 miles from the capital's outskirts, the Fifth Army was down to about twenty tanks and five reduced-strength rifle divisions barring the main highway. Thee days later, the 82nd Motorised Rifle Division began arriving from the Far East by rail, restoring at least one full-strength unit to the Fifth Army's order of battle. As Helmut Günther, with the *Kradschützen* Battalion *Reich*, saw it, 'We knew now that there would be no easy advance to Moscow.' Bloody fighting over the last six days suggested 'somewhere ahead of us, the Russians would make another stand'.[5]

German soldiers were acutely aware that Napoleon had passed through here 129 years before. Ludwig Horn's *Kriegs errinerungen* (wartime memories) recorded in his 10th Panzer photograph album shows a picture of men from his artillery battery huddled over a fire 'near Borodino'. 'A village known to us,' he notes, 'because of the narrow victory there of Napoleon's forces over the Russians led by General Kutuzov in 1812. The victory allowed Napoleon to occupy Moscow – just seventy miles away.'

Albrecht Adam, who accompanied the French General Eugène's IV Corps staff in 1812, observed what he called Zvenigorod Abbey in Mozhaisk on 10 September 1812. 'This abbey dominated the River Moskva,' he wrote; French soldiers were encamped outside. 'With its twenty-foot high and six foot thick crenellated walls and four towers on each corner of the battlements, it seemed a fortress.' German radio operator Wilhelm Schröder, with the 10th Panzer Division, likewise recalled, 'I was impressed by the beauty of the church,' when they occupied Mozhaisk on the evening of 18 October 1941:

which, standing in the snow-covered town at twilight, formed a wonderful picture, its outline etched against a stark winter sky. All around it the buildings were in flames.

It was quite likely the same structure.[6]

The German occupation of Mozhaisk was as uncompromising as the fighting. Nothing was allowed to get in the way. 'On the third day after the Germans occupied Mozhaisk,' recalled schoolteacher Mrs Nikoloyeva, 'my husband of 30 years was walking along the street when a group of German officers and soldiers arrested him on suspicion of giving signals to Soviet aircraft.' He taught mathematics at the Number One Secondary

School. 'Despite his explanations, he was taken to the nearest bomb shelter and cruelly shot,' she remembered. 'During the German occupation of our town we lived in total fear and humiliation. We witnessed all kinds of atrocities and abuse.'[7]

As darkness fell, General Fischer relocated the 10th Panzer headquarters to Novaya Derevnya, 3 miles away, in the village where Regiment 86 had assembled before its assault on Mozhaisk. The weather was getting worse. Since midday, temperatures had risen and snow turned from sleet to rain. The division headquarters vehicles finally struggled or were towed across muddy pothole-filled roads to Novaya Derevnya, satisfied they had achieved their operational objective. Throughout the night, artillery, anti-tank and an infantry headquarters all co-located their unit headquarters with that of the division. Joint planning was now needed to conduct a further advance.

The retreating 322 Soviet Regiment had lost up to 70 per cent of its personnel. Captain Sherbakov, who had previously defended at Shevardino, was tasked to counter-attack Novaya Derevnya to 'rout the enemy and draw together our own units'. Ivan Barchuk remembered, 'The Germans having captured the village, deployed as if they owned the place.' The Russians observed vehicles parked up on the east side of the village, loaded with rations and looted goods from the towns and villages through which they had passed. 'The "robber army" was moving forward almost with no hindrance,' he recalled grimly. Very flares shot up constantly from German outposts surrounding the village to provide security. The village was on a hill and Sherbakov's men approached stealthily through a hollow in a rye field, 'keeping quiet' having waded the Moskva river, removing boots and winding puttees around their bodies to keep them dry, 'ensuring mess tins, helmets and weapons did not bang together'. 'We enveloped the village in a half circle,' Barchuk remembered. The attack signal was the launch of two green flares. 'We could hear squeaks, the babble of people's voices, happy songs, laughter and humming.' Contrary to German accounts, claiming total exhaustion, Barchuk was convinced 'the Nazis had gathered the young women and girls and were reveling and drinking vodka'.

A reconnaissance group, who infiltrated forward to pick off the guards, preceded them. At 10 p.m. German sentries spotted movement and shadowy figures at the western entrance to the village and raised the alarm.

Grenades were posted rapidly through windows, which on detonation triggered the release of the two green flares. Russian soldiers scrambled into the houses from the north and west amid a flurry of rifle fire and more exploding grenades. Barchuk claimed some of the attackers drove in on vehicles. 'The order was not to take prisoners,' he recalled, 'and to set fire to the parked vehicles.' These burst into flames and illuminated the whole area. Russian soldiers quickly occupied most of the village, but fire was soon returned, according to the official 10th Panzer account 'from the general to the lowliest driver'. Crouched behind doorways and window-sills everywhere, officers, NCOs and soldiers grabbed their weapons and were soon engaged in bitter hand-to-hand fighting.

In the ambient light reflected from the burning buildings, German assault teams formed up and began to clear the village centre, supported by two armoured cars firing 20mm cannon point-blank against muzzle flashes spitting out from the shadowy houses. Amid the total confusion, General Fischer, the 10th Panzer commander, stood pistol in hand on the village street, trying to rally resistance. With ever-increasing numbers of Soviet attackers, Fischer summoned panzer support by radio from Mozhaisk, 3 miles away. The 2nd Panzer Company was alarmed from its billets in the city and dispatched, followed by another company at 2 a.m. when the situation was still not stabilised. *XXXX Panzer Korps* was informed at 1.35 a.m. that 'HQ 10th Panzer and other headquarters heavily engaged since 22.00'. They had suffered 'heavy casualties' and the 'headquarters is temporarily immobilised'.

Barchuk remembered, 'The enemy did not come to their senses imme-diately.' Panzers started to appear and as they 'began to break cover our 45mm anti-tank guns destroyed them'. Mortar and artillery fire rained down as 'light snow began to fall'.

'A difficult situation got even more complex,' as 'the Germans set up machine guns in house attics and began firing on their attackers with tracer rounds'. Terse radio messages received by *XXXX Korps* reported 'fighting still in progress around the division HQ' at 03.15. At 04.09 there were 'continued firefights' and 'two to three enemy tanks' reported. By 06.22 'heavy casualties' were becoming apparent, while other units were also being engaged, where 'attacks supported by tanks beaten off'. Finally, they were tersely informed, 'mopping up in progress'.

Barchuk remembered duelling with a German panzer that periodically forayed out from 'a bath house or a shed' and 'fired at us with its cannon and machine gun'. The confused battle raged on throughout the night, but with daylight 'the Germans were on top':

> Against an unbroken wall of fire, it was not possible to hold out. Command of the fighting broke down, ammunition had been consumed, guns and mortars lost and the majority of soldiers and commanders were dead or wounded.

Sherbakov ordered sheaves of corn set on fire to cloak the retreat with smoke. The only way to get out, Barchuk remembered, due to the isolated location of the village hilltop position, 'was by leopard crawling along the furrows that remained in the ploughed field … That is how we were protected from enemy fire and withdrew.'

It was a close call for the Germans; the headquarters had been complacent following its successful advance. They 'had saved their skins' the official report commented, 'but barely': fifty-eight men were seriously wounded, and there was no official count of dead. The village was completely wrecked and in the morning General Fischer led his chastened and badly mauled command post elements into Mozhaisk. They still retained the initiative for further eastward advances, but had been reminded the Soviets could still seriously bite.[8]

Generaloberst Hoepner felt utterly thwarted by the weather and the tenacity of the Soviet defence. A thaw was setting in and it rained all day on 19 October. *XXXX Korps* gave its two motorised divisions a day of rest and postponed the next planned attack until 21 October. 'I have been stuck here for the last six days,' Hoepner complained. 'With the roads in such a terrible state we can only move slowly.' The 10th Panzer's logistics officer had to form a towing detachment of open-topped obsolete Panzer I chassis, in effect tractors on tracks. 'According to various reports, there are approximately 1,000 vehicles stuck on the Juchnow-Gzhatsk road,' the logistics officer recalled, 'including about 100 belonging to the division.' They set to work five days later. His corps supply chief echoed the same concerns. Between Yelnya and near Mozhaisk:

There are muddy holes 5 to 6 feet deep. In most places the road surface is covered with mud 1½ to 2 feet deep, which means that not only are the vehicles up to the axles in mud, but in most cases up to the chassis.

Towing vehicles out created such resistance in the cloying mud 'that bumpers are torn off, radiators are pushed upward and oil tanks cracked etc'. Virtually all the vehicles pulled out were so damaged by the tow that they needed repairs before they could be used, further draining spare parts.

It was not just the weather slowing momentum, as Hoepner explained: 'The resistance from Moscow's defenders has been far stronger than I expected.' The heady days after the huge encirclement battles at Vyazma and Bryansk were gone. The Russians were retreating again, but were doing so in good order, a few miles at a time. Over these six days the Germans had only advanced 6 to 8 miles across a 6-mile front. From now on the daily advance, which had been 18 to 24 miles a day at the beginning of October, sank to some 3 miles a day after Borodino. Polosukhin's 32nd Division had acted as a brake. Hoepner complained:

> The Russians have brought up a fresh division from the Far East and thrown new tank brigades, containing hundreds of tanks, into the battle – it is quite incredible. I had a really tough fight on my hands at Moghaisk, on the main motor highway to Moscow, where the strongest defences are. The Russians here fought with remarkable courage.[9]

Colonel Polosukhin was ordered by the Fifth Army to withdraw his depleted remnants from the 113th and 322nd Rifle Regiments and what was left of the 18th, 19th and 20th Tank Brigades across the Moskva river. The 113th provided a rearguard. Further south, Vorbiev, the defender of Artyomki, fell back with the 17th Rifle Regiment survivors, the reconnaissance battalion, the remaining howitzers, anti-aircraft units and the Lenin Cadets across the Mzhum river, screened by the 36th Motorcycle Regiment. Despite being at only 40 per cent strength, the core remained intact and a new line was occupied from Teterino and Glasvovo, ready to resist any German attempts to cross the river.

And still it rained; snow transformed to slush and then to mud. Ironically, 129 years before, Napoleon had departed Moscow on 19 October in fine autumn weather. The *Grande Armée* headed west, out of the Kaluga Gate towards its eventual annihilation. The weather was so bad on the same day in 1941 that both 10th Panzer and *Das Reich* remained static, patrolling and improving positions. It rained again all the next day, so much so that those in shelter remained in their quarters, cleaning weapons, repairing vehicles and waiting for their logistics to catch up. *XXXX Korps* postponed any further advance until 21 October.

Men were exhausted and vehicles and equipment worn out.

Mozhaisk to Moscow, 8–14 September 1812

An inclement cloudy dawn with a cold northwesterly wind brought realisation, even to the rank and file of the *Grande Armée*, that their ordeal was far from over yet. It was a depressing start to the new day. An indecisive outcome to such an important battle so far from home was tantamount to a failed one. Those lost represented the cream of the combat arms, especially its quality leaders. Apart from the fallen forty-eight generals, well forward and almost by definition inspirational, eighty-six aides and thirty staff officers had gone. The initial leadership vacuum was especially acute in line units. Such men were not easily replaced. Of 316 line battalion or cavalry equivalent commanders, 103 had been wounded and another twenty-four killed, while thirty-seven colonels and sixty majors had fallen.

The shocked stupor that came with the sweeping away of so many comrades in the line was accentuated by the disorganisation that came with identifying who had survived and was suitable for promotion and who needed to be replaced. Albrecht Adam recalled poignant scenes the day after the battle: 'officers and NCOs, commanding handfuls of soldiers remained around the colours, clothes were battle torn and stained with powder and drenched with blood.' Moscow may have been only 75 miles distant, but there was little impetus to take up the pursuit of the Russians. 'I felt paralysed,' Adam recalled, viewing the battlefield at dawn. 'Only by calling to mind the countless other horrors I had been witness to in this frightful campaign, could I shake myself from my stupor.'[10]

It took the best part of the morning to assemble Murat's vanguard: two cuirassier divisions, some light cavalry regiments and two brigades, all that was left of – the now wounded – Friant's 2nd Infantry Division. The Russian army had pulled back about 8 miles to high ground behind Mozhaisk. By early afternoon the distant rumble of guns in that direction indicated the Russian rearguard was offering more resistance than anyone thought possible. The Russians may have been beaten, but they were not routed. Murat attacked recklessly with his much-depleted cavalry squadrons, convinced that taking Mozhaisk by the Moskva river, at the centre of a plain criss-crossed by ravines, would be a walkover. Russian grapeshot delivered at point-blank range suggested otherwise. 'The cavalry lost a lot of men in this affair,' recalled Colonel Griois, providing artillery support. The intention had been to base Napoleon's headquarters at Mozhaisk that night, but it did not happen. Two regiments pushed four *voltigeur* companies into its suburbs, but they were resisted bitterly by the Russian rearguard, who sought to evacuate as many of their wounded from Borodino as possible. When Napoleon arrived the town was blazing. 'So the Russians are still holding out?' he asked stoically. It was still 70 miles to Moscow and the campfires of some 40,000 men lit up the outline of the town from the high ground beyond. 'This sight proved both the incompleteness of his victory,' de Ségur observed, 'and the enemy's unshaken courage.' Flurries of snow started to come down in the ambient light; it was depressing. Napoleon spent the night at Kukarino, about a mile away.

His cold had worsened and he became increasingly introspect, 'very thoughtful and worried,' de Ségur remembered:

> He kept saying: 'Peace lies in Moscow. When the great nobles see us master of their capital they'll think twice before fighting on. The battle will open my brother Alexander's eyes, and the capture of Moscow will open his nobles.'

By dawn the Russian rearguard had broken clean again. After some fitful skirmishing, the French entered, capturing a large magazine and a store stocked with *eau de vie*, namely vodka. This was quickly shared out before the Imperial Guard purloined it. Russian wounded lay everywhere and dead bodies were tipped ignominiously out of windows to make room for even more fresh casualties. They were in such numbers, lying in rows inside the gardens, that the Russians did not set fire to the buildings. But when the French marched in, incendiary shells were lobbed in from the high ground, which did set fire to them. These being 'entirely built of wood,' de Ségur observed, 'roasted many of their own wounded'.

A group of fifty light infantrymen from the 33rd Line rashly scaled the heights behind Mozhaisk, to maintain the pursuit, much to the amazement of the *Grande Armée* assembled below. After 'taunting thousands of Russians with their fire', de Ségur recalled, they were immediately enfolded by masses of cavalry and 'disappeared from sight'. 'A tremendous groan rose from our ranks,' he remembered, and all craned their necks to see what would happen. 'Some cursed the distance, and wanted to go to help them.' It had been a reckless act, with the uncertainty prolonged by 'a few puffs of smoke rising from the centre of this mass'. This was superseded by some elation when it was realised the light infantrymen had formed square and were fighting back. 'As soon as the Russians saw that we were making serious preparations for a general attack,' de Ségur observed, 'they disappeared, without leaving a trace behind them, as they had done at Vitebsk and Smolensk.' The officer in charge of the light infantrymen had simply shot and killed the Russian officer, who approached with an offer of surrender. Napoleon's headquarters stayed in Mozhaisk for three days.[11]

Major C.F.M. le Roy, with the 85th Line, like many of his contemporaries, likened the advance towards Moscow to a respectful follow-up, rather than a speedy pursuit, with the Russians, 'at each position turning about and sacrificing some men to prevent a rout,' he assessed, 'which would have become unavoidable if he'd let himself be pressed too hard'. Lieutenant Faber du Faur, with the Württemberg artillery, remembered 'crowds of wounded from both armies scattered in countless villages after the battle of Borodino' lining the main road to Moscow from Mozhaisk.

> Sooner or later these villages, either by chance or deliberately, burnt to the ground. It was then that these unfortunates, unable to flee on account of their wounds, found themselves at the mercy of the flames. It was not unusual to find charred corpses laid out on floors in serried lines. Those that survived, some horribly mutilated, sought some means to prolong their pitiful existence.[12]

The army moved in three columns: Napoleon headed by Murat's vanguard pursued along the main Smolensk road. Prince Poniatowski's V Corps followed the Kaluga road and Eugène's IV Corps the Zvenigorod road on the left flank. 'For my part I was surprised to see the discipline, the good order reigning in a beaten army,' le Roy admitted:

> Being myself in the advance guard, I can affirm that I never once saw a single cart, not a horse, in a word not one single Russian soldier abandoned or straggling. [13]

The local infrastructure appeared to improve as they neared the capital. 'The road to Moscow is a masterpiece,' Cuirassier Captain Jean Bréaut des Marlots declared, 'you can march along it ten vehicles abreast.'

'We in the advance guard were making thirty to thirty-five miles a day,' Spanish Colonel Tschudi remembered. They had to be on their guard, because there were frequent clashes with Cossacks en route. 'In the evening we lay down regularly in square,' Tschudi explained, 'having two ranks alternating on their feet and one sitting down.' On 11 September three regiments of Russian cavalry suddenly attacked the 33rd Line's 2nd Battalion. The depleted 176 men remaining in the battalion formed square and unhorsed more than seventy-six Cossacks in a point-blank volley that left thirty-three bodies on the field.

Lieutenant du Faur felt they were 'approaching the great city' when they noticed houses 'which strongly resembled Swiss houses in architecture and decoration'. Unlike the majority they had passed, these 'had ornate glazed windows' and 'the interiors also suggested a certain level of opulence and a sophistication hitherto lacking'. Despite constant harassment and skirmishes from rearguards, there was no concerted second stand. Roads at 22 miles and then 19-mile points before Moscow were 'clogged with the wounded and the dying' from both sides, du Faur described. 'Few of the wounded would survive for long,' he explained:

> They would succumb to want of all kinds, or would die miserably in burning houses, or would fall under the blows of enraged peasants, bands of whom were roaming the area.

Du Faur recalled wounded or dismounted French Hussars, who 'unable to grasp the danger of their situation, and too short-sighted in their temporary security', refused his artillery detachment shelter for the night, and even 'rejoiced at our prompt departure'. The next morning he remembered 'a strong force of Cossacks descended on the village and massacred all those unable to flee'.[14]

On 13 September Napoleon temporarily halted the three columns. His cavalry, exhausted after Borodino, was incapable of conducting far-ranging reconnaissance. The Emperor was not only uninformed about Kutuzov's intentions, he did not know where he was. Napoleon had no idea what sort of dispatch Kutuzov had sent the Tsar after the battle. The Russians showed no indication they would stand and neither were armistice proposals forthcoming. It was perhaps conceivable the main Russian army was not even withdrawing on Moscow, but had turned south to Kaluga. Colbert's lancer brigade was sent to cut the road and investigate but found no trace of the enemy. Napoleon resumed the march, with some anxiety. If the Russians were indeed falling back on Moscow, why did they not offer battle?

Kutuzov openly voiced an opinion: 'The Russian Army must have another decisive battle under the walls of Moscow,' but was actually weighing his options. A potential battle site was identified near Poklonnaya Gora, a few miles from the capital. The area was, however, too wide for Kutuzov's diminished force, which had still to receive reinforcements. General Barclay de Tolly was dismissive about the cobweb of ravines and gullies being considered. 'You see what they want to do,' he complained to Rostopchin, the Governor of Moscow, who had anxiously come forward to ascertain the fate of his city. Pointing out the ground, de Tolly declared, 'The only thing I desire is to be killed if we are mad enough to fight here where we are.' Prior to Borodino such a position would not have been spared a glance, but now they were fast running out of options. Kutuzov cannily called a council of war at the nearby village of Fili, where the ten senior officers co-opted decided they should stand and fight. Kutuzov shrewdly invited comment, but opted for retreat, explaining 'the loss of Moscow does not mean the loss of Russia'. In hindsight, this was the only clear-sighted decision Kutuzov took throughout the entire 1812 campaign. If the Russian army continued to exist, hope of winning the war remained. The decision meant the army had first to traverse the capital itself, before moving south towards Kolamna, securing the fertile southern provinces and retaining the arsenal at Tula, the so-called 'Sheffield of Russia'. Moscow would be a sponge soaking up Napoleon's hitherto irresistible advance. General Miloradovich was appointed the commander of the rearguard to cover the move and the evacuation of about 250,000 of the city's inhabitants.

Without realising it, Moscow now lay at Napoleon's mercy. There are parallels relating to the situation in October 1941. Napoleon and Hitler were standing at the height of their respective European powers. Eighty-two days had passed since the *Grande Armée* had crossed the Nieman river. It had marched 825 miles, fought two major battles and several minor ones, including one of the bloodiest in modern times. Hitler's Army Group Centre had fought along Napoleon's same route towards Moscow, covering 600 miles in 106 days. Russian armies stood and fought at Smolensk and Borodino in 1812 and 1941, and both the invading armies arrived at the gates of Moscow wounded considerably by the pyrrhic victories they had fought to get there. The *Grande Armée* had shrunk from 450,000 men crossing the Nieman to fewer than 100,000 before Moscow. Hitler's *Ostheer* (Eastern Army) invaded the Soviet Union with some 3.6 million men and inflicted between 3 and 4 million casualties on the Russian defenders at a cost of 500,000 to itself. Another parallel was that, despite enormous losses inflicted on the Russians in 1812 and 1941, her seemingly inexhaustible manpower reserves enabled her to continue resistance to the very gates of Moscow. Similarly, despite the dismaying losses endured by the invaders, both the *Grande Armée* and *Wehrmacht* soldiers retained an unshakable faith in their Emperor and *unser Führer*. Statistics alone, however, do not reveal the fragile extent to which these casualties had eroded fighting power in both armies. It was not just about numbers. The losses had an insidious effect on willpower and motivation. Courage in battle is a bankable commodity, and commanders have to be sensitive about how much they spend and how to replenish it. In both September 1812 and October 1941 the psychological, physical and emotional reserves of both armies was tested severely – in essence they were being 'victored' to death.

Württemberger soldier Johann Wärncke wrote to his father from Mozhaisk in October 1812 describing how 'we are now a small army'. His regiment was down to 150 men, and 'the whole cavalry is lost':

> I don't know what else to write except that you will shortly see many cripples without arm and leg and so many must die pitifully of hunger and terrible dangers.

He ominously commented how the 'Russians appear all the time for the last battle. Let's end now.' Only 18,000 of Murat's 42,000 cavalry had made it to the outskirts of Moscow. The I Corps, originally 79,000 strong, was down to 29,000. Ney's III Corps lost 33,000 from 44,000, and Poniatowski's V Corps had only 4,844 infantry and 868 cavalry left from the 39,000 that crossed the Nieman river. Even the Imperial Guard, hardly committed to battle except its artillery, had only 17,871 men left from its original contingent of 50,000. Disease and the elements had taken the rest without a shot being fired. The army converging on Moscow in September 1812 was a shadow of the epic-sized force that had set off in June.

German losses in 1941, like the French and her allies in 1812, were mainly in the combat arms. They represented a force equivalent to thirty divisions in strength, greater than the twenty-six divisions that had invaded with Army Group North. The 'teeth' or fighting soldiers in an infantry division represented 64 per cent of the whole; the remainder was logistics 'tail'. Panzer divisions were just under 50 per cent teeth. Probably about one-third of the front-line leaders of German combat units approaching Moscow during Operation *Typhoon* had already succumbed as casualties, or through exhaustion or disease. The SS *Das Reich* Division, nominally 16,860 strong, had lost 8,039 men so far in the campaign, combining from three to two regiments after Borodino. The 10th Panzer Division had lost 12 per cent of its strength in the first five weeks of the Russian campaign. It was made up in tanks and 535 men prior to *Typhoon*, before it struck the Mozhaisk defensive line at Borodino, when it lost another 776 casualties and fifty of 175 tanks. Operation *Typhoon* was fast losing momentum in late October 1941.[15]

On 14 September, the day after Kutuzov's decision to give up Moscow, Prince Eugène, with Napoleon's central column, neared the city. He rode on to high ground to monitor progress:

Several hills veiled it from our sight and all we saw were whirlwinds of dust which, parallel to our route, showed the way the *Grande Armée* was marching.

In the absence of concerted resistance, columns made good time. Bavarian Chasseur Albrecht von Muraldt, with Murat's advance guard, passed 'only cheerful faces':

As the road was very broad, artillery and infantry were marching side by side, and everyone was hurrying on with winged footsteps. Here and there, especially in the Young Guard, the cry *Vive l'Empereur!* was heard. But the old bearskins were quieter and more serious.

In Moscow, the Fili conference conclusions had yet to emerge. Lieutenant Prince Nicholas Boris-Galitsin, wounded in the head at Borodino, had arrived at the city two days earlier. 'One had only to appear in military uniform to be accosted on all sides,' he recalled, 'questioned about events, the battle of Borodino, or the likelihood of a battle at the gates of Moscow.' Unable to respond, he remained deluded by Kutuzov's insistence at Borodino that he intended to counter-attack the next day: 'I could not conceive for a moment that Moscow would be sacrificed without firing a shot in its defence,' he insisted. Yet artillery began to roll through the suburbs during the evening of the 13th, followed in the early morning hours by the infantry.

General Bennigsen, who disapproved strongly of the Fili decision, described the problems of marching an army through the suburbs:

Imagine the difficulties attending this march across a town about six miles wide, with many narrow streets – a town which nearly all the inhabitants had left or were in the process of abandoning, where the doors of the cellars, especially those of taverns, had been left open or were broken into by soldiers, servants, cartiers, hauliers, and by the lowest classes of the population, and where the least damage to a team of horses stopped the entire column in the streets!

General Miloradovich, commanding the Russian rearguard, turned up just as the streets became clogged with artillery, wagons and horses, troops and drunkards. This coincided with Murat and Eugène's advance guard entering the town by the Smolensk–Ruza road, which confronted the Russian rearguard. Miloradovich shrewdly suggested an armistice on his own initiative, for several hours, to give time for the Russians to disentangle and evacuate the city. He added if Murat should not agree, according to Bennigsen, 'He would make him pay dearly for the possession of Moscow and would not let him enter except over corpses and ashes'. Onlookers were treated to the bizarre spectacle of Russian soldiers marching unmolested through French ranks. The majority of the French army held back, believing the war must now surely be over. Few doubted that Tsar Alexander would not sue for peace with Napoleon.[16]

By mid-morning of 14 September the rest of the *Grande Armée* was closing up. Sergeant François Bourgogne, of the Imperial Guard, remembered at about one o'clock in the afternoon, 'after passing through a great forest, we saw a hill some way off':

> Part of the army reached the highest point, signalling to us who were behind, and shouting 'Moscow! Moscow!'

Napoleon ascended the Poklonnay Hill about an hour later, overlooking the old city quarter, and after pausing for thirty minutes he made his way to the Dorogomiloyskaya Gate. There was no sign of the city penitentiaries.

The 'Moscow!' cry was soon taken up and some 'quickened their step to a disorderly run,' Napoleon's aide, de Ségur, recalled. Clapping hands, they called out 'Moscow! Moscow!' 'like sailors shout "land! land!"' Many French veteran's accounts dwelt on these memories of their first sight of Moscow's spires, as did *Wehrmacht* soldiers' in 1941. German soldiers later were almost obsessed with describing how close their particular units came within sight of the capital in December. Captain Heinrich von Brandt rode up to join Napoleon's entourage on the Sparrow hills west of the city:

> Seen from the top of this last hill, Moscow had an oriental or rather, an enchanted appearance, with its five hundred domes either gilded or painted in the gaudiest colours and standing out there above a veritable sea of houses. It was a magnificent sight.

'At that sight troubles, dangers, fatigues, privations were all forgotten,' recalled Sergeant Bourgogne, 'the pleasure of entering Moscow absorbed all our minds.' The city view represented winter quarters to the soldiers, and wine, women and song.

There was not the same exhilaration among Napoleon's entourage. Von Brandt 'noticed many anxious expressions among French officers'. No official deputation had arrived to meet them. 'They will wait a long time,' one veteran remarked. 'All those Russians will emigrate to Siberia rather than surrender.' De Caulaincourt recalled the vanguard 'hadn't discovered so much as a single prominent inhabitant. All had fled.' Moscow appeared deserted. Napoleon, 'normally so impassive, showed instantly and unmistakably, the mark of bitter disappointment'. There was no surrender. Anxious and 'greatly disturbed and impatient at having to wait two hours outside the city gate,' de Caulaincourt observed, 'This report undoubtedly plunged him into the gravest reflections.' Napoleon had failed to grasp that Alexander could not negotiate without the risk of assassination or dethronement.[17]

Major Baron von Löwenstern, on the Russian staff, was acutely aware of the emotional calamity the sacrifice of Moscow entailed. 'Whereas one man grieved over the loss of his house, another regretted the loss of houses belonging to his parents and friends,' he recalled, 'while others – and they were in the majority – were preoccupied with the humiliation at seeing this ancient capital occupied by foreigners.' Sergei Glinka, with a militia regiment, was fiercely patriotic. 'How the faces of the Russian soldiers had changed between morning and evening!' he remembered. As he watched Russian soldiers filing by Kutuzov, sitting on a *droshky* cart at the eastern city gate, he recalled with frustration that 'by evening anger and grief burned in their eyes'. 'Where are we being led?' were murmured mutterings coming from the ranks. General Yermolov, Barclay de Tolly's Chief of Staff, who similarly opposed the surrender, regarded the march past thoughtfully:

I observed very carefully the effect which the abandonment of Moscow had produced on the troops, and contrary to expectation I noticed that the private soldier had not lost heart and was by no means disposed to grumble, whereas chagrin was evident in the commanders and the loss of the ancient capital had dumbfounded them.

Soldiers had no possessions or property in Moscow. Since recruitment from serfdom, the army represented family and livelihood; they went wherever they were told. General Miloradovich came across two battalions of the Moscow garrison departing with a band playing. Normally imperturbable, he demanded indignantly, 'What blackguard gave you orders that the band should play?' Lieutenant General Brozin explained that this was the convention for a garrison leaving a fortress on capitulation, as 'laid down in the regulations of Peter the Great'. 'But where in the regulations of Peter the Great,' Miloradovich growled, 'does it say anything about the surrender of Moscow?'[18]

Napoleon expected to stay in Moscow for about two weeks, to negotiate the surrender and then withdraw to his logistics base at Smolensk and wait out the winter. Polish lancer Lieutenant Carl von Wedel's column found itself halted on the Sparrow hills before entering the city:

> Then the Imperial Guard *en grande tenue* went by as if to parade. 'There is the Guard who have not fought once throughout the campaign! They are going to show off in Moscow. As for us riff-raff, we shall not even be allowed to stick our nose inside! It's a disgrace, a scandal!' shouted the officers to one another. With suppressed rage we watched this splendid, envied, favoured Guard go past, and already our fine fantasies began to melt away.

When Colonel Toll reported to General Kutuzov that the French had entered Moscow, he answered simply, 'God be praised. That is their last triumph.'[19]

As the evening twilight deepened over the city's façade, the first flames appeared flickering near the Simonov Monastery. A boat had exploded on the Moskva river carrying army stores, in turn set off by flames from a wine shop that had caught fire on the other side. Within two days, and fanned by gale-force winds, the conflagration enveloped large areas of the most inflammable city in Europe. Of Moscow's 9,000 houses, only 525 stone and 1,797 wooden structures survived intact. Tin roofs flew off building tops, like so many hot-air balloons. 'The violence of the fire which engulfed Moscow was matched by the ferocity of the French soldiers as they watched the destruction,' remembered Albrecht Adam. Widespread looting, assault, rape and wanton destruction broke out. 'Most of the looters were drunk,' Adam observed, 'and this meant that they frequently fell to quarrelling over their booty, resulting in bloody and battered faces.' Discipline visibly broke down, much to Adam's indignation:

> It had been an army previously distinguished by its fine martial bearing and its appearance, its love of order, sentiments of heroism and honour. Now it was revolting to behold.

The fire reached the Kremlin, which transitioned to an island in a sea of flame. Napoleon was forced to evacuate. Guided by his accompanying Guard through a veritable storm of sparks, he followed the passage beneath the Taynitskaya tower, past the Vsekhvyatsky stone bridge and side streets to the Petrovsky palace, before crossing again over the Moskva river. Only the Kremlin and about a quarter of the city remained undamaged. Neither the disorder nor destruction had any effect on the Russian desire to make peace. Messages and letters sent by intermediaries received no response. Napoleon dismissed the destruction of so beautiful a city as 'atrocious and useless conduct'.

Nobody surrendered, and as Lieutenant Faber du Faur expressed it, 'Moscow became the grave of our every hope.'[20]

The 10th Panzer Regiment 7 continued the advance further east toward Psaryovo village and Tatarino, heading for Mozhaisk.

The 10th Panzer advanced along the Smolensk road past Gorki village towards Borodino, penetrating the rear of the line. A German half track passes by.

The advance along the Moscow highway towards Mozhaisk continued.

The Raevsky redoubt was likened to 'a volcano crowned with vapors'. Lieutenant Heinrich Vossler described ditches 'filled to the brim with bodies'.

Constant Russian counterattacks around Semy0novskoe village kept the crumbling Russian centre intact. (Borodino Battle Musuem Panorama)

Russian soldiers wait for action 'in constant fear of death', according to Leo Tolstoy. (Borodino Battle Musuem Panorama)

The sudden appearance of General Platov's Cossacks, wheeling north and rear of the French line, briefly unhinged Napoleon's plans for a final thrust at the centre of the Russian line, uncertain about his left flank.

The earthen walls of the Raevsky redoubt had been virtually levelled by French artillery by the afternoon. (S. Troshin, Moscow)

Postscript

Roads to Moscow and Back

Roads to Moscow, 1941

As German panzers fought among monuments at Borodino Field on 16 October 1941, an uneasy panic developed in Moscow. Newspapers failed to deliver, buses, trams and trolley buses ceased to run and the Metro ground to a halt. No policemen were seen. The wildest rumours began to spread: there had been a *coup d'etat*, Stalin had been arrested and the Germans had reached Fili, where the Mozhaisk highway enters Moscow – Fili, where Kutuzov summoned a council of war 129 years before, to consider the surrender of Moscow. Dense columns of vehicles moved through checkpoints east of the city, along the Highway of Enthusiasts, where 250,000 refugees had fled in 1812. Cars passed loaded with office files and middle-level bureaucrats, who overtook many of their fellow citizens labouring through the slush on foot. The backdrop was the constant grumble of distant artillery, gradually approaching from the west. Ten-year-old Yevgeny Gromov 'always associated the 16th October with gunfire, there should not have been any at that time,' he remembered:

> But even today it sticks in my memory. It was a frightening and dreadful day, my parents had a feeling that something was going to happen.

People rushed down nearby streets 'carrying sacks; and I even remember somebody carrying a children's bath, filled with something or other'. His mother worked in the local meat factory and remembered 'that people were looting from the shop floor, and people were walking about with strings of salami around their necks'. The bakery was ransacked. People stole because they were hungry, Gromov recalled:

> There was a general feeling that the Germans would be here at any minute anyway, and so people took the bread so that they would have something to fall back on.[1]

Thirty-one-year-old mother Maya Berzina was also convinced in mid-October that the Germans were about to enter Moscow. Her husband was Jewish: 'It meant we were doomed.' No trains were running, so they were advised to leave on foot. They were desperate: 'We had a three-year-old son and what could we do with him? He was too heavy to carry and too weak to walk.' Scenes of panic abounded. 'We heard there were people who put up posters that said "Welcome"':

> We were told by the conductor on the tram that she had seen Germans on another tram – I don't know if this was true … Directors of shops opened their shops and were saying to people, 'Take what you want. We don't want the Germans to get these things.'

On 16 October the NKVD shot more than 200 people: the biggest single-day figure since the peak of the political purges in 1938. Stalin's personal telegraphist, Nikolay Ponomariev, was warned the same day to pack up his signals equipment and get ready to leave. He was picked up by one of Stalin's security guards, who responded to his query on the destination, 'You'll see when you go,' and taken to a waiting car:

> We were driven away. Moscow was completely dark. The weather was wet. I saw we were heading for the railway station. I saw the armoured train and Stalin's guards walking to and fro on the platform. It became clear to me that I would have to wait for Stalin and go into evacuation with him.

Stalin, however, decided not to go. Four days later the declaration of a state of siege in Moscow was announced. Movement on her streets was forbidden between midnight and 5 a.m. 'Those disturbing the peace'

would be swiftly handed to military tribunals, alongside any agent provocateurs, and people 'engaged in the disruption of order [and] should be
shot on the spot'.[2]

Borodino Field represented the climactic point when Operation
Typhoon ran out of steam. After the dramatic news of the fall of Mozhaisk
on 19 October, the Russians were withdrawing again, but unlike the
previous debacle at Vyazma and Bryansk, they did so in good order, a
few miles at a time. Napoleon 129 years before had marched out of
Moscow the same day, to begin his disastrous winter retreat. What did
the *Wehrmacht* achieve during the continuing advances over the next six
weeks, in the teeth of deteriorating weather? It was the same weather
Napoleon had sought to avoid by departing earlier. Napoleon's pyrrhic advance had reduced his army from nearly 500,000 men to about
95,000 when he left Moscow. The *Wehrmacht* continued to advance
despite having lost thirty divisions' worth of casualties across all three
fronts – North, Centre and South – since June.

The *SS Das Reich* and 10th Panzer Divisions moved further east,
part of the northern pincer arm seeking to encircle Moscow, consist-
ing of *Panzergruppen 3* and *4* and Ninth Infantry Army. Guderian's
Panzergruppe 2, with the Fourth and Second Infantry Armies, approached
Tula seeking to enfold Moscow with the southern pincer arm in late
November and early December 1941. *Das Reich* and 10th Panzer moved
north from the main west–east Moscow highway through Rusa, crossing the river of the same name before turning east toward Nikolskoje
and Istra in late November.

Bitter Russian resistance intensified. A myth was born, propagated
by many German post-war accounts seeking to rationalise why defeat
occurred, despite virtually having the city in its grasp. The reason, it was
explained, was the unexpected arrival of fresh Soviet Siberian divisions,
dispatched from the Far East. Soviet spy Richard Sorge was able to assure
Stalin the previous September that Japanese expansion would be directed
towards the South Pacific rather than the Russian Far East. The Siberians
were formidable opponents, who gave little and expected no quarter. *SS Untersharführer* (Corporal) Ernst Streng with the *SS Deutschland*
remembered bitter resistance by Siberians in the woods west of Nikolskoje,
as they approached Istra. After one particularly costly setback, 'I saw one

of [our] severely wounded, creeping over the snow-covered field in front of us'. They were up against the 'superbly equipped Siberian 78th Rifle Division' and watched as:

> In his pain and need he had erred somewhat in direction and was now creeping directly toward the Russian position. A long trail of blood was visible in the snow. Metre by metre he crept along on his elbows, dragging his limp body behind him. I jumped up and waved him to me with my arms to divert him from his path to destruction. He heard us shout, lifted his head from the snow, and I could clearly see through binoculars how his face lit up when he saw us. With renewed willpower he continued to creep up the gentle slope on his elbows, his lower body dragging lifelessly through the snow.

The more urgently they yelled and called, waving to their position, the faster he crawled to the waiting Siberians. When he approached to within a few metres, they shot him twice in the head. 'There was nothing we could do,' just 30m away. 'We could have screamed with rage.' Effective enemy divisions were often labelled 'Siberian' in many German veteran accounts. Streng recalled, 'Siberians gave no quarter even to an obviously defenceless, severely wounded enemy in his life or death need.'[3]

Once spy Richard Sorge had convinced Stalin that Japan would respect their existing non-aggression pact, it is frequently alleged a decisive number of Soviet divisions were dramatically transferred west, from the Far East theatre, along the trans-Siberian railway. These reinforcements sufficed to bolster Moscow's defences and set up the ensuing Soviet winter counter-offensive. A total of twenty-eight divisions were transferred westward from the start of Operation Barbarossa, until the end of 1941. Only fourteen of these were, however, moved between August and September 1941 and only four ended up on the Moscow front. The 32nd Siberian Division that fought at Borodino had in fact been diverted from Leningrad in the north. The primary reason for the stiffening of resistance in front of Moscow was less the transfer of these many divisions, and more the expansion and formation of other divisions from within the overall Soviet mobilisation plan: men from across the whole of the USSR. In essence they were a factor of seemingly inexhaustible manpower reserves.

Both sides consistently underestimated the ability of their opponents to regenerate rapidly after setbacks, throughout the war in the East.

By the beginning of December, the *SS Das Reich* had pushed further east from Istra to Lenino, near the outskirts of Moscow. According to Helmut Günther with the *Reich* motorcycle battalion:

> In our opinion, it would only be a matter of days before the division would be at Red Square in Moscow. We attacked each day. One village after another between Istra and Moscow was taken from the Ivans. We counted the kilometres to the Red capital every day: 40, 35, 30. Boy, if we just kept that up!

They had driven forward despite relentless casualties and appalling weather. Temperatures fell to sub-zero, as low as -30° to -40°C. 'The depression that had hit us after the previous fighting in the cold and snow with inadequate clothing was swept away,' Günther recalled, 'by our drive to get to Moscow.' Unit élan, ideological commitment and having never lost an offensive to date, sustained them. 'We had been the first in Belgrade, why not the same in Moscow?' They had fought their way across 670 miles of Russia, with a major digression south to Kiev in the Ukraine, to reach the capital.[4]

Russia represented the *Wehrmacht*'s longest campaign to date. Poland had taken four weeks, the Balkans three and a half and France had lasted just six weeks. At the French parallel six-week point they had formed the Smolensk pocket, but with far greater casualties. Now after 166 days, compared with Napoleon's eighty-three, they were on the verge of taking Moscow. The Russians were numerically and technically the Germans' most heavily armed opponent to date. Unlike the Poles and western Allies, the Russians had recent experience of modern operations, having occupied the Baltic states, eastern Poland and fought a winter war against the Finns. Despite the crippling purges of the officer corps in the late 1930s, the Russians had demonstrated remarkable resilience in the face of crushing defeats on the western border the previous summer.

Das Reich captured Istra during 25–27 November. Russian civilians were caught between the appalling weather and remorseless German pressure to reach Moscow. Seventeen-year-old Ludmilla Kotsowa remembered how

'Everyone had to work for the Germans, even the children, and if a child refused, he was immediately shot'. The town was extensively bombed by both sides and Kotsowa recalled, 'They lived in holes made in the ground amid ice and snow at -20°C.' A German soldier stopped her music teacher on the street 'who wanted to take her coat'. She screamed, 'You bandit!' at the soldier, who promptly and calmly shot her in the mouth. 'She was killed instantly.' The Germans would hold the town for two weeks and when the Soviets returned 'where earlier the town was, only the chimneys from the houses were still standing'. Just two buildings remained, Kotsowa claimed, and 'in January the wolves prowled through the snow amid the ruins of Istra'.[5]

German veteran and unit accounts, almost without exception, seek to establish precisely how near their units got to the Russian capital. By 3 December *Das Reich* had moved from Istra, 18 miles from the capital, to Lenino, just 10 miles away. *SS Unterscharführer* Streng recalled looking out:

> Beyond the suburbs of Moscow, giant illuminating rockets hung like so many stars of Venus, and tight bundles of searchlight beams searched the sky, back and forth.

German bombers flew overhead on raids most nights. *Obersturmbann-führer* (Lieutenant Colonel) Otto Kumm, commanding the *SS Der Führer*, remembered:

> The men of the regiment believed they could count the number of days until they entered Moscow on the fingers of one hand. In clear frosty weather the towers of the city could be seen without binoculars. A forward-emplaced 100mm battery shot harassing fire into the city.

Streng was quartered with a woman in a village who worked in Moscow, coming back each evening by train. Helmut Günther watched 'fingers' of searchlight beams from the city 'over the edge of the woods', which seemed to beckon 'come on, come over here!' 'What was 18 kilometres anyway?' he asked. 'That was nothing in this broad gigantic land!' Günther's grossly optimistic assessment of their chances of success was becoming a minority view. Even he admitted the mental pressure of combat on the soldiers was remorseless. 'When we were in the midst of a tight spot, there was no time to think about it,' he recalled:

> When it was done, one started to contemplate what could have hap-pened, but soon swept all that away. You were happy to have come through it again alive. Nobody wanted to die.[6]

On 5 December both 10th Panzer and the *Reich* divisions were only at 40 per cent of their start-state strengths. Serviceable tanks amounted to eleven light Panzer IIs, seventeen medium Panzer IIIs and eight heavy Panzer IVs with two heavy and one light command vehicles. These were sufficient to field just two weak tank companies, from an entire panzer division. The logistic 'tails' of both divisions had, meanwhile, transi-tioned from the abbreviation *mot*, meaning motorised, to *hot*, an ironic title to denote horse-drawn – the small Russian Panye horses that pulled stores on carts. The 10th Panzer was nicknamed the *10th Panye Division* by the cynics. When Ernst Streng, with the *SS Deutschland*, regarded his comrades, he did not see the optimists Günther had referred to, counting off fingers as days to reach Moscow. 'The magnificent athletic combat-hardened soldiers of the summer months had become ema-ciated by constant strain,' he recalled. 'Men who were physically and mentally exhausted':

> Gaunt faces with dark shadows around the eyes and a bitter turn to the mouth, unshaven for weeks, frozen faces. A staff in one hand, a rifle in the other, their thoughts increasingly dominated by a longing for rest back home.

These were the survivors, the 'old hands' who 'subconsciously threaded their way through every danger as if they had some sixth sense'. Despite being too tired to bother about the lice crawling on and biting their bodies, 'their senses remained instinctively alert for any danger that threatened', which 'awakened the sleepers instantly'. Fresh replacements from the homeland, Günther recalled, lasted barely days before they were 'stricken from the company roster', killed or wounded.

The remnants of the 10th Panzer Division were due to be pulled out of the line the day before the Russian counter-offensive broke. Since 12 November half of the evacuated wounded, 256 in three days, were suffering from second- or third-degree frostbite. Its soldiers had been in uninterrupted combat since 2 October. Other units committed to left and right had at least been granted some days' rest. By the third week in November, company commanders were reporting:

> Many of their men, although they had previously shown the best will, have become apathetic from the exertions and fighting, and approach their duties with complete detachment.

The unit had reached Pawschino, 6 miles from the outskirts of Moscow and 11 from the Kremlin. Apathy was becoming rife. 'Neither kind words nor a hard attitude,' a report on 4 December read, 'nor even harsher means are capable of inducing them to carry out a proper attack. When the artillery fires they move forward several paces and then stop.' Temperatures at -30°C were causing frostbite cases inside tanks 'even though the engines are kept running'. Temperatures inside the refrigerated metal boxes were dropping to -15° to -16°C. Special tank-killing squads had to be formed to deal with Soviet T-34 tanks that broke through the line, because 'the self-confidence of the troops had been shaken in recent weeks,' another report read, 'by the ineffectiveness of our anti-tank guns'. The 10th Panzer was essentially broken.[7]

A brief weak incursion was made by an understrength motorised infantry regiment from the 7th Panzer Division across the Moskva–Volga canal near Yakhroma, supported by a few tanks. A 19-year-old museum guide, Valentina Belikowa, lived in one of the outlying villages. 'Suddenly we heard vehicle noises in the night,' she remembered. She had worked with the 6,000-strong labour group that had dug anti-tank ditches nearby, 'but they came from a direction that was completely unexpected'. Factory workers still turned up for work that morning. The Germans were ejected following bitter fighting between 27 and 29 November, and blew up the iron bridge when they fell back. This was the furthest the northern pincer got to envelop the city, 37 miles from the northern outskirts.[8]

On 1 December the 2nd Vienna Panzer Division, likewise understrength, got to within 10½ miles of the outskirts of the capital, pausing at an omnibus stop at Oserezkoje along the Solnechnogarsk–Moscow road. Three days later soldiers from the division could observe everyday life in the city for its Muscovites, through an artillery 'scissor scope' near Krassnaya Polyana. They saw Soviet soldiers disembarking in the suburbs from Lobnya station, but had insufficient artillery ammunition to do anything about it. A motorcycle and jeep detachment from *Panzerpioneer Battalion 62* was ordered forward to raid the railway station. In so doing they drove unopposed through the suburbs until they reached Khimki, a small river port on the north-west outskirts of Moscow, near the present-day motorway ring. Their appearance promoted panic among the local inhabitants. Cloaked by a steadily rising winter mist, the pioneers appreciated they were overextended and retraced their footsteps, without a shot being fired. The opening was immediately reported to *Panzergruppe 4* Headquarters, but there was insufficient combat power available to exploit their remarkable penetration. It was a fifteen-minute drive from Khimki to Moscow and another quarter-hour drive to reach the Kremlin. Four days later, a massive Soviet counter-offensive burst over the Germans.

Today, three huge steel Czech 'hedgehog' tank-trap memorials stand near Khimki, on the Leningradskoye highway at 'Kilometre 23', just outside the city. It commemorates the furthest point of the German advance in 1941. The epic monument was unveiled in December 1966 for the twenty-fifth anniversary of the Russian counter-offensive. Since then it has been immersed in residential building expansion, emanating from the densely populated Moscow metropolis, which has compromised its former epic impact. Dwarfed by the IKEA shopping centre nearby, any pause for reflection needs to compete with two lanes of traffic thundering either side, en route to St Petersburg or downtown Moscow.

In 1812, Moscow was surrendered without a second stand; in 1941 resistance continued up to the city's outlying suburbs. Hitler might well have been influenced by Napoleon's experience. Both he and Napoleon felt they would be able to force a decisive battle, despite the geographical vastness of Russia. Both failed. Moscow represents only one-seventh of the distance across the Russian land mass upon entering the interior. The canny Kutuzov appreciated 'the loss of Moscow is not the loss of the motherland', instinctively appreciating its symbolic rather than physical significance. He could not afford to lose the core of his army beneath its walls, knowing Russia's inexhaustible reserves of manpower would soon enable reinforcement. The power of the Tsar's regime in 1812 lay in the land, not in its cities. The ruling nobility officered the army and provided serfs as recruits. They had a traditional hierarchical and commercial stake in the land. Firing the city was a deliberate act, with intended moral outcomes. Baron von Löwenstern, on Barclay de Tolly's staff, recalled the blaze meant 'quite spontaneously everyone forgot his personal concerns and thought only of the affront the enemy had just inflicted on us'. As the Russian army departed the city, militia soldier Sergei Glinka recalled the ranks reflected sadly 'Mother Moscow is burning'. 'Far from being disheartened,' von Löwenstern explained, 'we felt more passionately determined than ever to continue the war and to make every conceivable sacrifice.' So far as he was concerned, 'the war is only just beginning!'[9]

German soldiers in December 1941 exhibited the same wilful optimism at first as Napoleon's soldiers on their entry into Moscow in 1812. Their problems would be solved: winter quarters and a negotiated surrender. There is, however, scant evidence to suggest that Stalin would have sued for peace, even if the *Wehrmacht* had entered the city at the end of 1941. On 24 November a Russian directive was issued to the military Soviets of the various armies offering guidance 'on the defence of population centres'. Resistance in cities 'should be stubborn', the order read, 'fighting for every street, for every building' while implementing a '*maximum* scorched earth policy'. Little documentary evidence indicates any desire to surrender the city.[10]

Stalin came to power by manipulating the power apparatus of the ruling Communist Party to his own advantage. Whereas in 1812 the Tsar's power lay in the land, in 1941 the power of the Communist Party – underpinning Stalin's regime – resided in the towns and cities. It is one of the ironies of history that Hitler, who had attained the leadership of the National Socialist Party in the same way, was blind to this power base. Besieging rather than taking Leningrad enabled the power of the party to remain in the north. Losing Smolensk and Kiev meant the Communist Party could only exert influence through partisan bands in the occupied surrounding rural areas. Moscow was an industrial hub, which the party could ill afford to lose. In 1940 it produced half the country's automobiles, half of its machine tools and instruments and 40 per cent of its electrical equipment. It was the party apparatus and Stalin's determination that was to hold the city, and with it the country, during the supreme crisis in November and December 1941.

On 17 November the Stavka High Command ordered that 'all populated areas in the German rear be utterly destroyed and burned for a distance of 40 to 60 kilometres in depth from the front and 20 to 30 kilometres left and right of roads' – not dissimilar to the Tsar's scorched-earth policy in 1812. Artillery and aviation were also ordered to assist in the achievement of this. Civilian populations were to be evacuated and population centres destroyed 'so that the enemy cannot make use of them'. Fighting in urban areas generally deteriorated to a disorganised scrap of man against man and was very manpower intensive. As there appeared little intrinsic advantage in attacking or defending cities, traditional military philosophy was to avoid it. The only factors promoting advantage were determination and a willingness to sacrifice men.[11]

Stalin's great-granddaughter, Galina Djugastivili, remembered, 'They arrested all the wives of the officers who had surrendered,' adding, 'It was of course a harsh law, but these were harsh times.' Stalin's own son, Yakov, was captured during the early stages of *Barbarossa*:

My mother spent two years in prison because of this law and was later released. My grandfather did help us again later, but there could be no allowances made for the law.

There would likely be no surrender of Russia, even if Moscow was taken. Much of the city's industrial capacity was already being migrated eastward to evade the German advance. NKVD officer Vladimir Ogryzko felt 'Stalin did well, for all his deep-seated shortcomings'. In his view:

A strong man was required. They used fear to crush fear. If it was right or wrong, so what? It was a time of war and there had to be certainty.

Ogryzko commanded an NKVD unit that provided such certainty, preventing soldiers from running away by apprehending them with 'rearguard detachments'. The front was to be held whatever the cost. It was not about brutally subduing civilian panic in Moscow, although it played a part. He explained:

> These rearguard detachments played, I would say a psychological, morale-supporting role including a sense of responsibility and bolstering the front line. Once you're in battle, then it's no longer desertion, it's treason. The order went out: 'Moscow is behind us, there's no falling back!'

The battle for Moscow was to swirl over a territory the size of France and last six months, from September 1941 to April 1942. The cost, some 926,000 soldiers killed, was greater than the combined British and American totals for the entire war.[12]

Artillery Lieutenant Mark Ivanikhin marched in the 7 November annual Red Square parade that commemorated the Bolshevik Revolution, even though the German advance was near. It was a measure of Stalin's determination that he insisted the parade take place. 'It was bitterly cold and it was dark,' Ivanikhin remembered:

> I was somewhere in the fifth line on the right flank ... And I was surprised to see Stalin looked so short in his hat and ear flaps, not at all like the man we had seen in the portraits.

Alexei Rybin, part of Stalin's personal security team, remembered the march being set up. 'What parade Comrade Stalin?' asked Colonel General Pavel Artemiev, who commanded the Moscow Defence Zone. He was told to organise it, but asked, 'Where are we to get the tanks and troops?' 'You mean to tell me you haven't got any?' Stalin demanded. Artemiev tried to be more circumspect. 'Comrade Stalin, what if they bomb the parade?' he enquired. Stalin responded testily, insisting no bombers should be allowed to get through. Even so, Artemiev persisted, 'Supposing they do start bombing?' 'Then clear away the dead and the wounded and continue with the parade,' he was informed coldly.[13]

Roads Back from Moscow, 1812 and 1941

In October 1812 the French gradually realised there would be no surrender. 'During our stay in Moscow, the tomb of our hopes,' artillery Lieutenant Faber du Faur recalled:

> Those few inhabitants remaining in the city kept well away from us, as though we carried some contagious disease. They hid in the ruins or churches and spent their days like us, in worry and care, hoping for better days to come.

The surprise Russian attack that came in on 18 October 1812 was every bit as disturbing for the invaders as the sudden Russian counter-offensive in December 1941. Murat's cavalry, shaken by their losses at Borodino, had been recovering amid a beautiful landscape of oak woods and fields of standing corn when masses of Cossacks and regular cavalry, supported by artillery, burst in on their encampment at Tarutino. General Sébastiani, the new commander of the I Cavalry Corps, caught off guard, was slopping around in slippers clutching a volume of Italian verse. The badly mounted French cavalry field watch was overwhelmed quickly by the suddenness of the attack. A Prussian officer with the 1st Light Cavalry recalled, 'Only the infantry were left to withdraw in tight formations over the plain, surrounded by thick masses of Cossacks who kept up a terrible yell.' It was a debacle. 'Sometimes our troops disappeared in the throng altogether,' he recalled. Murat's vanguard was badly mauled, suffering 2,500 casualties and losing 2,000 prisoners, and thirty-eight of its 187 guns.

Under pressure from the setback, Napoleon brought forward the day of retreat. 'Victory now seemed to smile on the Russians for the first time,' du Faur recalled. 'News of these events caused joy to the inhabitants.' The following day the *Grande Armée*, reduced to 95,000 men, filed out of Moscow, with 500 guns, laden with useless booty, swarms of camp followers, 2,000 wagons and countless carts and vehicles of all kinds. They headed south-west, because Napoleon was aiming to retreat through the undevastated Ukraine. The sun shone on a fine autumn day, but there was unease. 'As we became discouraged,' du Faur remembered, 'new hope was born among the Russians.'[14]

The roads now led from Moscow. Both Napoleon and Hitler's fortunes changed at the pinnacle of hegemony over Europe. The shock was equally bad for the *Ostheer* when, starting on 6 December, three newly formed and unidentified Soviet armies, First Shock, the Twentieth and Tenth – formed from the Stavka reserve – swarmed across 60 miles of front before Moscow. The German pincer incursions north and south of the city collapsed and the Soviet air force established local air superiority, operating from the city's hardened runways. The initial intent was to eliminate the immediate threat to the capital, and then advance west, and conclusively break up the German advance so it would have no chance to regroup or dig in near the city. 'The Russians are fielding everything they've got,' revealed one captured German field post letter home, 'because around here at Moscow – the devil is loose.' It was a total surprise for the German soldier: the first major reverse of the war to date.[15]

What began now in 1812 was a catastrophic defeat for Napoleon's disintegrating *Grande Armée*, while the German *Ostheer* withdrew 60 to 150 miles in similarly painful circumstances. The haphazard nature of the Russian advances and German resistance in 1941 produced innumerable salients and encirclements for cut off units – an uncontrolled nightmare for the General Staff to control and co-ordinate. Rolling retreats and withdrawals, suddenly outflanked, produced numerous crises of confidence to conduct. Vehicle-borne troops were better off than their foot-borne infantry counterparts. Mixed up with green logistic troops, the fighting soldiers were caught up in extensive traffic jams at demolished bridges or withdrawal bottlenecks, and suffered heavily. 'One look at the infantry,' declared one 20th Panzer soldier, 'was enough to change our minds if we felt compelled to complain.' He added:

> It was astonishing what was expected of and done by them. Worst was the cold. Temperatures could change from four days at -15°C to -20°C by day and -35°C at night and then go up and be followed by a snowstorm. Those who endured it would remember it for the rest of their days. They lay in the open and were unprotected on the roads.[16]

'My God, what is this Russia going to do to us all?' asked *Gefreiter* Fritz Siegel, just as the Soviet offensive broke near Tula, in temperatures of -35°C.

'Our superiors must at least listen to us on one occasion, otherwise in this state we are going to go under.' German soldiers were tactically unused to the concept of withdrawal, having never practised it during the pre-war years. Now they had to do it in a fast-moving crisis situation. 'Discipline is beginning to let up,' reported a retreating *Panzergruppe 3* north-east of Moscow and heading west:

> There are more and more soldiers separated from their commands walking westward without weapons, leading cattle by ropes or pulling walking sledges filled with potatoes. Men killed by air bombardment are no longer buried … A psychosis bordering on panic, has gripped the baggage trains, unaccustomed to retreat, being only used to rapid advance. Service troops, too, are without rations and are cold. They are retreating in utter confusion. Among them are wounded who could no longer be sent to the rear … Traffic control elements working day and night can hardly cope any more. The Panzer Corps' most difficult hour has begun. [17]

Napoleon's 1812 retreat was not across a wide front, but down a single road. The battle at Maloyaroslavets on 26 October barred his intent to follow the more southerly route. He was obliged to turn north and retrace his footsteps along the twice-devastated approach route to Moscow from Smolensk. Borodino once again presented a deeply depressing scene, where most of the decomposing dead remained unburied. 'Here one saw again,' Württemberger foot soldier Jakob Walter remembered, 'in what numbers the dead lay.' The columns struggled on, now down to about 90,000 men. There had been an untidy start to the overladen retreat; traffic jams had led to wagons being abandoned even shortly after leaving Moscow.

By late October the Cossacks, instinctively aware of the increasingly disorderly nature of the withdrawing columns, began to actively harass them. 'Those who were too weak to carry their weapons or knapsacks threw them away,' Jakob Walter recalled, 'and all looked like a crowd of Gypsies.' The steadily diminishing *Grande Armée* fought its way through a succession of roadblocks the Russians placed in their way. The first was at Vyazma on 3 November, which resulted in the town being burned down. Then it began to snow. In the first week of November 'the army disbanded and melted away', recalled Lieutenant Faber du Faur, as 'the Russian winter finished off what starvation, exhaustion and retreat had been unable to accomplish'.[18]

The French cut their way through the second major roadblock at Krasnyi in desperate fighting between 15 and 17 November. Marshal Ney barely escaped with the remnants of his cut-off and hard-fought rearguard, during confused fighting in blizzard conditions at sub-zero temperatures. By now the army was reduced to 60,000 men. 'The greatest misery fell upon the poor sick,' Walter remembered at Krasnyi, 'who usually had to be thrown from the wagons, just to keep us from losing horses and wagons entirely.' Discarded clumps of wounded were soon obscured by snow and 'left to freeze among the enemies'.

The present-day Russian 1812 Museum located off Red Square in Moscow was established for the bicentenary in 2012. It possesses a mobile French field kitchen, one of sixty that belonged to Davout's I Corps. Most were abandoned with the cannon and baggage trains before reaching the Berezina river. It carried a stove to heat water in a boiler, placed upon a fire that burned in a metal box on the carriage. Food was prepared and placed in containers heated by water, which did not burn the contents. Cooking and reheating could be done while the army was on the move. The whole assembly was held on a two-wheeled cart and towed by a horse, with the cooking apparatus stabilised by wooden posts attached to the wagon shafts.

Wehrmacht infantry had a similar mobile equivalent that they nicknamed the *Goulash-Kanon*, or 'soup cannon'. It was more purpose-designed for cooking, with a smoke stack that resembled the barrel of a cannon. The apparatus was pulled by two horses with another two-wheeled cart attached, which was the food container. The mobile kitchen was regarded as the most important vehicle with the company *trost* baggage train. The huge 175-litre or two 60-litre kettles were filled with the available meat and vegetables in the morning and stewed as the soldiers marched. A glycerin liner inside the kettle prevented burning.

Like the 1812 equivalent, it developed an unforeseen role as the morale-boosting social collection point for infantry soldiers after a battle. Dejected survivors would gather after a bruising encounter with the enemy and commiserate. Soldiers not only came to eat, but also to bond; remnants could confide with each other and share information. It offered a haven in a perpetually hostile environment where the emotional pressures of the day might be assuaged. This was also the place where letters were handed out and announcements made. Soldiers would fight to retain their mobile kitchens as much as they might for any other piece of important military hardware.

Both armies suffered in the harsh climate. Atrocities were committed against Russian prisoners, shot or left unfed, as also were French stragglers and those unfortunate camp followers left behind. Walter recalled the treatment of Russian prisoners during the advance on Moscow, who were shot by the rearguard if they failed to keep up. 'Every fifty to a hundred paces I saw another who had been shot with his head still smoking,' he remembered. This was a deliberate policy so 'no robber corps could be formed behind us'. Those that fell out in the retreat therefore expected scant sympathy from their Russian captors. General Sir Robert Wilson, serving with the Russian staff, recalled seeing sixty dying naked men, prisoners taken at Vyazma on 5 November. Their necks had been laid out on a felled tree and they were being brained by Russian men and women with large faggot sticks, 'singing in chorus and hopping around' as 'with repeated blows' they 'struck out their brains in succession'. He was especially moved at the sight of:

> A French woman, naked to her chemise, with black, long, dishevelled hair, sitting in the snow, where she had remained the whole day and in that situation, had been delivered of a child, which had afterwards been stolen from her.[19]

Napoleon burned his pontoon train at Orsha and was then confronted with an unexpected thaw, just as he was about to extricate his army across the Berezina river. The tricky operation was compromised by a Russian column led by Tchitchagov coming up from the south-west threatening to converge with another under Wittgenstein moving in from the north. Closely following up his line of retreat was Kutuzov's force. French pioneers remarkably stood waist to neck deep in frozen water to construct a timber pontoon bridge opposite the village of Studianka. Successful deception cloaked the French army escape between 26 and 28 November, for the loss of 25,000 battle casualties and perhaps 30,000 non-combatants. Only twenty-five guns were lost.

Adolf Hitler confounded the plans of his hard-pressed General Staff on 18 December 1941 when he dispatched a teletape to Army Group Centre, which read:

> Commanding Generals, commanders and officers are to personally intervene to compel troops to fanatical resistance without regard to enemy, that may break through on their flanks or the rear.

Hitler based his decision on his First World War trench experience, aiming to minimise fluidity during the withdrawal. Soldiers caught up in the fast-moving situations that characterise a precipitate retreat are more easily controlled when instructed to stand fast. Dismayed at the impending collapse of the front, his generals were denied command initiative. In the midst of the crisis, Hitler relieved thirty generals, corps and division commanders and senior officers from command. The 'Hold Order' was regarded with incredulity at battalion level. Soldiers were told to fight and if necessary to die in place; there would be no more retreat. '*Vorwärts Kameraden, wir müssen züruck!*' (Advance men, we've got to get back!) was the black-humoured catchphrase that was voiced by desperate, embittered veterans. The front gradually coalesced and stabilised where it was, creating vulnerable salients and encirclements. Conditions in the fighting line were almost untenable. Comradeship mattered to the exclusion of all else, and inspirational leadership held units together. Draconian discipline and mutual suffering bonded men together in an inexplicable and intangible way.

Company commander *Oberleutnant* (Lieutenant) Breck-Broichsitter, with the *Gross Deutschland* Regiment, was tasked to hold a 4km-wide stretch of front with just 200 men. Despite exhaustion, he personally checked his perimeter, where on one occasion he found an isolated grenadier still heroically manning his foxhole. Twenty-four dead Russians were sprawled all around the lone trench. He had shot them with his rifle:

> He had remained completely alone at his post during a snowstorm. His relief had not turned up and despite dysentery and frostbitten

toes he stayed there a day and a night and then another day in the same position.

'I promoted him to *Gefreiter* [Corporal]', the impressed company commander remarked wryly. A campaign medal was awarded to mark the winter crisis, which had tested the stamina of the *Ostheer* to virtual breaking point. The soldiers immediately christened it 'the order of the frozen flesh'.[20]

During the 1812 and 1941 retreats both invading armies were especially susceptible to the cold during two of the severest winters recorded in Russia. Cold is indifferent in its impact, also affecting the Russians, but being native they were more familiar with its extremes. The effect was pronounced on the *Grande Armée* and Germans, denied food, shelter and most forms of sustenance. As temperatures plummeted at times to -40°C for sustained periods, alternating with brief periods of soaking thaw, everything slowed down, reducing combat capacity. Extreme cold reduced weapon muzzle velocities on both occasions. Gunpowder and propellant burns more slowly in such conditions, impairing accuracy and range. Lethargy slowed human activity. Men did not get enough to eat. The calorific intake was not enough to fuel the bursts of energy required to fight and maintain body resistance against exposure in sub-zero temperatures. Ironically, men became dehydrated even though surrounded by snow, because of their exertions and the difficulty of melting snow for water. Exhausted and inadequately clothed soldiers are more likely to freeze to death in their sleep, whereas a fit man will awaken before reaching the danger point. Junior leadership and personal grit comes to the fore. Interestingly, well-equipped modern NATO armies train soldiers to operate in temperatures down to -30°C, but discontinue activity if temperatures fall below that point. More primitively clothed soldiers endured these temperatures in 1812 and 1941, having to endure marching and fighting at -40°C and worse with the accompanying wind chill factor.

Napoleon's soldiers fighting rearguards and roadblocks in the winter of 1812 saw slow-burning artillery charges consistently drop short. Musket mechanisms jammed and froze, while barrels were susceptible to clogging up with 'fir' from unburned powder residue, causing misfires. 'Continuing the march was a terrible effort every single day,' remembered artillery

Lieutenant Faber du Faur, and 'for the gunners it was especially tough as they tried to look after their horses and save their guns'. Wheeled vehicles such as artillery caissons in 1812 or lorries in 1941 can barely move in about a foot of snow, unless it is compacted or strenuously cleared by shovel. The first artillery pieces were being abandoned on 7 November, according to du Faur, who also described the impact of rain and sudden thaws on snow conditions. 'Horses found the going difficult on the icy surface and gave up,' he recalled. Accompanying infantryman Jakob Walter remembered, 'The road became as smooth as a mirror from the rain, so that the horses fell down in great numbers and could not get up again.'[21]

Napoleonic soldiers recognised the obvious effects of extremely low temperatures, but their only solution was to wrap up more, light fires or gain access to shelter, all of which was in short supply. 'At night one could really see how much space the army still occupied,' Walter remembered. 'The fires were always visible about a two hours' march in length and about an hour's in breadth.' There was little understanding of the medical characteristics of trench foot, frostbite, hypothermia, snow blindness or dehydration, except obvious visible effects. Soldiers' faces, noses and ears – the extremities – became disfigured by frostbite and the resulting sores often turned gangrenous. They were not schooled to identify the first telltale signs of frost-nip, the precursor to frostbite, and the need to immediately thaw the affected area with a comrade's body warmth, before serious tissue damage set in. The drunken and apparently drugged antics of men affected by hypothermia were identified as either alcoholic inebriation or craziness, or simply individuals fatally succumbing to the cold. Walter saw his face in a mirror for the first time after surviving the march:

> The washing of my hands and face proceeded very slowly because the crusts on my hands, ears and nose had grown like fir bark with cracks and coal black scales.

Blackness and scales are characteristic signatures of untreated frost-nip and these ugly scars were to distinguish the Russian campaigners of 1812 and 1813 when they got back home.

'Every soldier was like an officer now,' commented Walter, because everybody was totally cocooned in clothing, 'since none of the uniforms showed any distinction in rank and no superior could command a private.' Command and control was breaking down. Walter remembered, 'Officers were beaten away from the fire just as a privates whenever they tried to press forward without merited claim,' which meant they had food or gathered firewood. Clothing is an insulator, trapping body warmth between layers, but the tight-fitting jackets and breeches of Napoleon's soldiers were totally unsuited to the temperatures. They were unable to trap warmth in between and shoes had also to be encased with insulating rags. German officers in the winter of 1941, likewise, soon ditched tight-fitting, stylish, calf-length boots for captured Russian footwear. Walter described how the army marched in this remarkable array of clothing:

> It was not possible to recognise another except by voice. Everyone was disguised in furs, rags and pieces of cloth; they wore round hats and peasant caps on their heads, and many had priest's robes from the churches. It was like a world turned upside down.

Men dressed in layers quite by chance, but sweat clogged the airspace between unwashed fibres with moisture. Marching through thick snow was the equivalent of wading through soft sand, and was as demoralising as it was exhausting. Men sweated by day in column and then froze at night. Few considered venting or opening their clothing in the extreme temperatures. Walter explained:

> I was so enwrapped that only my eyes had an opening out of which I could breathe. From time to time I had to break off from this opening the ice that would immediately form again from my breath.

They sat on the dead at night, 'converted into cushions', to insulate themselves from the snow. 'Only by marching did I overcome freezing,' he recalled. Lice lurked beneath these muffled layers of clothing. An officer companion on the march begged Walter to 'kill the tormentors in his shirt collar' as they warmed themselves by a fire. When Walter checked he looked away in disgust because 'his raw flesh showed forth where the greedy beasts had gnawed in'. What was even more dismaying was 'these pests were no less to be found on me, thousands of them'. Mass graves discovered in 2002 excavated at Vilnius in Lithuania were found to contain many dead from the *Grande Armée*. On investigation, scientists concluded that mass lice infestations and fleas likely felled more soldiers in Napoleon's retreating columns through typhus and trench fever than General Winter did.[22]

Excessive layers of clothing also complicated the process of having to defecate in freezing conditions. Jakob Walter suspected his officer companion likely froze to death when he disappeared because 'he had not been able to put on his pulled down trousers again because of the cold'. Many others had succumbed in similar fashion, 'when they had sat down because of weakness or necessity, that their clothing had been brutally torn from them and, where they could not defend themselves, they froze to death naked'. Walter had fought off one such attempt himself. Dehydration, the consequence of insufficient fluids from melted snow, caused the constipation that exposed the weak and vulnerable to such attacks. The opposite extreme was diarrhoea, caused by tainted horsemeat or impurities picked up in the snow they swallowed. Lieutenant J.L. Henckens, who temporarily commanded the remnants of the 6th Regiment of *Chasseurs à Cheval*, only ate small quantities of horsemeat, which he seasoned with gunpowder rather than salt, to neutralise the adverse effect on his bowels. His solution when he became loose was, 'I decided to slit my breeches.' Despite the impropriety:

> I had seen so many poor devils who, after performing their natural functions, were unable to pull up and fasten their breeches, while their companions either could not or would not help them.

He recalled, 'Several others followed suit.'

During the winter of 1941, infantry doctor Lieutenant Heinrich Haape saw men afflicted in the same way. Dysentery, he diagnosed, was brought on by poor food, unhygienic conditions and lice bites. The loss of copious amounts of fluid could be a death sentence in certain conditions. He observed how 'these poor fellows' despite their weakness and affliction attempted to keep up with their comrades as best they could. 'If they exposed themselves more than three or four times a day to the demands of nature,' he recalled, 'they lost more body warmth than they could afford to lose.' Soiled wet clothing could cause frostbite and death.

Without regard for the niceties, therefore, we cut a slit 10–15 centimetres long in the seat of their trousers and underpants so that they could relieve themselves without removing their garments.

Stretcher-bearers or comrades tied up the slit with string or wire until the next time. 'All the men had lost weight' by this time, Haape remembered, 'so the trousers were roomy enough to permit this solution'. History had bleakly repeated itself.[23]

Panzer soldiers were beset with problems by the intense cold. Slow-burning propellant, on firing, decreased the gun muzzle velocity and accuracy of the main armament and machine guns. Superior German telescopic sights, finely manufactured, misted up, unlike the more simple Russian variants. Visibility in snow flurries, fog and icy mist was poor in any case. Depth of snow could be an issue if ground clearance was low and depended on the weight of the armoured vehicle relative to its engine power. Wide-tracked T-34 tanks benefitted from less ground pressure and were more mobile, with more reliable diesel engines. Wearing gloves clumsily impeded fire missions involving any rapid or dexterous finger adjustments of instruments and when reloading ammunition. Carelessly placing bare hands on metal could result in torn skin left welded on to frozen hulls and surfaces. The resulting sores and flesh wounds might produce gangrenous infections if not doused in disinfectant. Tank tracks lost traction on loose snow slopes and slipped and skidded on icy roads, causing accidents by vehicle collisions or running over the tired or unwary. The only way to get tank engines to turn over in extreme cold was to light a fire beneath to thaw out the oil sump, working parts and transmissions. Petrol and oil leaks made this a vulnerable option, which in any case severely reduced the pace and tempo of operations. Fuel was in short supply and reduced the time engines could be kept running while tow-starting vehicles frozen stationary invariably damaged them. Artillery officer Lothar Fromm lamented that 'the weapons did not work any more':

Let me tell you about the recoil mechanisms of the guns. Minus 30° was seen as the lowest temperature at which efficiency could be maintained. They were frozen up. Crews stood there and tried to make them work time, and time again. It didn't happen, the barrel would not come back and the recoil mechanism was unable to move. That was really depressing.

It was worse for the infantry. Brittle metal split small-arms firing pins and it was so cold that weapons could only be 'dry cleaned' with petrol. Getting wounded in any fast-moving situation was a virtual death sentence. One infantry officer with *Schützen* Regiment 6 described the desperate retreat westward from Klin:

> Dead tired, we went from village to village. Time after time it was 'Halt! Occupy positions! Prepare to move – march!' One did not even consider rest.

They were operating in a totally alien and unknown tactical environment in sub-Arctic conditions. Condensation clouds from firing and the light mist emitted by body heat and breath was sufficient to give positions away to enemy reconnaissance. Even the noise could give them away; fighting in woodland had an unusual sonorous quality that carried for long distances in the Arctic-cooled air. Combat degenerated into bitter fighting for shelter as night fell, because failure might compromise survival if refuge was not attained.

The roads leading from Moscow in 1812 and 1941 were a virtual *Via Dolorosa* for both invading armies. 'The wind was forever blowing into our faces,' recalled infantry machine gunner Walter Neustifter, 'it crystallised the ice all over the face, in front and behind, on the nose ...' 'The most soldiers,' he recalled, 'froze to death – not shot – froze.' At temperatures below -30°C he was breaking icicles off his nose, and 'fingers', he demonstrated, tapping his hand, 'the finger was away! Real shitty!'[24]

Ironically, despite enormous suffering, both armies kept faith with their Emperor or *Führer*. Moreover, both armies in 1812 and 1941 were changed perceptibly by the ordeal. Napoleon issued his famous 29th Bulletin on 17 December, one day ahead of his eventual arrival in Paris. Regimental Commander Colonel Fezensac recalled it 'had abruptly informed France that the *Grande Armée* had been destroyed'. He described the consequences:

The emperor was invincible no longer. While we were dying in Russia, another army was perishing in Spain, and in Paris an obscure conspirator had tried to seize power.

Prussia would soon defect from Napoleon and the Austrian Alliance was shaky. Napoleon had lost his cavalry: between 130,000 and 175,000 horses had perished. This lack of cavalry was to contribute to his defeat in 1813 by Austria, Prussia, Sweden and Russia. Even at Waterloo in 1815, the French cavalry arm was a poor shadow of its former glory and effectiveness. Some 9,380 officers were lost in Russia, 2,965 of which died. Seven division generals were killed and thirty-nine wounded, twenty-two brigadier generals died and another eighty-five were wounded, as also were five marshals. This loss of high command experience was simply the tip of the iceberg alongside the moral impact of the catastrophic loss of the largest army ever before fielded in Europe. Not counted in these figures was the myriad of junior leaders and veterans – the core of Napoleon's combat effectiveness – forever lost. Those remaining were barely sufficient to form the nucleus of a future field army. This started to form up in January 1813 when Napoleon called up 250,000 conscripts. He was to admit to his minister Molé that:

> I'd been commanding the finest army of modern times. Next day, nothing of all that was left.[25]

Hitler was, likewise, not blamed for the debacle of the winter retreat of 1941. The soldiers blamed 'those at the top'. Faith remained in the *Führer*, whose actions in sacking over thirty top generals and implementing the 'Hold Order' finally stabilised the front. His innate faith in his own powers of deduction and decision that resulted was to seriously compromise the efficiency of the General Staff during the later fateful Stalingrad campaign. Blind belief in the invincible prowess of the *Wehrmacht*, which had formerly invariably delivered the impossible, was at an end. Hitler appointed himself overall commander of the *Wehrmacht* and in the process weeded out the better-trained former *Reichswehr* officers who originally crafted it and produced the instrument of *Blitzkrieg*. Men now owed allegiance to Adolf Hitler and National Socialism if they were to advance. The last vestige of Weimar and General Staff influence was gone. The *Ostheer* and *Wehrmacht* became the military arm of the National Socialist *Reich*.

Casualties in the German Army by early 1942 included about one-third of the army's junior leadership, the vital seed corn of veteran experience previously built up over two years of campaigns since Poland in 1939. National Socialism was now accepted in the loose peer pressure sense. Virtually all the veterans and leaders that had fought in the 1914–18 war had fallen out as casualties or physically and mentally infirm and been replaced. A new generation of leaders emerged in the *Wehrmacht* after 1941, primarily schooled in the unforgiving years of National Socialism rather than democratic Weimar Republicanism. Cynicism went in tandem with losses alongside the moral debilitating impact of widespread atrocities in the East, which had been extensively witnessed. This tarnished the cause for the idealistic while leaving the ideologically motivated indifferent or supportive. The main impact would be on the tactical flexibility and initiative of junior leaders that were left and those emerging. It diminished the effectiveness of *Auftragstaktik*, or mission-controlled tactics, a flexible style of command and a war winner to date. The ability to pass on risk to higher commanders prepared to salvage daring commanders, who may have overreached themselves, was gone, as was demonstrated by the decisions taken in the following year at Stalingrad. From now on, experience in the army that changed on the road to and from Moscow, was to lose ground to the Soviet ability to learn.

Infantryman Jakob Walter marched more than 1,400 miles in 1812, fought at Borodino, reached Moscow, endured the retreat, and made it back to Württemberg. Helmut Günther, with the *SS Das Reich*, probably rode the same distance as a motorcycle dispatch rider, also fought at Borodino and just fell short of reaching Moscow. His summing up of his 1941 experience probably paralleled his 1812 contemporary when he admitted, 'Most of us were so scared our assholes had slammed shut.' Walter covered the second leg of his epic march in sub-zero conditions, on shoes swaddled with rags. He complained he was unable to sleep at night 'on account of the cramps in my feet', which meant 'I could not lie still for a quarter of an hour'. One of the skeletons from Napoleon's *Grande Armée* recovered from the mass grave at Vilnius in September 2002 showed he was around 5ft 9in in height. Forensic checks revealed a healed fatigue of the third metatarsal in the long bone of his right foot. This 'march foot' was the very symptom Walter complained of, and in the case of the skeleton was thought to have been sustained during the long retreat from Moscow. The deterioration would have produced a painful swollen bulge on the foot. When Helmut Günther finally took off his boots in December 1941, he knew he was in trouble, because he could not move his toes. 'In the blink of an eye, my feet had swollen so much that I would have needed a size 27.' He had severe frostbite, 'in spite of having used the *Völkischer Beobachter*', a well-known propaganda newspaper, he wryly observed, to wrap his feet. He was evacuated on one of the last trains to escape his sector of front before it was overrun.

The experiences of Walter in 1812 and Günther in 1941 were not dissimilar. Disabled Napoleonic soldiers were to emerge begging in Western European cities with characteristic red swollen eyes from snow blindness and disfigured frostbitten noses, ears and cheeks. Only 20,000 of them made it out of Russia. Probably as many as half the starving soldiers that managed to reach temporary haven at Vilnius in mid-December died shortly after arrival. Many over-ate to assuage a hunger their digestive tracts were unable to cope with, or drank themselves into a fatal stupor. Frostbite turned gangrenous and many simply froze to death outside, on the doorsteps of many inhospitable civilians. The remains of 3,000 soldiers and camp followers were found in 2002, offering data that on occasion was quite poignant:

> Some of the men were so exhausted that they died in a crouching position, frozen on their heels. One officer was still wearing his shako on his head, decorated with a red, white and blue rosette.[26]

By the third week in January 1942 the story of Borodino and Moscow had reached full circle. Mozhaisk was liberated on the 20th after bitter hand-to-hand fighting. The next day, the Soviet 210th Motor Rifle Regiment captured Gorki, the site of Kutuzov's rather languid headquarters during the Battle of Borodino in September 1812. The obelisk commemorating the site was still standing. Artillery fire was brought down on the Russian advance from a German group covering the eastern edge of Borodino village. Soviet skiers bypassed them, but they escaped. On the 21st the villages of Artyomki and Yelnya, desperately fought over by *Das Reich* and 10th Panzer in October, were finally recaptured. Shevardino, the site of Napoleon's 1812 headquarters, was overrun the same day, as the advance continued, and they were followed by Doronino and Rogachyovo, where the *Das Reich* had first penetrated the Mozhaisk line. The Germans pulled back further from the bullet- and shrapnel-scarred monuments on Borodino field.

The museum where Colonel Polosukhin had pledged – in the visitor's book – to defend the battlefield was burned when the Germans retreated; it had been used as a slaughterhouse. They also set fire to the Monastery of the Mother Superior, established by Margarita Tuchkov in memory of her husband, General Alexander Tuchkov, whose body was never recovered in the fighting for the *flèches* in September 1812. The 32nd Rifle Division, who had conducted the second epic defence of Borodino Field, returned in resurrected form, and was still commanded by Colonel Polosukhin. They attacked south of the Moscow highway. Fifth Army's westward offensive continued until April 1942, but the German defence zone rapidly reinforced at Gzhatsk held firm. On 18 February, the 32nd Division commander, characteristically well forward conducting a reconnaissance against Gzhatsk, was killed near Ivanniki. He was buried in Mozhaisk with full military honours. He was awarded the Order of the Red Flag. General Zhukov appraised the division's fight at Borodino, 'that field, which for a long time has been a national sacred place to the immortal memory of Russian soldiers'. He added, 'the battles of the 32nd Rifle Division did not detract from this glory but enhanced it.' The unit was later awarded 'Guards' Division status, in recognition of its hard-fought reputation.[27]

The 10th Panzer Division was not relieved. Its remnants were broken down into individual 'fire-brigade' quick-reaction tank units, and used to shore up the crumbling Moscow front. It had shrunk to 50 per cent of its strength, about 8,000 men and a score of tanks, when it was withdrawn to France in April 1942, after the Moscow front had been stabilised. By this time the *SS Das Reich* Division numbered just a few hundred men when it entrained at Rzhev for Germany and reconstitution, departing two months later. The shadow of Napoleon permeated the black humour of the *Kradschützen* (motorcycle) battalion, who sang this song to the strains of 'Lili Marlene' during bleak days around Lenino and Istra in mid-December 1941:

Auf der Strasse von Moskau zieht ein Bataillion,
es sind die letzen Reste von unsrer Division.
Wir sah'n Moskau schon von ferne stehn;
Jedoch wir mussten stiften gehn,
Wie einst Napoleon, wie einst Napoleon.

On the road from Moscow comes a battalion,
It is the last of our division.
We once gazed at Moscow from afar,
Then had to bolt to save our skins,
Just like Napoleon, just like Napoleon.[28]

By early December *Das Reich* had reached Lenino, just west of Moscow, and could see the city's spires and searchlights by night.

Living conditions in the line were virtually untenable: this picture of a dugout was taken in temperatures approaching –50° Centigrade.

The Soviet winter offensive of early December 1941 fell upon a totally unsuspecting *Wehrmacht*.

The defeated columns were lashed by the coldest winter in decades.

All signs in 1812 and 1941, like this poignant picture taken in December 1941, led to Moscow. (Museum of the Great Patriotic War, Moscow)

Notes

Prologue

1   R. Braithwaite, *Moscow 1941*, Profile Books, 2006, p. 224.
2   J. Russell, TV interview, *The World at War*: 'Barbarossa', Thames TV, 1973.
3   Braithwaite, *Moscow 1941*, pp. 129–30, 133.
4   Russell and Tokati, interviews, *World at War*.
5   Figures from A. Mikaberidze, *The Battle of Borodino*, Pen and Sword, 2010, p. 218.
6   Braithwaite, *Moscow 1941*, p. 232.

The Road by Vyazma

The Vyazma Pocket, 8–9 October 1941

1   H. Günther, *Hot Motors, Cold Feet*, J.J. Fedorowicz, 2004, p. 128 and 82, 28 and 118.
2   Hümmer, Diary 7.10.41, Regimentskameradschaft , *Frontkämpfer-Hart wie Stahl, Das Regiment Deutschland 1934–1945*. Nation Europa, 1999, p. 115.
3   Hümmer, Diary 8.10.41, *Ibid*.
4   Uwe Timm, *In My Brother's Shadow*, Bloomsbury, 2005, pp. 9–10, 13, 52, 82–4, 89–90. Günther, *Hot Motors, Cold Feet*, p. 74.
5   Viewpoints and casualty figures, S. Neitzel and H. Welzer, *Soldaten*, Simon and Schuster, 2012, pp. 293–4, 296–8 and 300. 10th Pz Casualties 22 Jun–30 Sep, A. Schick, *Combat History of the 10th Panzer Division 1939–43*, J.J. Fedorowicz, 2013, p. 263. *SS Deutschland*, 24 Jun–30 Sep, O. Weidinger, *Das Reich Vol. III*, J.J. Fedorowicz, 2002. p. 68.

6   Schick, *Combat History*, p. 295.
7   Kristakov, P. Kohl, *Ich wundere mich dass ich noch lebe*,Verlaghaus Gerd Mohn Gütersloh, 1990, pp. 151–3.
8   Strazdovski, L. Rees, *War of the Century*, BBC Books, 1999, p. 65 and 67. Fuchs, Letter 9 Oct 41, *Sieg Heil!* p. 140. Schaefer-Kehnert, Rees, *War of the Century*, p. 65.
9   Horn, L. Rees, *Their Darkest Hour*, pp. 70–1, and *War of the Century*, p. 67.
10   Fuchs, Letters 12 and 15 Oct. 41, pp. 142–3. Schaefer-Kehnert, Rees, *War of the Century*, pp. 65–7. Horn, Photo album entry,Time-Life series: *The Third Reich*. Barbarossa,Time-Life, 1988, p. 140.

'A Feast of Church Towers', Vyazma, 29–31 August 1812

11   J.Walter, *The Diary of a Napoleonic Foot Soldier*, Ed. M. Raeff, p. 41 and 53.
12   Von Brandt, Ed. A. Brett-James, *1812: Eyewitness Accounts*, p. 106. De l'Ain and von Suckow, Brett-James, *1812: Eyewitness Accounts*, p. 108 and 51.Walter, *Diary*, p. 53.
13   Heinemann, P. Britten Austin, *1812:The March on Moscow*, p. 221.Walter, *Diary*, p. 43.Von Roos, Brett-James, *1812: Eyewitness Accounts*, p. 67.
14   Walter, *Diary*, p. 52. De Laugier, Britten Austin, *1812:The March on Moscow*, p. 238. A. Adam, *Napoleon's Army in Russia:The Illustrated Memoirs of Albrecht Adam 1812*, p. 120.
15   De Caulaincourt, Brett-James, *1812: Eyewitness Accounts*, pp. 109–10.
16   Walter, *Diary*, p. 45 and 47. Zotov, D. Boland, *Recollections from the Ranks*, p. 59 and 61.
17   Wilson, Brett-James, *1812: Eyewitness Accounts*, p. 73. Radozhitsky, Mikaberidze, *Russian Eyewitness Accounts of the Campaign of 1812*, p. 52 and 76. Bagration, Mikaberidze, *Russian Eyewitness*, p. 40.
18   Lejeune, Britten Austin, *1812:The March on Moscow*, p. 235. Adam, *Napoleon's Army in Russia*, p. 62.
19   Nazarov and Menshoy, Boland, *Recollections*, p. 13, 48 and 50.
20   Radozhitsky, Mikaberidze, *Russian Eyewitness*, p. 45 and 51. Antonovskii, Mikaberidze, *Russian Eyewitness*, p. 37. Nazarov, Boland, *Recollections*, p. 17.
21   Le Roy, Britten Austin, *1812:The March on Moscow*, p. 47. Dejean, Britten Austin, *1812:The March on Moscow*, p. 48. De Ségur, C. Duffy, *Borodino*, p. 33. Napoleon, Britten Austin, *1812:The March on Moscow*, p. 48.
22   H.Vossler, *With Napoleon in Russia 1812*, p. 30, 41 and 25.
23   Von Scheler, Brett-James, *1812: Eyewitness Accounts*, pp. 54–5. Fare, Brett-James, *1812: Eyewitness Accounts*, p. 63.
24   Wärncke, Letter 13 Oct 1812, Ed. M. Raeff, Appendix to *The Diary of a Napoleonic Foot Soldier*, p. 147.Von Suckow, Brett-James, 1812: *Eyewitness Accounts*, p. 51.Vossler, *With Napoleon in Russia 1812,* p. 58.
25   Du Faur, Ed. J. North, *With Napoleon in Russia, Illustrated Memoirs*, Plate Nos 41 and 42.

The Road by Gzhatsk (Gagarin)

The Moscow Highway, 8–11 October 1941

1   Hümmer, Diary 9.10.41, *Frontkämpfer-Hart Wie Stahl*, p. 123. Battalion quotes, Weidinger, *Das Reich* Vol. III, p. 91.
2   Hümmer, Diary 8.10.41 and 9.10.41, *Frontkämpfer*, pp. 122–3.
3   Windisch, Weidinger, *Das Reich* Vol. III, p. 97.
4   Günther, *Hot Motors Cold Feet*, p. 170.
5   Landgraf, audio sound recording, 9.10.41, *Auf der Autostrasse vor Moskau*. Recording from *Tief im Feindesland*, audio collection *Das Dritte Reich* German magazine series, 1975. Also Imperial War Museum Catalogue No. 8357.
6   Recce flight, W. Paul, *Die Schlacht um Moskau*, 1941–42, p. 164. Braithwaite, *Moscow 1941*, pp. 222–3.
7   Bodnar, A. Drabkin interview, *I Remember* website.
8   Hümmer, Diary, 10.10.41, *Frontkämpfer*, p. 124.
9   Heinrici, M. Jones, *The Retreat*, p. 60.
10 Veteran, Interview *Red Empire*, Yorkshire TV, 1995, from R.J. Kershaw, *War Without Garlands*, pp. 201–2.
11 Dr W. Wüster, Arty Regt 171, training in May 1942, *An Artilleryman in Stalingrad*, pp. 4–5.
12 Hümmer, Diary 11.10.41, *Frontkämpfer*, pp. 125–6. Günther, *Hot Motors, Cold Feet*, p. 79.
13 Leadership casualties, Kershaw, *War Without Garlands*, pp. 169–70 and 176.

'The Pretty Little Town of Gzhatsk', 31 August–5 September 1812

14 Napoleon and Lejeune, P.B. Britten Austin, *1812: The March on Moscow*, Vol. 1, p. 247.
15 Labaume, Britten Austin, *1812: The March on Moscow*, p. 248, P. de Ségur, *Napoleon's Russian Campaign*, pp. 47–8.
16 Interview, *The World at War: Barbarossa*, Thames TV, 1973.
17 Daru and de Ségur, Britten Austin, *1812: The March on Moscow*, p. 159.
18 Old Guard quotes, Line Officer, Anon, *Journal of the Three Days of the Battle of Waterloo*, p. 25. Joke, M. Aidken, *Waterloo Companion*, p. 197. Barbero and Hayden, Joke, M. Aidken, *Waterloo Companion*, p. 199. Numbers of Guard, Mikaberidze, *The Battle of Borodino*, p. 52. Immortals, Britten Austin, *1812: The March on Moscow*, p. 45.
19 Dupuy, Brett-James, *1812: The March on Moscow*, p. 99.
20 Yemelov, Mikaberidze, *Russian Eyewitness Accounts*, p. 158.
21 Yermelov, Mikaberidze, *Russian Eyewitness Accounts*, p. 159. Officer 16th Regt, Brett-James, *1812: Eyewitness Accounts*, pp. 100–1.
22 Von Clausewitz and Bagration, Mikaberidze, *The Battle of Borodino*, p. 24 and 25.
23 Von Clausewitz, Brett-James, *1812: Eyewitness Accounts*, pp. 112–13. Tsar, Mikaberidze, *The Battle of Borodino*, p. 21.

24   Suvorov, Mikaberidze, *The Battle of Borodino,* p. 21 and von Clausewitz and Kutuzov, p. 23. Wilson, Brett-James, *1812: Eyewitness Accounts,* p. 111.

25   Borodino site dilemma, de Tolly and Yermelov, Mikaberidze, *Russian Eyewitness,* pp. 155–6 and 161 and *Borodino,* de Tolly, pp. 25–6.

26   Du Faur, *With Napoleon in Russia,* notes plates 43, 44, 46 and 48. Von Brandt, Mikaberidze, *Borodino,* p. 22. De Ségur, *Napoleon's Russian Campaign,* pp. 53–4.

27   Durnonceau, Britten Austin, *1812: The March on Moscow,* p. 253. Vossler, *With Napoleon in Russia 1812,* p. 59.

28   Fire incident, Britten Austin, *1812: The March on Moscow,* p. 252.

29   Anon soldier, Britten Austin, *1812: The March on Moscow,* p. 253. Walter, *Diary,* p. 53. De Ségur, *Napoleon's Russian Campaign,* p. 53. French major, Aide to Gen. Louis-Pierre Count Montbrun, 2nd Cav Corps, Brett-James, *1812: Eyewitness Accounts,* p. 99.

The Road from Gzhatsk to Borodino

Moscow Behind Us! 11–14 October 1941

1   A. Drabkin, *The Red Army at War,* p. 21.

2   A. Gorbunov, Russian translated title *Moscow is Behind Us!,* Barchuk, p. 160, Kazmirov, pp. 34–5. Nechaiev, p. 127.

3   Golbraikh, Drabkin, *Red Army,* p. 22. Barchuk, Gorbunov, *Moscow is Behind Us!,* pp. 162–3.

4   Ogryzko, Rees, *War of the Century,* pp. 73–4. Beria Doc, Doc 48 to the people's Commissar of Internal Affairs SSSR General Commissioner of State Security Comrade Beria, Oct 41. Ed. A. Hill, *The Great Patriotic War of the Soviet Union 1941–45, Documentary Reader,* pp. 68–9.

5   Barchuk and Kazmirov, Gorbunov, *Moscow is Behind Us!,* p. 161 and 35.

6   Bodnar, A. Drabkin interview, *I Remember,* website.

7   Ogryzko, Rees, *War of the Century,* p. 74. Nechaiev, Gorbunov, *Moscow is Behind Us!,* p. 128. T-34 crewman, Drabkin, *Red Army,* p. 22. Tsarist General, Braithwaite, *Moscow 1941,* p. 94.

8   Alexeev, author interview, 29 Jul 2006. Kozlov, author interview, 30 Jul 2006. Malyeshev, D. Richards and L. Rees, 1st Guards Division interview, *Mother of All Battles, Kursk 1943,* BBC Timewatch, 2006.

9   Pushin, Mikaberidze, *The Battle of Borodino,* p. 27. Von Bittenfeld, Kershaw, *War Without Garlands,* p. 142.

10   Semjonowa, Diary 10 Oct 41–27 Jan 42, Kohl, *Ich wundere,* pp. 163–5. Yermolov and Glinka, Mikaberidze, *Russian Eyewitness,* p. 19 and 27.

11   Neuman, Kershaw, *War Without Garlands,* p. 142. PW figures and B. Zeiser, *In Their Shallow Graves,* Elek Books, 1956, p. 139 and 140.

12   1812 comments, Gorbunov, *Moscow is Behind Us!* Nechaiev, pp. 127–8 and 141–7, Kazmirov, p. 161. Günther, *Hot Motors, Cold Feet,* p. 134.

13   Running distances, T. Jentz, *Panzertruppen 1933–42*, Vol. 1, p. 208. Photo,
      J. Restayn and N. Moller, *The 10th Panzer Division*, p. 104.
14   Hümmer, Diary 12.10.41, *Frontkämpfer*, p. 126. Bodnar, Drabkin, *I
      Remember*, website.
15   German tactical lessons 1941, 1st and 4th Pz Div reports (22 Oct 41) and 6th
      and 33rd Pz Regts, C.J. Sharp, *German Panzer Tactics in World War II*, pp. 42–4.
16   Hümmer, Diary 12.10.41. *Frontkämpfer*, p. 126. Casualty figures, Weidinger,
      Das Reich, Vol. III, p. 109. Kazmirov, Gorbunov, *Moscow is Behind Us!*, p. 35.

Ground of 'No Particular Advantage', 5 September 1812

17   Golitsyn, Mikaberidze, *Russian Eyewitness*, p. 172. Kutuzov, Duffy, *Borodino*, p. 75.
18   Von Clausewitz and Yermolov, Mikaberidze, *The Battle of Borodino*, pp. 27–8.
19   Norov, Mikaberidze, *The Battle of Borodino*, p. 27. Mayevskii, Mikaberidze,
      Russian Eyewitness, p. 175.
20   Bogdanov, Mikaberidze, *Russian Eyewitness*, p. 166.
21   Von Clausewitz, Mikaberidze, *The Battle of Borodino*, pp. 26–7.
22   Adam, *Napoleon's Army in Russia*, p. 124. Würtemberger, Mikaberidze, *The
      Battle of Borodino*, p. 30. Von Leissing, Duffy, *Borodino*, pp. 75–6.
23   Dumenceau, Mikaberidze, *The Battle of Borodino*, p. 33.
24   Glinka, Mikaberidze, *Russian Eyewitness*, p. 185. Griois, Duffy, *Borodino*, p. 78.

The Road by Rogachyovo, Yelnya and Shevardino

Break-In, 13–14 October 1941

1   Lohaus, After-action report recce conducted by reinforced 3 Pl of 5/PzRegt 7
      and 9/SS Inf Regt 'D', 13 Oct 41, Weidinger, *Das Reich*, Vol. III, p. 110.
      Description, *Kriegsberichter* Gert Habedanck, *Die Wehrmacht* Magazine, 3 Dec 1941.
2   Lohaus, Weidinger, *Das Reich*, p. 111. Order, Weidinger, *Das Reich*, Vol. III, p. 113.
3   Ops Diary 32 Rifle Div 22.30 13 Oct. V Kroupnik translation.
4   Hümmer, Diary 13.10.41, *Frontkämpfer*, p. 127.
5   Nechaiev account, Gorbunov, *Moscow is Behind Us!*, pp. 127–47, 13 Oct, p. 2.
6   Selin, Kravchenkova OV, *Participation of the 17th Infantry Regiment in the battle
      of Borodino in Oct 1941, and memories of Veterans.* Taken from *Battles for Moscow
      on Mozhaisk Direction. Studies, Documents, Memories.* Kroupnik Trans.
7   Windisch, Weidinger, *Das Reich*, Vol. III, p. 113. Bodnar, interview, *I Remember*,
      website.
8   Selin, Kravchenkova, *Participation of the 17th Infantry Regiment*, p. 98.
9   Hümmer, Diary 13.10.41, *Frontkämpfer*, pp. 127–8.
10   Kolmakov, Kravchenkova, *Participation of the 17th Infantry Regiment*, p. 99.
11   Hümmer, Diary 13.10.41, Ivasenko and Kolmakov, Kravchenkova, *Participation
      of the 17th Infantry Regiment*, pp. 99–100. Kazmirov account, Gorbunov, *Moscow
      is Behind Us!*, p. 2.

12 XXXX Pz Korps War Diary 14 Oct 41, Weidinger, *Das Reich*, Vol. III, p. 120.
13 Windisch, Weidinger, *Das Reich*, Vol. III, p. 119. Günther, *Hot Motors, Cold Feet*, p. 171.
14 Hümmer, Diary 14.10.41, *Frontkämpfer*, pp. 128–9.
15 Op diary 32nd Rifle Division 14 Oct 41, Kroupnik trans. Baromykin, Jones, *The Retreat*, p. 61.

'What a Sham!', Shevardino, 5–6 September 1812
16 Landgraf, Imperial War Museum (IWM) sound catalogue No. 8358.
17 Yermolov, Mikaberidze, *The Battle of Borodino*, p. 34.
18 De Ségur, *Napoleon's Russian Campaign*, p. 55. Löwenstern, Mikaberidze, *The Battle of Borodino*, pp. 38–9. Observers, Duffy, *Borodino*, p. 21. Gourgourd, Mikaberidze, *The Battle of Borodino*, p. 39 and Duffy, *Borodino*, p. 79. Gorchakov, Mikaberidze, *The Battle of Borodino*, p. 40.
19 Gardier, Mikaberidze, *The Battle of Borodino*, p. 42.
20 Lamothe, Mikaberidze, *The Battle of Borodino*, p. 45. Labaume, Duffy, *Borodino*, p. 80.
21 Napoleon, Bagration and veteran, Mikaberidze, *The Battle of Borodino*, p. 47, 45 and 48. Biot, Brett-James, *1812: Eyewitness Accounts*, p. 119.
22 De Ségur, *Napoleon's Russian Campaign*, pp. 56–7.
23 Glinka and soldiers, Mikaberidze, *The Battle of Borodino*, pp. 84–5.
24 Rapp, Brett-James, *1812: Eyewitness Accounts*, p. 120 and Duffy, *Borodino*, p. 89. De Ségur and Rapp, *Napoleon's Russian Campaign*, pp. 61–3. Le Roy, Britten Austin, *1812: The March on Moscow*, p. 262. Boulart, Britten Austin, *1812: The March on Moscow*, p. 264.
25 De Ségur, *Napoleon's Russian Campaign*, p. 58. Glinka, Mikaberidze, *The Battle of Borodino*, p. 71, 76 and 87. Mitarevsky, Mikaberidze, *The Battle of Borodino*, p. 86. Capt Fritz [surname unknown], Brett-James, *1812: Eyewitness Accounts*, p. 123.
26 Brandt and Linsingen, Britten Austin, *1812: The March on Moscow*, pp. 268–9. Bourgogne, *The Retreat from Moscow*, p. 14.
27 De Metz, Mikaberidze, *The Battle of Borodino*, p. 89. Bogdanov, Duffy, *Borodino*, pp. 92–3.

The Road by Artyomki, Utitsy and Borodino Railway Station

The Stop–Start Advance, 14–15 October 1941
1 Landgraf, sound recording, *Auf dem Schlachtfeld von Borodinow*, 14 Oct 1941, IWM Catalogue No. 8358. Windisch, O Weidinger, *Das Reich*, Vol. III, pp. 113–14.
2 SS Secret Report, Ed. H. Boberach, *Meldungen aus dem Reich*, 6 Nov 1941, p. 2950.
3 Landgraf, IWM sound catalogue No. 8358.
4 Official history, Schick, *Combat History*, p. 302.

5   Chevgus, Gorbunov, *Moscow is Behind Us!*, pp. 42–3.
6   Ivasenko, Kravchenkova, *17th Regiment and the Battle of Borodino*, from *Battles for Moscow on Mozhaisk Direction*, trans. Kroupnik, p. 100.
7   Abortive Balloon Project, Mikaberidze, *The Battle of Borodino*, pp. 30–1. De Ségur, *Napoleon's Russian Campaign*, p. 91.
8   Chevgus, Gorbunov, *Moscow is Behind Us!*, pp. 42–3.
9   Kesselring, *Memoirs*, p. 95. H.U. Rudel, *Stuka Pilot*, Bantam, 1979, p. 45.
10   Kesselring, *Ibid.*, p. 96 and 97. Mahlke, *Memoirs of a Stuka Pilot*, Frontline Books, 2013, p. 249.
11   Mahlke, Ibid., pp. 238–9, 55–6 and 239–40.
12   32nd Div War Diary 14 Oct 41, trans. Kroupnik, *Battles for Moscow on Mozhaisk Direction*, pp. 133–4. Kazmirov, Gorbunov, *Moscow is Behind Us!*, p. 39.
13   Chevgus and Nechaiev, Gorbunov, *Moscow is Behind Us!*, pp. 43–6 and 132–3.
14   Barchuk, Gorbunov, *Moscow is Behind Us!*, pp. 164–5. Ivasenko, Kravchenkova, *Participation of the 17th Infantry Regiment*, p. 101.
15   Chevgus, Gorbunov, *Moscow is Behind Us!*, p. 48.
16   Kesselring, *Memoirs*, p. 96 and 97.

The Battle of the Giants, 7 September 1812

17   Tolstoy, *War and Peace*, pp. 933–4.
18   Mitarevsky, Grabbe, Yermolov and Liprandi, Mikaberidze, *The Battle of Borodino*, pp. 93–5.
19   De Tolly, Mikaberidze, *The Battle of Borodino*, p. 96.
20   Lejeune and eyewitness, Mikaberidze, *The Battle of Borodino*, p. 98.
21   De Laugier, Britten Austin, *1812: The March on Moscow*, p. 274. Petrov, Mikaberidze, *Russian Eyewitness*, p. 180. Walter, *Diary*, p. 54.
22   Petrov, Mikaberidze, *Russian Eyewitness*, p. 179.
23   Radozhitsky and Dreyling, Mikaberidze, *The Battle of Borodino*, p. 91.
24   Russian officer, Mikaberidze, *The Battle of Borodino*, p. 81. Lejeune, Britten Austin, *1812: The March on Moscow*, p. 274.
25   Lejeune, Britten Austin, *1812: The March on Moscow*, p. 275. La Faye, Mikaberidze, *The Battle of Borodino*, p. 110. Walter, *Diary*, p. 54.
26   Dutheillet and de l'Ain, Britten Austin, *1812: The March on Moscow*, pp. 275–6. Rapp, Brett-James, *1812: Eyewitness Accounts*, pp. 129–30.
27   Vorontsov, A. Zamoyski, *1812: Napoleon's Fatal March on Moscow*, pp. 268–9. Glinka, Mikaberidze, *Russian Eyewitness*, p. 187. Bagration, Mikaberidze, *Russian Eyewitness*, p. 176.
28   Poniatkowski and Karpov, Mikaberidze, *The Battle of Borodino*, p. 137 and 138.
29   Baggovut, Duffy, *Borodino*, p. 100.
30   Rostworowski and Soltyk, Mikaberidze, *The Battle of Borodino*, p. 138 and Britten Austin, *1812: The March on Moscow*, p. 308.
31   Witness, Duffy, *Borodino*, p. 106. Mayevsky, Mikaberidze, *The Battle of Borodino*, p. 123 and *Russian Eyewitness*, p. 176.

32   François, Mikaberidze, *The Battle of Borodino*. p. 124 and Austin, p. 281.
      Mitarevsky, Mikaberidze, *The Battle of Borodino*, p. 123. Raevsky, Mikaberidze,
      The Battle of Borodino, p. 124.
33   De Laugier, Griois and François, Britten Austin, *1812: Eyewitness
      Accounts*, pp. 280–1.
34   François and Griois, Britten Austin, *1812: Eyewitness Accounts*, p. 282.
      Wolzogen, Duffy, *Borodino*, p. 108.
35   Dessaix, Mikaberidze, *The Battle of Borodino*, p. 140.

The Road Through Borodino Field

The Fight Among the Monuments, 15–16 October 1941
1   Landgraf, *Auf dem Schlachtfeld von Borodino*, 29.10.41. *Wochenschau* 582.
2   Sherbakov, Gorbunov, *Moscow is Behind Us!*, pp. 134–6. German reports,
      Great Patriotic War Society research for author. 32 Div Ops log, 15 Oct,
      trans. Kroupnik.
3   Barchuk, Gorbunov, *Moscow is Behind Us!*, pp. 166–7 and Jones, *The Retreat*, p. 64.
4   Walter, *Diary*, pp. 53–4.
5   Landgraf, *Wochenschau* 582. Straub, *Geschichte des Panzer-Regiment 7*,
      unpublished manuscript, from Weidinger, *Das Reich*, Vol. III, p. 123.
6   Conditions, Weidinger, *Das Reich*, Vol. III, p. 144. Kumm, Weidinger, *Das Reich*,
      Vol. III, p. 125. Berlin Report, Weidinger, *Das Reich*, Vol. III, p. 138.
7   Barchuk, Gorbunov, *Moscow is Behind Us!*, pp. 170–1.
8   Barchuk, *Moscow is Behind Us!*, pp. 178–9. Landgraf, *Wochenschau* 582.
9   Baromykin, Jones, *The Retreat*, p. 65. 32 Div. Ops Diary, 16.10.41. Trans.
      Kroupnik. Sverdlov, Rees, *War of the Century*, p. 84.
10   German movements, Schick, *Combat History*, pp. 303–4. Sherbakov and
      Nechaiev, Gorbunov, *Moscow is Behind Us!*, p. 140, Lermontov pp. 141, 142–3
      and 145–7.
11   Sverdlov, interview, Rees, *War of the Century*, BBC TV, 1999. Barchuk,
      Gorbunov, *Moscow is Behind Us!*, pp. 173–4 and 176.
12   Barchuk, Gorbunov, *Moscow is Behind Us!*, pp. 174–9. 32 Div. Ops Diary,
      16.10.41, Kroupnik trans.
13   *SS* Berlin Report, Weidinger, *Das Reich*, Vol. III, p. 133.
14   Hoepner, Jones, *The Retreat*, p. 62.

Indecision in the Centre, 7 September 1812
15   Tolstoy, *War and Peace*, pp. 959–60. De Tolly, Mikaberidze, *The Battle of
      Borodino*, p. 106. De la Faye, Brett-James, *1812: Eyewitness Accounts*, p. 128.
16   De Brack, *Cavalry Outpost Duties*, pp. 31–2. Des Marlots, Brett-James, *1812:
      Eyewitness Accounts*, p. 129. Morgenstern, Mikaberidze, *The Battle of Borodino*,
      p. 104. Schreckenstein, Britten Austin, *1812: The March on Moscow*, p. 296.

17 Dumenceau, Britten Austin, *1812: The March on Moscow*, pp. 286–7. Divov, Mikaberidze, *Russian Eyewitness*, p. 178.
18 Von Roos, Brett-James, *1812: Eyewitness Accounts*, p. 126.
19 Wärnicke, letter Mozhaisk 13 Oct 1812 to Master Stonemason Wärnicke, Mannsfeld, Dept of Saale. From Walter, *Diary*, pp. 147–8.
20 Griois and des Marlots, Brett-James, *1812: Eyewitness Accounts,* p. 135 and 129. Bourgogne, *The Retreat from Moscow*, pp. 16–17.
21 Radozhitsky, Mikaberidze, *Russian Eyewitness*, p. 148. Glinka, Mikaberidze, *Russian Eyewitness*, pp. 145–6. Mitarevsky, Mikaberidze, *Russian Eyewitness*, p. 148. Kutuzov and Yermolov, Duffy, *Borodino*, pp. 120–1.
22 Flize and Lejeune, Britten Austin, *1812: The March on Moscow*, p. 285.
23 Von Meerheim, Duffy, *Borodino*, p. 112. Von Schreckenstein, Brett-James, *1812: Eyewitness Accounts*, pp. 124–5.
24 Konovitsyn, Mikaberidze, *Russian Eyewitness*, p. 157. Timofeyev and Glinka, Mikaberidze, *Russian Eyewitness*, p. 158.
25 Murat and 48th Line Colonel, Duffy, *Borodino*, p. 115. Ney, Mikaberidze, *Russian Eyewitness*, p. 161. Napoleon, Duffy, *Borodino*, p. 116.
26 Glinka, Mikaberidze, *Russian Eyewitness*, p. 186. De Ségur, Duffy, *Borodino*, p. 117. Zotov, Boland, *Recollections*, pp. 75–7.

The Road by Raevsky, Gorki and Tatarinovo

Supreme Effort, 17 October 1941

1   Hoepner, Jones, *The Retreat*, p. 66.
2   Günther, *Hot Motors, Cold Feet*, p. 175, 136 and 185.
3   Casualties, Kershaw, *War Without Garlands*, p. 251. *SS* Reports, Ed. H. Boberach, *Meldungen aus dem Reich*, No. 233, 30 Oct 41, p. 2929 and 2939. Also No. 234, 3 Nov 41, p. 2948.
4   Gratz, Kershaw, *War Without Garlands*, p. 175. *SS* Report, *Meldungen* No. 231, Oct 41, pp. 2914–16.
5   Barchuk, Gorbunov, *Moscow is Behind Us!*, p. 180.
6   Chevgus, Gorbunov, *Moscow is Behind Us!*, pp. 49–50.
7   Iulianovich, Interview, A. Drabkin and I. Kobylyanskiy, *Red Army Infantrymen Remember the Great Patriotic War*, pp. 75–7.
8   Günther, *Hot Motors, Cold Feet*, pp. 171–3.
9   Chevgus, Gorbunov, *Moscow is Behind Us!*, p. 50.
10 Loktionov, Gorbunov, *Moscow is Behind Us!*, pp. 51–2.
11 Landgraf, *Wochenschau* 582, 29.10.41. Chevgus, Gorbunov, *Moscow is Behind Us!*, p. 48.
12 Landgraf, Ibid.
13 *Deutschland* Numbers, *Frontkämpfer*, p. 129. Günther, *Hot Motors, Cold Feet*, p. 180. Chevgus, Gorbunov, *Moscow is Behind Us!*, p. 52.

'A Volcano Crowned with Vapours', The Raevsky Redoubt, 7 September 1812

14   Vossler, *With Napoleon in Russia 1812*, p. 67. Combe and De Metz, Mikaberidze, *The Battle of Borodino*, p. 164 and 165. Griois, Duffy, *Borodino*, p. 123. Aubry and Des Loches, Britten Austin, *1812: The March on Moscow*, p. 296.

15   Lejeune, Griois and Bertrand, Britten Austin, *1812: The March on Moscow*, p. 302.

16   Von Meerheim and Russian officer, Duffy, *Borodino*, pp. 126–7 and Mikaberidze, *The Battle of Borodino*, p. 174.

17   Griois, Zamoyski, *1812: Napoleon's Fatal March*, pp. 278–9. Berthier, Napoleon and Eugène, Britten Austin, *1812: The March on Moscow*, pp. 303–4.

18   Saxon Curassier, Britten Austin, *1812: The March on Moscow*, pp. 304–5. Napoleon, Duffy, *Borodino*, p. 131.

19   Thiron, Britten Austin, *1812: The March on Moscow*, pp. 307–8.

20   Von Clausewitz, Mikaberidze, *The Battle of Borodino*, p. 197. Von Wolzogen, Brett-James, *1812: Eyewitness Accounts*, pp. 132–3. Napoleon, Duffy, *Borodino*, p. 131.

21   Petrov, Mikaberidze, *The Battle of Borodino*, p. 198. Corner, Britten-Austin, *1812: The March on Moscow*, p. 309. Von Wolzogen, Brett-James, *1812: Eyewitness Accounts*, pp. 133–4.

22   Von Clausewitz, Zamoyski, *1812: Napoleon's Fatal March*, p. 287.

23   Bertrand and von Schreckenstein, Britten-Austin, *1812: The March on Moscow*, p. 313 and 319.

24   Günther, *Hot Motors, Cold Feet*, pp. 176–8.

25   Berthier and Murat, de Ségur, *Napoleon's Russian Campaign*, p. 78 and Duffy, *Borodino*, p. 136. De Caulaincourt, Britten-Austin, *1812: The March on Moscow*, p. 310.

26   Casualty numbers, Zamoyski, *1812: Napoleon's Fatal March*, p. 287 and Duffy, *Borodino*, p. 148. Dumonceau, Britten-Austin, *1812: The March on Moscow*, p. 311.

27   Adam, *Napoleon's Army in Russia*, p. 142. Montesquiou, Brett-James, *1812: Eyewitness Accounts*, p. 139. Labaume, Britten-Austin, *1812: The March on Moscow*, p. 316. Des Marlots, Britten-Austin, *1812: The March on Moscow*, p. 314.

The Road to Mozhaisk

The Capture of Mozhaisk, 18 October 1941

1   Baromykin, Jones, *The Retreat*, p. 67. Pastushenko, Kravchenkova, *Participation of the 17th Infantry Regiment*, p. 100 cont.

2   Horn, Ed. G. Constable, *Time-Life series: The Third Reich*. Barbarossa, Time-Life, p. 141. Wüster, *An Artilleryman in Stalingrad*, p. 18.

3   Baromykin, Jones, *The Retreat*, p. 67. Barchuk, A. Gorbunov, *Moscow is Behind Us!*, pp. 180–1.

4   Günther, *Hot Motors, Cold Feet*, pp. 181–6.

5   10th Panzer start state was 173 tanks, J. Restayn and N. Moller, *10th Panzer Division*, p. 74. Other casualty figures, R. Forczyk, *Moscow 1941*, p. 57. Günther, Jones, *The Retreat*, p. 70.

6   Adam, *Napoleon's Army in Russia*, pp. 152–3. Schröeder, Jones, *The Retreat*, pp. 69–70.

7   Nikoloyeva, Interview, P. Galan, I. Gootman, I. Grigouriev and I. Gelain, *Blood Upon the Snow*, IPB Films, 1995.

8   10th Panzer radio traffic, Schick, *Combat History*, p. 307. Barchuk, Gorbunov, *Moscow is Behind Us!*, pp. 187–9.

9   Hoepner, Jones, *The Retreat*, p. 69. 10th Pz Logistics Officer and Corps Supply Chief, Schick, *Combat History*, p. 311 and 316.

Mozhaisk to Moscow, 8–14 September 1812

10   Casualty figures, Mikaberidze, *The Battle of Borodino*, pp. 215–16. Adam, *Napoleon's Army in Russia*, p. 144 and 146.

11   Napoleon and Ségur, Britten Austin, *1812: The March on Moscow*, p. 321. De Ségur, *Napoleon's Russian Campaign*, pp. 83–4.

12   Du Faur, *With Napoleon in Russia*, Plate 54.

13   Le Roy, Britten Austin, *1812: The March on Moscow*, p. 329.

14   Des Marlots and Tschudi, Britten Austin, *1812: The March on Moscow*, p. 329. Du Faur, *With Napoleon in Russia*, Plates 55–6.

15   Casualty Figures, 1812, Britten Austin, *1812: The March on Moscow*, p. 385. 1941, Kershaw, *War Without Garlands*, p. 25 and 251. Weidinger, *Das Reich*, Vol. III, pp. 148–9. 10th Panzer, Schick, *Combat History*, p. 263 and 345.

16   Eugène and von Muraldt, Britten Austin, *1812: The March on Moscow*, p. 337. Boris-Galitsin, Brett-James, *1812: Eyewitness Accounts*, pp. 161–2. Bennigsen, Brett-James, *1812: Eyewitness Accounts*, p. 159.

17   Bourgogne, *The Retreat from Moscow*, p. 18. De Ségur, *Napoleon's Russian Campaign*, p. 97. Von Brandt and veteran, Brett-James, *1812: Eyewitness Accounts*, p. 172. De Caulaincourt, Britten Austin, *1812: The March on Moscow*, p. 345.

18   Löwenstern, Brett-James, *1812: Eyewitness Accounts*, p. 164. Glinka, Brett-James, *1812: Eyewitness Accounts*, p. 165. Miloradovich, according to A.A. Scherbinin, Quartermaster officer, Brett-James, *1812: Eyewitness Accounts*, p. 160.

19   Von Wedel and Kutuzov, Brett-James, *1812: Eyewitness Accounts*, p. 167 and 165.

20   Adam, *Napoleon's Army in Russia*, p. 164. Napoleon, Brett-James, *1812: Eyewitness Accounts*, p. 146. Du Faur, *With Napoleon in Russia*, Plate 60.

Postscript

Roads to Moscow, 1941

1 Moscow scenes, Braithwaite, *Moscow 1941*, p. 245 and 247. Gromov, Interview, *Blood Upon the Snow*, IPB Films, 1995.
2 Berzina, interview, Rees, *War of the Century*. NKVD figures, Braithwaite, p. 258. Ponomariev, L. Rees, interview, *Ibid.*, Soviet Siege Decree 19 Oct 41, Hill, *The Great Patriotic War of the Soviet Union 1941–45 Documentary Reader*, Document 51, p. 71.
3 Streng, *Frontkämpfer*, p. 132.
4 Günther, *Hot Motors, Cold Feet*, p. 207.
5 Kotsowa, interview, Kohl, *Ich wundere*, pp. 177–8.
6 Streng and Kumm, Weidinger, *Das Reich*, Vol. III, p. 222 and 224. Günther, *Hot Motors, Cold Feet*, p. 235.
7 Unit figures, Weidinger, *Das Reich*, Vol. III, p. 228 and Schick, *Combat History*, p. 365 and 319. Streng, Weidinger, *Das Reich*, Vol. III, p. 213. Company Comds, Report to XXXX Korps, Schick, *Combat History*, pp. 358–9. Apathy, Major Bürker Ops Offr 10th Pz to Organizational Department Army General Staff Berlin, 4 Dec 41, Schick, *Combat History*, p. 368.
8 Belikowa, Kohl, *Ich wundere*, p. 176.
9 Kutuzov, Glinka and Löwenstern, Brett-James, *1812: Eyewitness Accounts*, p. 165 and 164.
10 Directive, Hill, Documentary Reader, Doc 56, 24 Nov 41, p. 77.
11 Directive, Ibid., Doc 55, 17 Nov 41, p. 77.
12 Industry figures, Braithwaite, *Moscow 1941*, p. 22. Djugashvili, interview, *Blood Upon the Snow*, IPB Films, 1995. Ogryzko, interview, Rees, *Their Darkest Hour*, p. 156. Casualties, Braithwaite, *Moscow 1941*, p. 7.
13 Ivanikhin and Artemiev, interviews, *Blood Upon the Snow*.

Roads Back from Moscow, 1812 and 1941

14 Tarutino Prussian Officer, Duffy, *Borodino*, p. 151. Du Faur, *With Napoleon in Russia*, Plate 70.
15 Field Post letter, Golovchansky, Osipov, Prokopenko, Daniel and Reulecke, *Ich will raus aus diesem Wahnsinn*, p. 47.
16 20th Panzer Soldier, R. Hinze, *Hitze, Frost und Pulverdampf*, p. 101.
17 *PzAOK 3 Gefechtsbericht Russland 1941–42*, 22 Dec. 41. From Kershaw, *War Without Garlands*, p. 228.
18 Walter, *Diary*, p. 62 and 60. Du Faur, *With Napoleon in Russia*, Plate 74.
19 Walter, *Diary*, p. 68. Wilson, Brett-James, *1812: Eyewitness Accounts*, p. 222.
20 Hitler and Beck-Broichsitter, Kershaw, *War Without Garlands*, p. 232 and 236.
21 Du Faur, *With Napoleon in Russia*, Plate 74. Walter, *Diary*, p. 68.

22 Walter, *Diary*, pp. 90, 100–1, 75, 71–2, 87, and 78. Mass Graves, Vilnius, D. Raoult and P.E. Fournier, National Scientific Research Centre Marseille, *Guardian* News Media, 2008.

23 Henckens, Brett-James, *1812: Eyewitness Accounts*, p. 272. H. Haape, *Moscow Tram Stop*, p. 213 and 233.

24 Fromm, interview, *Der Verdammte Krieg*, ZDF German TV, 1991. Infantry Officer, Kershaw, *War Without Garlands*, p. 229. Neustifter, interview, Ibid. ZDF German TV.

25 Fezensac, Brett-James, *1812: Eyewitness Accounts*, pp. 293–4. Napoleon, Britten Austin, *1812: The March on Moscow*, pp. 448–9.

26 Günther, *Hot Motors, Cold Feet*, p. 235. Walter, *Diary*, p. 87. Vilnius data, R. Osgood, *Unknown Warrior*, pp. 168–9.

27 Zhukov, Russian Borodino Museum Publication, *Borodino Field – Memorial to Two Patriotic Wars,* Map Pamphlet, trans. J. Badgery.

28 Song, Weidinger, *Das Reich,* Vol. III, p. 248.

Bibliography

General Published Sources

Braithwaite, R., *Moscow 1941*. Profile Books, 2006.
Brett-James, A., *1812: Eyewitness Accounts of Napoleon's Defeat in Russia*. Macmillan, 1973.
Britten Austin, P., *1812: The March on Moscow*. Greenhill Books, 1993.
—— *Napoleon in Moscow*. Greenhill, 1995.
—— *The Great Retreat*. Greenhill, 1996.
Chandler, D.G., *The Campaigns of Napoleon*, Vol. II. Folio, 2002.
Cooper, L., *Many Roads to Moscow*. Hamish Hamilton, 1968.
Drabkin, A., *The Red Army at War*. Pen and Sword, 2010.
Duffy, C., *Borodino: Napoleon Against Russia 1812*. Sphere, 1972.
Forczyk, R., *Moscow 1941*. Osprey, 2006.
Jones, M., *The Retreat*. John Murray, 2009.
Kershaw, R., *War Without Garlands*, Ian Allan, 2000.
Mikaberidze, A., *The Battle of Borodino*. Pen and Sword, 2010.
—— *Russian Eyewitness Accounts of the Campaign of 1812*. Frontline Books, 2012.
Osgood, R., *The Unknown Warrior*. Sutton Publishing, 2005.
Rees, L., *War of the Century: When Hitler Fought Stalin*. BBC Books, 1999.
Sharp, C.C., *German Panzer Tactics in World War II*. George Nafziger, 1998.
Time-Life, *The History of the Third Reich*. Time-Life, 1988.
—— *The SS*. Time-Life, 1988.
—— *Barbarossa*. Time-Life, 1990.
Tolstoy, L., *War and Peace*. Folio Society, 1971.
Yerger, M.C., *Otto Weidinger*. Schiffer, 2000.
Zamoyski, A., *1812: Napoleon's Fatal March on Moscow*. HarperCollins, 2004.

Personal Accounts

Albrecht, A., *Napoleon's Army in Russia: The Illustrated Memoirs of Albrecht Adam 1812*, Ed. J. North. Pen and Sword, 2005.

Boland, D., *Recollections from the Ranks*. Helion and Co., 2017.

Bourgogne, *The Retreat from Moscow: The Memoirs of Sgt Bourgogne*. Folio, 1985.

Coignet, J.-R., *Captain Coignet*. Leonaur, 2007.

Dollinger, H., *Kain, wo ist dein Bruder?* Fischer Verlag, 1987.

Faur, F. du, *With Napoleon in Russia: The Illustrated Memoires of Major Faber du Faur 1812*, Ed. J. North. Greenhill Books, 2001.

Fuchs, K., *Sieg Heil! War Letters of Tank Gunner Karl Fuchs 1937–41*. Archon Books, 1987.

Günther, H., *Hot Motors, Cold Feet*. J.J. Fedorowicz, 2004.

Haape, H., *Moscow Tram Stop*. Collins, 1957.

Kesselring, *The Memoirs of Field Marshal Kesselring*. Greenhill, 1988.

Rees, L., *Their Darkest Hour*. Ebury, 2007.

Ségur, P. de, *Defeat: Napoleon's Russian Campaign*. New York Review Books, 2008.

Sevrek, V., *Moscow Stalingrad, Recollections, Stories, Reports*. USSR Pub, 1974.

Timm, U., *In My Brother's Shadow*. Bloomsbury, 2005.

Vossler, H., *With Napoleon in Russia 1812*. Folio, 1969.

Walter, J., *The Diary of a Napoleonic Foot Soldier*. Penguin, 1991.

Zhukov, G.K., *Errinerungen und Gedanken*, 2 Vols. Moscow, 1974.

German Sources

Bekker, C., *The Luftwaffe War Diaries*. Macdonald, 1967.

Boberach, H., Ed., *Meldungen Aus dem Reich*. Band 8 18 Aug–15 Dez 41, Pawlak Verlag Herrsching, 1984.

Haupt, W., *Die Schlachten der Heeresgruppe Mitte 1941–44*. Podzun-Pallas, 1985.

Hinze, R., *Hitze, Frost und Pulverdampf, Der Schicksalweg der 20 Panzer Division*. Heinrich Pöppinghaus Verlag, 1981.

Kohl, P., *Ich Wundere Mich dass ich noch lebe, Sowjetische Augenzeugen berichten*. Verlaghaus Gerd Mohn Gütersloh, 1990.

Neitzel, S. & Welzer, H., *Soldaten*. Simon and Schuster, 2012.

Paul, W., *Die Schlacht um Moskau 1941–2*. Ullstein, 1990.

Piekalkiewicz, J., *Die Schlacht um Moskau*. Lübbe, 1981.

Regimentskameradschaft Deutschland, *Frontkämpfer-Hart wie Stahl, Das Regiment Deutschland 1934–1945*. Nation Europa, 1999.

Restayn, J. & Moller, N., *The 10th Panzer Division*. J.J. Federowicz, 2003.

Schick A, *Combat History of the 10th Panzer Division 1939–43*. J.J. Fedorowicz, 2013.

Weidinger, O., *Das Reich*, Vol. III. J.J. Fedorowicz, 2002.

—— *Comrades to the End, 4th SS Pz Gren Regt Der Führer*. Schiffer, 1998.

Wüster, W., Dr, *An Artilleryman in Stalingrad*. Leaping Horseman, 2007.

Zeiser, B., *In Their Shallow Graves*. Elek Books, 1956.

Russian Sources

Bodnar, A., *Borodino Account 1941*. Heroes Website.

Borodino Field, *Borodino Field Map*. Trans. J. Badgery.

Drabkin, A. & Kobylyanskiy, I., *Red Army Infantrymen Remember the Great Patriotic War*. Authorhouse, 2009.

Gorbunov, A., *Moscow is Behind Us! [Москва за нами!]*, Moscow, 2007, extracts trans. Badgery.

Hill, A., *The Great Patriotic War 1941–45*. Documentary Reader, Routledge, 2009.

Battles for Moscow on Mozhaisk Direction: Studies, Documents, Memories [БОИ ЗА МОСКВУ НА МОЖАЙСКОМ НАПРАВЛЕНИИ]. August 2017, extracts trans. V. Kroupnik.

—— Kravchenkova OV, *Participation of the 17th Infantry Regiment in the battle of Borodino in Oct 1941*.

—— *Operations Summary 40th Panzer Corps 14.10–23.10. 1941*.

—— *Operations Diary of the 32 RD (Sep 1941–1 Jan 1941)*.

Sharp, C.C., *Soviet Order of Battle*, Vol. VIII. 1995.

Periodicals

Jordan, J.W., 'Thunder at the Gates of Moscow'. *Military History Quarterly Review*, Vol. 12 No. 4, Summer 2000.

Signoli, M. and 14 Various Contributors, 'Discovery of a Mass Grave of Napoleonic Period in Lithunia (1812 Vilnius)'. *Human Palaeontology and Prehistory*, Elsevier, April 2004.

Signal, various issues of the German propaganda magazine Oct 41–Jan 42.

Stolfi, R.H.S., 'German 10th Panzer Division's Eastern Front Offensive Near Vyazma During World War II'. *World War II* Magazine, Sep 1997.

Die Wehrmacht Magazine, No. 25, 3 Dec 41.

Film, TV and Audio

Galan, Gootman, Grigouriev and Gelaine, *Blood Upon the Snow, Russia's War*. IBP films, 1995.

Isaacs, J., *The World at War*. Thames TV, 1973–74.

Knopp, *Der Verdammte Krieg*. ZDF German TV, 1991.

Landgraf, H., *Fighting on the Borodino Position*,

——*9 Oct & 14 Oct 1941*, Imperial War Museum, Audio Catalogue No. 8357 and 8358.

—— *Die Deutsche Wochenschau, 26 Oct 41. Auf dem Schlachtfeld von Borodinow*. No. 2948.

Rees, L., *War of the Century*. BBC TV, 1999.

Index

By the same author

978 0 7509 8888 9

'Robert Kershaw's *24 Hours at Balaclava* has to be one of the finest books on the battle ever written. Indeed, as an evocation of the visceral human experience of combat, it ranks high among books on battle in general.'

Neil Faulkner,
Military History Matters

Shortlisted for the *MHM* Book of the Year 2020 award